With quiet eloquence, Katie Eberhart delicately teases away layers of the natural world and human history to explore how people adapt to landscapes and landscapes to people. The homestead at the heart of this story is a time portal that invites her to excavate the mysteries and meanings embedded within its log walls—sometimes literally. Her keen attention to the surrounding environment unveils the intricate connections between slugs and glaciers, wells and rivers, gardens and forests, settlement and abandonment, timelessness and transformation. The result is a compelling mosaic of meditations that illuminates the extraordinary within the commonplace.

—Sherry Simpson, author of *Dominion of Bears*

Katie Eberhart's well-constructed memoir reminds me of my favorite kind of house, an old house that's been added onto over the years, a bedroom here, a family room there, each addition reflecting the style and available materials of the period as well as the eccentricities of the owners, while maintaining an overall harmony. A house still cared-for, still full of life. As with this lovely book, when you step inside, you feel immediately at home.

—Charles Goodrich, writer, poet. Former director of the Oregon State University's Spring Creek Project

CABIN 135

CABIN 135

A MEMOIR
of ALASKA

KATIE EBERHART

University of Alaska Press, Fairbanks

Text © 2020 Katie Eberhart

Published by
University of Alaska Press
P.O. Box 756240
Fairbanks, AK 99775-6240

Cover, interior, and map art by Ruth Hulbert.
Interior design by 590 Design.
Photos by Katie Eberhart.

Library of Congress Cataloging-in-Publication Data

Names: Eberhart, Katie, author.
Title: Cabin 135 : A Memoir of Alaska / Katie Eberhart.
Description: Fairbanks : University of Alaska Press, 2020. | Summary:
"Cabin 135 was built near Palmer, Alaska in 1935 for the Matanuska Colony, a New
    Deal resettlement project. The author and her husband took possession of the
    house many years later and went to work tearing out and digging around the
    aged structure, discovering evidence of changes made by prior residents and
    layering their own adaptations. Through the lens of these activities—uncovering
    the past and modifying the future—the author muses on questions of the nat-
    ural world, migration, and settlement, the connections forged and abandoned
    between people and places. Cabin 135, A Memoir of Alaska offers a journey of
    wonder and curiosity through the renovations of an old house, looking to the
    garden and greenhouse, the forest, and beyond to grapple with persistent worries
    regarding habitation, nature, and the planet. It is a story of life."—Provided by
    publisher.
Identifiers: LCCN 2019058777 (print) | LCCN 2019058778 (ebook) | ISBN
    9781602234208 (paperback) | ISBN 9781602234215 (ebook)
Subjects: LCSH: Eberhart, Katie. | Matanuska River Valley
    (Alaska)—Biography. | Farm life—Alaska—Matanuska River Valley.
Classification: LCC F912.M3 E34 2020 (print) | LCC F912.M3 (ebook) | DDC
    979.8/3—dc23
LC record available at https://lccn.loc.gov/2019058777
LC ebook record available at https://lccn.loc.gov/2019058778

for Chuck

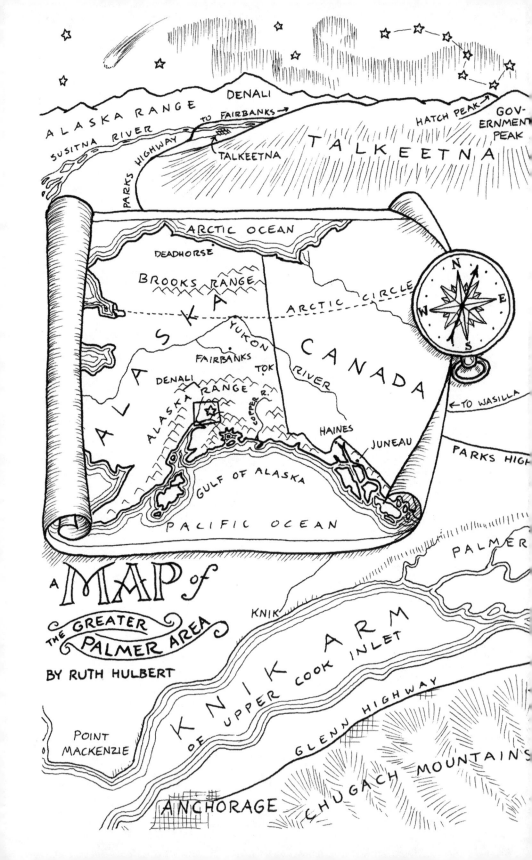

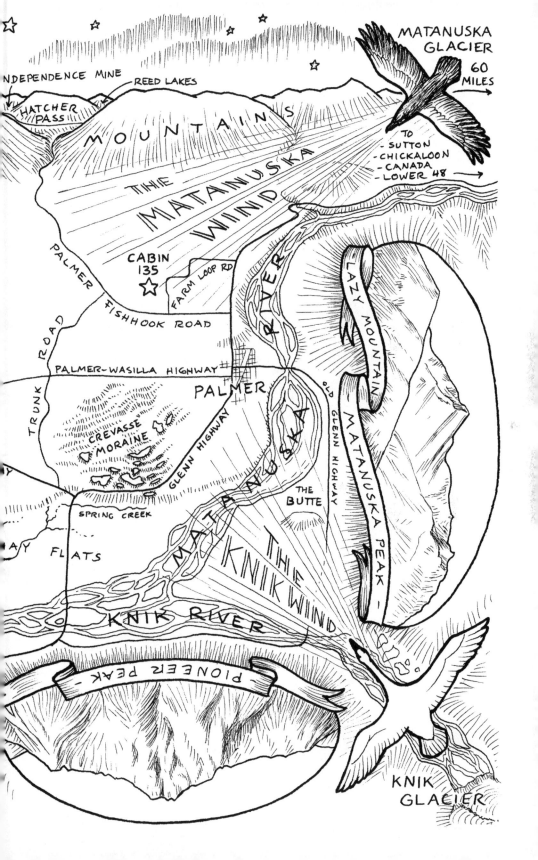

BEGINNINGS

C A B I N • If you had come to visit us that evening, you couldn't have discerned from outside the ambience inside our house, what with the windows steamed up and the aromas of cooking trapped behind them.

A pan of caraway seeds, toasting on the stove, released the scent of licorice, reminding me of a trip with my parents to Alsace, where my father had fought in World War II and where I first remember tasting anise. The seeds were for a vinaigrette. For the hot-and-sour soup, I peeled the papery skin from a couple of Oregon garlic cloves. The onion was an Ailsa Craig that Chuck started from seed nine months earlier, on Super Bowl Sunday. It surrendered to the knife in thin, glassily translucent rings. No tears. I poured a thin pool of oil into the pan and added the diced onions, garlic, and dried hot pepper. They sizzled in the hot oil.

I peeled and sliced a carrot, thick and dark orange, from our garden. Even with an end broken off, the carrot weighed nearly a pound. I tossed the carrots and a few mushroom slices into the pot with the frying vegetables, then poured in chicken broth. Ten minutes later, after a few more additions, the soup simmered, clear and thick.

That summer collards had grown large because the moose favored brussels sprouts and russian kale. Before the first frost, I picked and stored armfuls of collards, the leaves like elephant ears threaded with heavy white veins. One of those ears, sliced into shreds, was enough for the chiffonade the soup needed. The shredded collards floated in the pot, turning bright green, then dark as seaweed, but simmering into a sweet-tasting tenderness. Perhaps the sweetness came from soil accumulated from eons of glacial silt—loess—deposited by the Knik and Matanuska winds, or from the abundant subarctic daylight, or because we shunned chemicals, or because rainfall watered the plants. Or maybe all these conditions contributed to the delectable nature of the vegetables that grew in our garden plot, a rectangle of land that had been a garden when we arrived in 1983, and probably for decades before that.

T I M E • It was the end of the 1970s when Chuck and I met while studying at Washington State University. A year later we married and moved to Alaska. In Anchorage our first residence was a small unremarkable apartment, our second home a flat-roofed house better suited to California.

Having lived in that house for not quite a year, one morning, still half asleep, I sat up and swung my legs over the edge of the bed. My feet plunged into icy water. I yanked my feet up, hoping I was dreaming but I wasn't. The carpet was underwater.

"Chuck! Wake up. We're flooded!"

We sloshed across the bedroom to our shoes and pieced together what had happened. While we slept, a Chinook wind had arisen, bringing warm temperatures and rain—and, like a giant anvil, the accumulation of soggy snow pressed meltwater through the roofing and into the house.

Over the following weeks, we dealt with the insurance company and hired a contractor to repair the roof of a house we couldn't love. Some months later, we started looking for a house outside Anchorage, in the Matanuska Valley. We valued a view and good water as well as space for a garden and a horse. We weren't daunted by the idea of an old house or acreage without fences or a barn.

During the first few weeks, our house-hunting pilgrimages produced no results. The places we looked at felt hemmed in by neighbors or the land was too steep or the house oddly remodeled.

❧

C A B I N • One day, rather than driving west, we motored north, eventually ending up on Farm Loop Road, where we noticed a faded For Sale sign. At the end of a long driveway, a house with a steeply pitched roof and a wide dormer resembled a quaint cottage. The exterior was painted red, accented with white trim and narrow shutters. That afternoon, when we got home, I called the realtor who had the listing for our Anchorage house. She called back with more information and an appointment to view the property. The next weekend, with considerable anticipation, we returned to the valley, this time turning into the driveway with the weathered For Sale sign.

The owner, Mrs. Webb, tall and attractive, met us at the door. She and her husband had lived there for twenty years, raising their children but, she explained, since retiring, they had decided to move to Oregon. A truck-sized shipping container beside the house was being loaded with furniture.

Mrs. Webb led us through the front door into her cozy rooms. Perhaps she was seeing the house through our eyes— us the age of her children, her children grown and gone. She seemed reconciled, if a little wistful. When you prepare to leave a place you've lived in for many years, memories and routines, once snug and secure, become unhinged.

Inside the living room, picture windows to the south framed Pioneer Peak and to the east, Lazy Mountain and Matanuska Peak.

Pointing to the wide windowsills, Mrs. Webb commented, "The walls are log and sturdy. The house was built for the colony."

T I M E • During the Great Depression, the federal government created new agricultural settlements in a number of
states, including Alaska. Farmers who had run out of other
options applied for the chance to start over in one of these
government-sponsored colonies. In 1935 over two hundred
families were accepted for the Matanuska Colony. They traveled by train from Minnesota, Wisconsin, and Michigan to
Seattle or San Francisco, where they boarded ships bound for
Seward. The last leg of their journey, from Seward to Palmer,
was by train.

C A B I N • The compact kitchen, dining area, living room,
and bathroom were on the main floor. In the hallway past
the kitchen, we tromped downstairs into the basement. The
ceiling was low, and only two tiny windows, the edges tightly
sealed, let in daylight. Sheetrocked walls, painted a crisp
white, would have been unremarkable except, in a niche
behind the furnace, the concrete block foundation was visible—painted an unsettling minty green. With furniture moved
out, the basement appeared quite spacious.

I asked about the washing machine and dryer.

"We're taking those," Mrs. Webb said as she pulled open
a door, revealing a closet-sized room. Shelves lining the walls
would hold many jars of home-canned jelly and jam, fruit,
and pickles. I would call this the cold room because that's
what my mom called the unheated room lined with shelves
where she stored her home-canned produce.

The floor in the cold room was cement except for a patch
of earth in one corner where a pipe protruded. Plastic tubing

snaked from the pipe to a squat metal pump that sat on the floor. An electrical cord connected the pump to an outlet near the ceiling.

"That's the well," Mrs. Webb said. "It's just over thirty feet deep and the water tastes good."

Exiting the small room, Mrs. Webb pulled open another door, revealing plank steps hitched between concrete walls and leading up to an exterior door. Daylight streamed through windows and translucent roof panels.

"In the spring, I start plants here. It's my second green-house," Mrs. Webb said, indicating a wide ledge and shelves within reach of the steps.

Chuck and I both wanted to garden. Another ledge suitable for starting seeds and hardening off vegetables would be advantageous. During the quick tour, we were already falling in love with the house, or at least with how we imagined it.

We traipsed after Mrs. Webb, returning through the basement and climbing the stairs.

"Watch your step," she said as she turned along the back hallway and started up the stairs to the second floor. Semi-triangular bottom steps required a quick turn like the start of a spiral staircase. Mrs. Webb paused, as if sinking into a distant memory.

"There used to be a landing here," she mused. "The stairs went into the living room, but I didn't want them there. One day, I tore out the lowest steps. When my husband came home from work, before he could go to bed that night, he had to build new stairs."

Balanced on a narrow step, I imagined walking through the front door and seeing a staircase, not a wall. The bedrooms were upstairs, the bathroom downstairs. Anyone getting up in the night would trek down the stairs and through the living room, dining area, and kitchen to reach the bathroom. The rebuilt stairs were not rectangular, nor were they strictly triangular. The bottom steps formed a curve that intersected the rectangular upper stairs.

Touring the house that day, the story of the stairs was interesting but not gravely important. Chuck and I also didn't take much notice of the dark paneling, worn appliances, or flattened carpet. Nor did we care about the inconvenience of having a bathroom downstairs and bedrooms upstairs. What attracted us was the house's location atop a small hill with a grand view of fields, forests, and mountains.

On the west side of the house, we walked across a wooden deck that had a birch tree growing through a cut-out hole and a planter whimsically shaped like a wishing well. A small greenhouse, painted dark red with white trim like the house, crouched between the deck and the steeply sloped lawn.

"The vegetable garden," Mrs. Webb indicated, pointing expansively toward a broad square of soggy soil surrounded by winter-parched lawn.

She might as well have said, you know you're going to make an offer. How can you not? A unique house. Acreage for your horse. Exquisite views. A ready-made vegetable garden. A separate plot for potatoes and a raspberry patch in a swale north of the house. Chuck and I glanced at each other with a look that said "this is it." We didn't consider there might have been reasons that the place hadn't sold during a year on the market.

Driving back to Anchorage, there were many things that Chuck and I did not discuss. We didn't talk about the cabin's steep, narrow staircase, out-of-date wiring, decrepit plumbing, the roof coated with urethane, lack of insulation, or log crib instead of a septic tank. We also didn't consider the cost or difficulty of fixing any of that—but if we had, we wouldn't have cared. We planned to fence a corner of the field, build a barn, and grow vegetables.

The owners accepted the offer we soon tendered. In May 1983 we moved into the house that had been built forty-eight years earlier for the Matanuska Colony. Chuck was returning to the community where he'd grown up. I was yet another person in a long procession of migrants to Alaska.

T I M E • I have compared every place I have lived to my grandparents' impeccably maintained house even though family stories recall a place that wasn't always so delightful. My grandmother Violet would say matter-of-factly: "I found my house in a dream . . ."

In the late 1930s, she described the house she had seen "in a dream" to a realtor. He knew of a structure that matched her description. His advice, though, was as officious as a tent preacher's: "You wouldn't want that house. It's old and rundown."

"I insist," she said, smiling sweetly.

Violet's dream house was indeed neglected, but she saw only possibilities and thought rehabilitation would be manageable.

After moving into that house, the sagging and crumbling ceiling over the living room and dining room attracted Violet's attention. My mom remembers her mother balancing on a stepladder, with her neck craned back, wielding a screwdriver. For weeks, Violet perched on the ladder and methodically twisted one tiny screw after another, reattaching plaster to a vast ceiling.

As a child, I heard this story told and retold. Much later, I began to understand the lessons being conveyed. The story paired the sad state of the house with Violet's stubborn intentions and inclination toward perfection. Eventually, I suspected that story, of my grandmother fixing a deteriorated ceiling with a screwdriver and thousands of screws, contributed to my obliviousness to difficulties related to an old house.

I suspect my grandparents' garden similarly imprinted my youth. Their garden, which faced Puget Sound, and the red-tile balcony along the west side of the house offered both near and far views. Below the balcony, tall rhododendrons (Grandma called them "the rhodies") were blanketed in lavender blooms and beyond that, the lawn sloped toward a bluff. The effect was of a garden buttressed by shimmering waters and, in the far distance, on the Olympic Peninsula, snowcapped mountains. The garden offered my grandmother an antidote to hardships on the Canadian prairie. Her stories often featured hellacious winds, blizzards, and blistering fires.

My mom was a sophomore in high school when her family moved to the house overlooking Puget Sound. She said a lot of trees surrounded it, even a large redwood that her parents cut down. That was long before my birth, but I do remember my grandmother's rose garden.

"Grandma liked to have two of each rose," my mother recalled. "She planted the roses in pairs and all the roses in each block were the same color. Gardening wasn't hit-or-miss for her. She kept an index card for every plant. She even mixed her own fertilizer."

Violet talked about the roses as if they were her close friends—Theresa Bugnet, Mr. Lincoln, Peace—but my sisters and I fancied ourselves unicorns and peeled thorns from a stem to stick on our noses.

When my mother was a teenager, people would park on the dead-end street beside her parents' house. The visitors carried picnic baskets and blankets onto neatly mowed grass beneath tall silver poplars. Mom said her parents explained to the interlopers that they were on private property.

"The picnickers," my mom recalled, "always said, 'This place is so beautiful, we thought it was a park.'"

Gardening, except growing food out of need, is an avocation of a person with time and a willingness to learn. Perhaps my fascination with plants came from being exposed at an early age to my grandparents' garden and glimpsing my grandmother's attitude toward landscaping and plants. Violet loved her garden, and family stories imply a reciprocity. When she became too ill to tend her roses, they died.

C A B I N • When Chuck and I moved into the log-built house, I wanted a rooted existence like my grandparents had and like, eventually, my parents found. I felt that legitimacy attaches to spending a long time in one place. On the other hand, I had mixed feelings about Alaska. I was enthusiastic about the adventure, but I had a poor sense of time. I missed rambles across the arid desert steppe.

T I M E • By the time I was a teenager, my family had moved to the country and I had a horse. East of the Washington Cascades, we lived a half mile from an irrigation canal that drew a sinuous line between farmland and rangeland. After crossing a wooden bridge over the canal, I slid to the ground and pried open a barbed-wire gate. With reins draped over my arm and mindful of the needle-sharp barbs, I led my horse through the opening. After my sister rode through, I tugged the gate closed and fastened it with a loop of stiff wire.

Writing, I debate which horse I was riding and what year it was. If I was as young as I claim, then I was riding Stepper, a large pony. If I was older, then I was riding Sham, a sure-footed Arabian often wiser than me. In between, I tended a Thoroughbred-Appaloosa gelding that was fast and unreliable and would have been an unlikely choice for traipsing across wild land. Another problem with filling in the details is that I don't precisely recall the route. However, these questions hardly interfere with the story that is not about horses or journeys but rather memory and imagination.

Once past the gate, the horses trod cattle trails across ground mostly hidden by clumps of sagebrush. Climbing toward a parched ridge, we crossed beneath the interstate highway. The tunnel was cool and dark, and hoofbeats echoed.

We emerged uphill, into bright sunlight and the sound of trucks and cars whooshing above us on the built-up freeway. Farther uphill, near a saddle in the ridge, several paths split off toward a water tank—it appeared as if cows couldn't agree on which track was best. At a slow walk, we crossed to the south side of the ridge where sagebrush grew taller and denser and the landscape appeared more luxuriant. Far beyond farmland, the only sounds were dust-muffled hoofbeats and our voices as we angled the horses across a dryland plateau toward a deep canyon carved by the Yakima River.

The freeway, Interstate 82, which takes a straight-line route over the ridges, wasn't completed until 1971. Before that, to travel south, you would drive a two-lane highway that snaked along the river. As a passenger in the backseat of a car, speeding around perpetual curves, I looked up at steep hillsides—in spring, cloaked with wildflowers, and during autumn, a patchwork of fiery red sumac. Most of the time, though, the vista was basalt outcrops laced with parched grasses. At each loop of the river, I leaned left or right, moved by centrifugal force as the car turned and turned, but the journey was quick—thirty or forty minutes—and many magnitudes of time less than the eons it takes a river to erode volcanic terrain.

Our horses swished flies with their tails, and a couple times, we stopped and untied canteens from the saddles to swallow sun-warmed water. It was a long ride for a view—a few hours each way—but when we reached the canyon rim where the ridge dropped off steeply toward the river, we gazed across a neck of basalt that the river flowed around, almost completing a circle but not quite.

Sitting on warm horses on a sunny day, we weren't calculating how to cross a deep river canyon. We were there only for the view and to imagine what happens in a lifetime. Children, really, looking forward and entertaining the idea of a far-off future when the river breaks through the rocks, imagining rushing water, imagining a magnificent semicircular lake disconnected from a straight channel. Or water flowing around a new island. We considered many possibilities but, even so, no glimmer came to me that I would live in Alaska and, several decades later, rekindle my search for nature.

❧

TERRAIN • Two decades before the Matanuska Colony was established, the U.S. government hired surveyors to ready the territory for homesteading. It was early autumn 1913, perhaps with snow already dusting the mountains, when a surveyor worked not far from the future site of Cabin 135. Satisfied with his measurements, he hefted a short-handled sledgehammer, pounding an iron rod into the ground to mark the southwest corner of Section 19, Township 18 North Range 2 East.

The surveyor paused and pulled a notebook from his pocket, jotting a description of the land: "Level. Soil, rich, black and sandy loam, 2 feet deep on gravel subsoil 2nd rate." He added a comment about vegetation: "spruce, birch and cottonwood" and dense undergrowth, "willow, fireweed and wild rose bushes."

A century later, I contemplate the surveyor's map on the screen of my computer, scrolling from south to north, following the Matanuska River from where the channel narrows between rock outcrops—near the place where Palmer eventually developed. I imagine the surveyor standing on the bluff and gazing across the gray river toward snow-streaked peaks. Far to the east, a glacier shimmered. The surveyor leaned his canvas pack against a log and took out the map he had been revising. Multiple streams gleamed in the late afternoon sun as he sketched parallel lines to illustrate the braided river and dabbed clusters of dots to represent islands.

On the map, tightly spaced lines signify steep bluffs alongside the river—a familiar landscape to me. Sometimes, driving home, I pull off at the overlook where a dune, with the soft resistance of beach sand, fills the asphalt path. At the bluff promontory, wind shoots grit upward, peppering my face. To the south, low clouds split into pale streamers above a gleaming fogbank that obscures the lower slopes of Pioneer Peak. Streaks of bluish and silvery mist linger over the gray river channel, and for the first time, I notice a distant scarp banded with yellow. Above the yellow stripe, an atmospheric effect causes Bodenburg Butte to appear detached from the earth, like a drifting ghost ship.

Below the bluff, a trail traces the railbed where, until the early 1960s, trains hauled coal from upriver, near Sutton and Chickaloon, to Anchorage. In my memory, though, no scheduled trains rolled into Palmer. The train station had been transformed into a community center.

On top of the bluff, a dune nearly buries a fence intended to keep visitors back a safe distance. Stepping over the ankle-high barrier, I inch toward the edge but, far down the bluff, stones rattle spookily. I retreat, stepping back across the mostly buried fence to where I recall a layer of hard asphalt before the dune encroached.

TIME • Farther west, where Cabin 135 was eventually built, the 1913 surveyor's map shows the land flattening out. The surveyor sketched trees and shrub-brush as bumpy-edged circles interrupted by swatches of horizontal lines with clusters of short vertical marks indicating marshes, or shallow lakes. On a section farther west, he drew two black squares, one labeled "rancher cabin" and annotated:

"There is one settler living in Township 18 North Range 1 West about the center of Sec. 25, on Govt. wagon road. Has about ½ acre cleared and set to garden, 1 house 20 × 15 ft., log, as well as out buildings."

After the government survey was completed, more home-steaders arrived. Charles A. Larson, following an unsuccessful attempt at mining near Nelchina, staked a homestead west of the Matanuska River. Larson built a cabin and chopped trees. He lived there and farmed long enough to prove up and gain title to the land. The public record shows that, on November 8, 1921, President Warren G. Harding signed the patent that transferred ownership of the land to Larson.

Larson stayed on the homestead for another fourteen years, until 1935, when agents of the Matanuska Colony bought forty acres from him, along with another forty acres to the east, for $5.03 per acre. The combined eighty acres was identified as Tract 135 and put in "the hat" for one of the Colony land drawings.

In the movie *Alaska Far Away*, a train rolls into Palmer. The expressions of hopefulness on the colonists' faces dissolve into disappointment as they realize that their first Alaska home will be a canvas tent in a long row of identical tents. But now that they were here, their course was to turn around or get on with it.

C A B I N • Clystia and Henry LaRose were accepted as colonists because they knew how to farm. They arrived in Palmer on one of the colonist transport trains. During the land lottery on May 23, 1935, Henry picked Tract 135. Clystia and Henry leafed through a catalog of houses and selected one of the log cabin plans. That summer, workers hired by the U.S. government began building Cabin 135. The LaRoses moved in even before construction was finished.

On an overcast day in 1935, the photographer, Willis T. Geisman, stood slightly downhill from Cabin 135. He set up a wooden tripod with a large camera on top and carefully inserted a frame holding film. He opened the shutter to expose the film, documenting the nearly complete construction of Cabin 135 for the Matanuska Colony.

T I M E • Seventy years later I study the photograph, gleaning what I can of time and place.

With no obvious foundation and a dozen logs splayed across the slope, the cabin appears to have risen organically from the ground. Scaffolding—used as a platform to reach the steeply pitched roof—remained attached to the log walls.

I didn't realize, the first time I saw this photograph, that it was of our house. The picture could have been any cabin built atop a roughly cleared knoll.

I was struck by the idea that stumps in the adjacent forest were from trees used to build the house. Later, I learned that logs for the colony cabins were harvested and milled elsewhere in the valley. The logs were likely white spruce (*Picea glauca*), a common tree in southcentral Alaska. Spruce grows slowly, the timber dense and straight-grained.

In the 1935 photo, no one stands outside in view of the camera; no one even peers out a window. Perhaps the photographer asked everyone to step away because his job was to document structures, not families. Despite the scaffolding and absence of people, the cabin appears inhabited. Curtains hang in the windows and a chimney protrudes through the roof. A tall narrow window in the east-facing gable indicates a second floor, or at least plans for one.

C A B I N • Looking at the colony-era photograph of Cabin 135, I imagine myself inside the cabin, as if a doorway through time remained ajar. The cabin smells of new logs. Woodsmoke backdrafts from an iron cookstove. A ladder leans against a ceiling joist. I scramble up to investigate the upstairs. The steeply pitched roof and unfinished walls make the attic seem small and claustrophobic. A narrow window in each gable contributes light that is largely absorbed by the roof boards. The flooring is familiar but unpainted. Tongue-and-groove boards, solidly laid. My footsteps echo in the hard-edged space. Sooner rather than later, a staircase will replace the ladder. After that, walls and doorways will separate two bedrooms, each with a single window. Eventually, someone will create a third room by hacking off a section of roof and installing a wide dormer. The dormer will face south with a tremendous view of Pioneer Peak through a heedlessly small window.

T I M E • The government album documented colony house interiors, but not Cabin 135's. An interior photo of another dwelling, Cabin 31, shows a steep staircase rising to the second floor. The walls are slab-sided logs, the only furnishing a small plank table—perhaps a washstand—beneath one window. In the middle of the floor, the top rung of a ladder protrudes from an open cellar hatch.

Perhaps Cabin 135 also had a root cellar dug into the ground beneath the floor. That would have been handy in the winter. No need to tromp outside in a blizzard to retrieve stored food from a cache built on stilts.

Henry and Clystia LaRose began their new life in Cabin 135, but if anyone had asked Clystia "What is home?" I imagine she would have described houses she knew in Wisconsin and the gardens—her mother's and grandmother's—with a profusion of vegetables and a prolific orchard. Perhaps she reminisced about the chores, her memories settling on springtime and the poignant fragrance of lilacs.

C A B I N • By the time we moved in, nearly a half century later, Cabin 135 had been fitted with a foundation and basement. A wide dormer protruded from the south side of the roof, and an oversize garage was attached to the north wall. The logs were hidden—outside by cedar shake siding and inside by paneling, wallboard, and fake bricks. Narrow windows had been replaced with wide picture windows. An arctic entry and new front door had been added at the northeast corner of the house. The original front door, in the center of the south wall, had vanished beneath siding, paneling, and large windows.

The arctic entry had a closet and a window with a view of the driveway. The windowsill was narrow and scratched, suggesting that the ledge had once been favored by a cat. The light that hung from the ceiling didn't have a wall switch, instead you had to reach up and twist a little knob to turn it on or off. The front door, heavy varnished wood with diamond-shaped panes in the top half, offered the only view to the north.

Having only one window on the north side of an Alaska house strikes me as odd. (I would have liked an entire wall of glass facing north and a room with comfortable furniture—dubbed the Aurora Observatory.) I suspect that Cabin 135 once had windows in the north wall but that they had been covered when the garage was built.

W I N D • In the Matanuska Valley, mention the "Knik" or the "Matanuska" and the context conveys whether you're speaking of the wind or the river. During winter, the Matanuska wind blasts subzero chill off the Matanuska Glacier, ricocheting along the mountain-hemmed river for sixty miles. Both river and wind come into the valley to the northeast. The river mostly keeps to its channel, but the wind surges upward like a beast released from shackles. Having escaped the river canyon, wind erratically pummels forests, fields, and houses.

The Matanuska hauls loads of talc-fine silt. When wind speed falters, the glacial loess drifts downward, sifting into even the tiniest cracks and crevices. The arctic entry was the first place I noticed a slim line of silt had settled indoors, on the cat-clawed windowsill.

The Matanuska River supplies the wind with an endless source of pulverized earth. Warm weather melts glacial ice, releasing particles that contribute to the silty river flow. Thunderstorms, or the tail end of Asian typhoons, pummel the mountains, sending melted snow churning along the tumultuous river. During winter, melting slows and the Matanuska flows translucently green.

As winter moderates toward spring, the wind shifts to the southeasterly Knik. Like the Matanuska, the Knik wind is never a gentle breeze. It rampages off glaciers and blusters along a river channel, lofting plumes of silt and grit that from a distance resemble a tornado tipped sideways.

Neither wind enhances comfortable living. Both sport a teeth-gritting misery—subzero chills or throat-scratching air, or both. Yet over centuries and millennia, wind built up topsoil—loess—that, along with abundant daylight and rainfall, provides exceptionally productive earth for gardens and farms.

TERRAIN • During the night a crash woke me bolt upright. The noise happened instantly, unlike the slow crescendo of an earthquake, which begins with rattling like a distant drum corps, gradually increasing in timbre and intensity and accompanied by the whole house swaying. The house was not shaking. I climbed out of bed and peered through the window, my eyes adapting to the darkness. In the backyard, I discerned the tall white trunks of the two birch trees, and the two remaining trunks of the candelabra-shaped birch splayed outward in their usual gravity-defying position. Mystified as to the source of the loud sound, I went back to bed.

The next day, while filling the bird feeder suspended between the two straight-trunked birch, I noticed down the hill, beyond the raspberries, a cottonwood had uprooted. Not the largest cottonwood but still a lofty tree, reposed awkwardly across a knoll, balanced between the turned-up root mass and the top branches entangling the neighbor's wire fence.

A tree falling at any particular moment is enormously unlikely unless it's leaning or rotten, and perhaps with encouragement of a strong wind. Being hit by a falling tree also seems unlikely, not worth a second thought or energy spent worrying. Except I acquired a more circumspect attitude toward the upright inclination of trees.

TIME • One summer we embarked on a camping trip. The first night we camped at the Tok Campground. With plentiful daylight, Chuck and I casually pitched our tent among spruce, and about fifty feet away, Ben and Michael put up theirs. Chuck and I had a nylon dome tent with fiberglass poles. The boys' tent was a newer half-dome with aluminum poles. The camp-ground was nearly full, with motor homes at one end and tent campers scattered among trees at the other end.

About four o'clock the next morning, daylight seeped through the tent fabric. Half awake, cocooned in my sleeping bag, I listened to wind rustling spruce and willows. An explosion of wood shattered the air nearby. As a thick spruce crashed onto our tent, ripping nylon and tearing fiberglass, instinctively, I rolled one direction and Chuck rolled the other.

I was stuck, encapsulated in an envelope of tent fabric.

"Chuck," I shouted. "Are you all right?"

"Yes," he said. "Are you?"

"Yes. The boys?"

Surely the tree hadn't hit their tent too.

"Help!" Ben shouted. "Michael's trapped."

The tent zipper ripped open and Chuck shouted, "I'm coming."

I twisted and reached, finally retrieving a pocketknife stashed at the foot of my sleeping bag.

Chuck shouted for help and then another voice answered, and I heard Chuck saying, "If we both lift."

I opened the knife blade and sliced the tent. Crawling out, I ran toward the boys' tent just as Chuck and another camper strained to lift the tree.

Michael shouted, "I'm out from under it."

A tree that was too large to carry lay across the boys' tent.

A man rushed over from one of the motor homes. One look, and he said, "I have a chainsaw." He hurried back to his camper and, a few minutes later, returned with the saw and cut through the spruce. Everyone lifted the now shorter log off the tent. The boys rushed out.

Still early morning, we packed our car and drove into Tok, stopping at a restaurant, where we ate pancakes for breakfast as if everything was normal, but that night we stayed in a hotel, and later when we ventured into another campground, we carefully considered the inclination of the trees before deciding where to pitch the tents.

⚜

T E R R A I N • After moving into the house, Chuck and I installed an electric fence and I trailered my horse, Sham, from a boarding stable to his new home in the electric-fenced paddock. Later that summer we built a three-sided shed to provide shelter for Sham until we could build a barn. I nailed recently milled cottonwood planks to the sides of the shed. After a few months, the boards dried and shrank, leaving gaps in between. I cut and nailed narrow batten strips over the gaps as if that was what I had intended all along. Someone with more experience could have predicted that green cottonwood would shrink. I was annoyed by the extra work, but I was learning that natural forces proceeded irrespective of my intentions.

With a horse on the premises, we also needed a pasture fence. "Wood," I commented to Chuck, "not barbed wire."

T I M E • When I was thirteen, my family moved to a place with a hayfield but no fences. We built fences. Our dad showed us how to hammer in metal posts, brace the corners, and stretch wire using a come-along. What he didn't know, and what my sisters and I learned, was how easily horses cut themselves on barbed wire. The horses leaned into the wire or rubbed against it. Sometimes the needle-sharp wires, intended to discourage cattle from bashing through fences, cut the horses' skin. We spread salve or daubed purple antiseptic onto the wounds and waited for them to heal.

T E R R A I N • In the early 1980s, the State of Alaska sold agricultural rights at Point MacKenzie, a largely forested landscape southwest of Palmer. One new farmer agreed to sell me posts from black spruce she cut down while clearing her land.

I drove to Point MacKenzie. The black spruce logs I bought turned out to be entire trees, with the limbs lopped off, and too long for my pickup. A handsaw proved no match for the slow-growing spruce, wood that resembled hardwood or, I mused, iron. My arms ached as I pushed and pulled the narrow blade through the dense spruce. After sawing a half dozen logs, I gave up, driving home with fewer posts than I expected. On my next trip, I stopped at a hardware store and bought a chainsaw. Faced with the same pile of logs, I revved the chainsaw and quickly sliced through a log. The saw was noisy and effective, and I only stopped when I noticed the pickup settling beneath the weight of the timber.

After having accumulated a sufficient number of post-length logs, Chuck and I planned to use a drawknife to peel off the bark.

A drawknife is likely the most nostalgic non-motorized tool. The knife has a wooden handle at each end, at right angles to the blade. I imagine this tool was used by homesteaders across North America, preparing posts for fences and barns and accommodating their lives in a new location, as if taking up where they left off somewhere else, and certainly changing the environment.

Propping a log crosswise between two other logs, I grasped the handles, angling the blade against the log, and pulled. Long strips of bark fell from the log. Sometimes, though, the bark adhered tightly and the drawknife wouldn't slide. Then, the effort became akin to whittling. My tugging only scraped off flakes of bark.

Building the ideal fence with wooden posts and planks became an ongoing project. We had much to learn. The hardware store owner said we ought to treat the posts to prevent rot. He recommended soaking the ends in creosote, which sounded like a good idea at the time.

T I M E • It feels like an aside when I bring horses into this story, but my relationship with horses was deeply rooted in my past and my psyche, and without the nudge to acquire acreage for a horse, Chuck and I probably would not have ended up at this house. Our lives would have been different. We would have had different stories, encounters, and places. There would have been no Cabin 135 memoir.

The stories I tell here root around in nature. Rediscovering illuminating experiences also connects to my youth when, with a pony and later a horse, I wandered—leaving behind place, time, family. For an afternoon, I inhabited a landscape of forest or sagebrush, noticing wildlife— jackrabbits, badgers, rattlesnakes—and the weather and terrain and beginning to comprehend how a horse traverses slopes, swales, and cutbanks. A steel canteen hung from the saddle. (Plastic water bottles had not yet appeared.) My habit of exploring began when I was twelve and I learned that on horseback I could vanish into the hills—beyond the sound of my mother's voice.

T E R R A I N • The previous owners had an arrangement with the neighboring farmer to harvest hay off the hillside beside the house. Mowing kept the forest from reclaiming the slope. Grazing would have the same effect. Chuck and I pounded stakes to mark the corners of the pasture fence. We stretched string between the corners and measured where to locate each post.

We didn't rent a powered auger, although now I wonder why. We dug holes with posthole diggers—hinged shovels with double handles you manipulate like you're a robotic mastermind. Sometimes the digging went quickly, the blades biting easily through the soft loess, but in other spots the shovels clanked against rocks. Chuck brought home a railroad bar—a six-foot chunk of steel. Lifting and dropping the heavy rod loosened buried cobbles. Manipulating the posthole digger like giant forceps, I plucked stones from the narrow posthole.

Like the shed walls, the fence boards were green, uncured cottonwood from a local mill. The planks were supposed to be the same length, but they weren't. Or else we hadn't spaced the posts evenly. Extension cords stretched from the house and powered a saw that sped the trimming of the fence boards. We nailed the boards, butted end-to-end, onto the posts.

Last, we hung a gate at the corner nearest the house. After that, each morning I led Sham from the shed to the pasture. Every evening I led him back to the paddock and shed. Interacting with the same horse year after year, a bond grows. This sensibility between human and horse results in an attentiveness like mind-reading, or shared anticipation.

TIME • I worked for the State Division of Agriculture in the early 1980s when the agency was evaluating land for agriculture potential on the Kenai Peninsula. The study team visited one such site—east of Deep Creek—on horseback. Mostly, people rode horses provided by a local rancher, but I brought Sham, a horse wise to the desert steppe but not to marshes. We had to cross several wetlands to reach the potential farmland. Halfway across the first bog, Sham's forefeet broke through the vegetation mat. He panicked. This horse that barely deigned to notice rattlesnakes bunched his muscles and leaped. Landing with that much force drove his hooves deeper into the soggy peat. I slid off, hoping that without my weight the horse wouldn't sink as much and would calm down. The bog vegetation supported me and I started walking toward dry ground. As soon as I was slightly ahead, Sham leaped again and landed practically on top of me. His intention seemed to be to occupy the same "safe" patch that supported my feet. I jumped sideways. Finally, by leaps and stops, we reached dry ground.

The other people, mounted on bog-wise horses, watched our perilous crossing. Finally on safe ground, I asked the cowboy leading the expedition how his horses managed to stay on top of the fragile plant mat. He replied, "They walk lightly, like on tiptoes."

At the bottom of the next hill, faced with another wetland, I cued Sham for collected walk, the light-walking we'd practiced for dressage. That horse trusted me and I trusted him. As if he knew there was a new plan, he stepped onto the bog path like he was stepping onto eggshells and after that crossed every stretch of marsh like an old pro—or a Zen master, who had learned the art of not sinking.

E A R T H • When we moved in, the house was surrounded by gardens, more than an acre of lawn, and a fragment of hayfield. Mountain ash trees, honeysuckle shrubs, and a lilac hugged the house. A Siberian crabapple grew a short distance away beside a fence with white planks nailed in a pattern of Xs. The fence was decorative, striking a line across the lawn and enclosing nothing.

Fences ought to be definitive—creating an enclosure. Or marking a property line—separating neighbors' lots. The fanciful X-patterned fence accomplished neither, although looking out the front window during our first winter there, the fence delineated a narrow yard beside the house from an expanse of snowy lawn that merged with an equally snowy field. In winter, the landscape appeared seamless, and timeless, and yet Mrs. Webb's comment that they had lived there when it was the best stuck in my mind like a harbinger of change.

Tiger lilies, columbines, and delphinium had been planted next to the house during some undeterminable time before we arrived. Each summer, masses of lilies—orange-hued and stippled with black, four to a stalk and as large as my hand— flourished beneath the front windows, as did clumps of delphiniums. By midsummer, the delphiniums stretched upward into head-high spikes laced with pale blue florets. Near the edge of the lawn, columbines paraded long-spurred blooms in pastel shades of lavender, pink, yellow, and creamy white. I appreciated the columbines' capacity to survive. With deep roots, the plants tolerated drought and freezing. Any spent bloom that went untrimmed developed a prodigious quantity of seeds. Much like the lilac.

Despite their showiness, these flowers could not upstage the lilac, what with its substantial architecture and insistent fragrance. The aged lilac hugged the house with branches up to the eaves. In early June, its leaves burgeoned. Panicles of miniscule buds opened until the tree-sized shrub resembled a lavender cloud with a syrupy aroma that engulfed the yard.

T I M E • The lilac did not emerge independently from the boreal earth. It was deliberately planted. I am certain of that even though I am speculating because, unlike my grand-mother's garden, this garden had no provenance and no doc-umentation. No catalog of index cards recorded the history of each plant, but I noticed which plants were here when we arrived and I knew which we planted.

In the garden, two kinds of time exist: seasons and years. Surely each season is unique, but after so many, my memories entwine like a thicket. When planting a tree, I imagine how large it will grow in a decade, or two. I wait, hoping that noth-ing happens to the transplanted tree, that it survives without injuries or diseases or attacks by predators—insects, rodents, rabbits. Or moose. Watching a tree grow over twenty-plus years is a different experience than marveling at the height and girth of a mature tree encountered in an arboretum or forest. A well-established tree chronicles conditions over many decades (or even centuries) of warmth, sunlight, and precipitation.

In 1983 a tall spruce with spreading branches cast a long shadow between the garden and house. If we had measured the tree's height and breadth, twenty years later we would have realized it had grown larger. Without data points to gauge growth, that spruce always looked the same to me, as if I had lost my ability to recognize the passage of time.

Trees have a knack for overshadowing the span of a human life. When I was a child, a deodara cedar in my grandparents' yard stretched to the sky. I asked my mom, and she said it was already a large tree when she was a girl.

C A B I N • I suspect the old lilac at the corner of the house was planted by colonist Clystia LaRose. Maybe, soon after moving into Cabin 135, Clystia visited a friend with a more established yard. The two women might have talked about where they'd come from, the families they left behind, the houses where they grew up. Circling the topic of what they missed the most, her friend insisted that she missed roses the most. Clystia replied, "What I'd do to get a lilac that blooms sweetly every spring." Perhaps, a few weeks later, someone dropped off a package at Cabin 135. Inside, was a slender sprout, woody and rooted, wrapped in damp newspaper and tin foil, with a note, "A lilac for your new garden."

Clystia dug a small hole beside the house, unwrapped the sprout, and knelt, spreading the slim roots. She gently filled the hole with soil and wrapped a scrap of chicken wire around the seedling to protect it from hungry moose or care-less footsteps. When the ground dried, she poured water on the little lilac, leftover dishwater or water she hauled from the well her husband and some other men dug by hand.

By the time we arrived, the lilac didn't need much watering. It survived on rainfall that flowed off the eaves.

W A T E R • When Chuck and I walked through the house and around the yard with Mrs. Webb, she did not mention a hand-dug well. In fact, I don't think she knew there had been one. Our first hint of the well was when Chuck was mowing the lawn one summer, and he noticed an unusual depression. The turf hadn't torn, but between the large spruce and the Siberian crabapple, a patch of lawn drooped.

Many years later I asked Chuck if he remembered when the sinkhole appeared.

"I have a photo in a box somewhere," he said. "The slump happened at least fifteen years before we got our first digital camera."

Good luck finding that in our boxes of photos printed from film.

"Any other ideas?" I wondered.

"David Kincaid was still living at the corner of Fishhook when I called to ask him if he would dig a hole with his backhoe so we could bury the horse."

I winced at the memory of the young horse that had broken his leg and had to be put down. That was 1986, but I think the sinkhole showed up a year after that.

As if reframing my question, I again stated the sequence of events. "Toward the end of the 1980s, you were mowing the lawn, and from the riding mower you noticed that the lawn had settled—not a big area but like the impression on a soft chair after someone gets up. What did you do?"

"I got off the mower and stomped on the sunken spot and it broke through a bit. I got a shovel and dug around. There seemed to be a sinkhole so I laid a piece of plywood over it."

Disorganized imagery percolated my mind.

"Yes. I remember the plywood was weighted down with a tire."

Chuck reminisced, "I called Kincaid and eventually he drove over on his backhoe. He dug into the lawn and opened up a hole."

"How deep was it?"

"Hard to tell, but deep, and the hole was square with boards shoring up the inside. Just how a hand-dug well would have been."

I didn't recollect all these details, but I remembered a backhoe digging the lawn and a hole being filled.

"Where did Kincaid get the fill dirt?"

"From the old silage pit," Chuck said.

(We didn't really know whether the trench carved into the hill beside the driveway was ever used by a farmer to ferment grass into silage for cattle feed. The pit was probably the source of soil and rocks used to level the land around the house and I had transposed—onto this landscape—memories of farms where I grew up.)

"So Kincaid scooped dirt from the slope beside the driveway and dumped that into the hand-dug well?"

"Yes," Chuck said. "There's a photo somewhere of a scruffy garden we planted after the hole was filled."

T I M E • One of the first tasks would have been to dig a well. The 1935 photo of Cabin 135 shows the front door in the center of the south wall. The hand-dug well would have been about twenty feet from the door, an interesting choice since a well on top of a hill would likely have been deeper than one dug at a lower elevation where, presumably, the aquifer was nearer the surface. A deeper well would have needed more timber shoring up the sides to prevent cave-ins. Trade-offs would have been considered and choices made. A well at the bottom of the hill likely would have required less digging, but every gallon of water would have had to be lugged farther—uphill—to the house, until electrification came and a pump was installed.

I imagine Clystia, pleased with that first well and glad to have it finished with no one injured. She smiled as she stepped out the door on the south side of the cabin, only a dozen steps from the well. After hauling up a bucket of water and before returning to her many tasks, she poured some onto the newly planted lilac.

E A R T H • Heralding spring, the first bumblebee buzzes single-mindedly toward the bergenia I planted in front of the house. An ankle-high plant with rubbery leaves, bergenia barely changes except in early spring when hot-pink blooms jut from tubular stems. Alighting, the bee lumbers, as if punch-drunk, between the flagrant blossoms. Juncos and robins drop from skyways—joyously trilling and yodeling—while the Knik wind casts a silty pall across the face of Pioneer Peak.

Bergenia is often the first bloom in the garden. As transformation to summertime continues, Siberian irises split pale green wrappers, first dark purple like elfin robes, neatly pleated, then flaring into a trio of wide petals striped cream and burgundy like fantastical birds tethered by green cords. The Himalayan poppy, stems clad with wiry hairs, bears frail flowers as gently blue as the morning sky. I once started Himalayan poppies from seed and only learned later that first-year buds must be heartlessly plucked if the plant is ever to bloom again. Indeed, my seed-grown poppies only bloomed once.

Gardening proceeds as tyranny beneath an umbrella of optimism. Four summer months bustling with daylight-inspired mania offset by eight winter months spent planning and dreaming. This seasonal way of life seemed normal to me. Or normal enough. The Pacific Northwest, where I grew up, was far enough north that seasons were obvious: winters cold and snowy. Summers stiflingly hot.

I suspect if I had spent my youth far to the south where not much changed from summer to winter, I would have thought the seasonal swings in Alaska extreme rather than just an edgier version of normal.

The word *gardening* is code for shovels and soil, clippers and trimmings, moths and bees, flowers unfurling, seeds dropping. Chickadees pecking insects from crevices in bark. The invisibility of pollen. A flock of butterflies flitting among lilac blooms. Routine tasks remembered and retackled each summer, year after year.

Garden work falls into a dichotomy of nurturing and eradicating. In an untended garden, chaos thrives. Vetch entwines lilies and irises, claiming surface and subsurface, light and dark, bane as in the Old English—*slayer* or *destroyer*. Thin-stemmed and rambling, vetch overwhelms the columbines and invades the densely branched cotoneaster hedge.

I sit on the ground surrounded by graceful pink and white columbines. Gently, I unwrap vetch clutching a columbine. Like a blind surgeon, I prod the earth with my fingers searching for rootlets, trying not to break any because even a fragment may regrow.

C A B I N • There's a difference between living in a place and a quick walk-through. On our tour with Mrs. Webb, much went unnoticed, or we quickly forgot as if selective amnesia was necessary for us to decide to make an offer.

We had lived in the house for only a few months when I freed the living room from a carpet, green as pine needles, that spread wall to wall with a path worn from front door to kitchen. Wielding crowbar and hammer, I ripped it off tack-strips and tossed the chunks out the door, onto the driveway. Underneath the carpet was straight-grained wood. Chuck would be pleased, I thought, when he got home from his fishing trip.

While prying, yanking, and slicing carpet, I imagined the floor as elegantly gleaming, like my grandmother's floors had been, that is, until I reached the corner where, in Mrs. Webb's story, stairs had descended into the living room. In that corner, the carpet hid a constellation of steel disks—big nails or bridge spikes. Scars dimpled the honey-hued wood, chronicling every missed hammer stroke. Why? Were the spikes an artifact of an argument over a creaky floorboard? Was it a ripple of consequences related to switching the stairway to the back hallway? Did someone just grab a hammer and a handful of large nails, muttering "I'll fix that squeak once and for all."

The floor was marred, but I was certain we would figure out a solution.

"What the heck?" Chuck asked when he got home and saw the bulging sacks and piles of carpet outside and bare floor inside.

"I tore out the carpet. The floor isn't in too bad of shape—except for spikes in the corner."

"Hmm," Chuck said, skeptically. "Do you have a plan?"

"Refinish the floor? Just not carpet." I didn't consider at the

time that we might end up installing an entirely new floor—
and begin our own reenvisioning of the house.

F O R E S T • When the homesteaders arrived in the early
twentieth century, the terrain was mostly forested—spruce,
birch, cottonwood, scrubby willows, and alders—like now,
more or less. Where the forest was undisturbed, spruce grew
tall and straight and slimmer than I expected. From a distance,
birch formed a leafy tent-top canopy punctured here and
there by spires of black spruce.

After a beetle attack in the 1990s, dead spruce lingered,
needles gradually browning. Eventually, the desiccated needles fell. For several years after that, woodpeckers and nut-
hatches marched up and down the snags drumming the bark,
raining fragments to the ground.

Eventually, the dead trees fell. Not all at once, but now
and then.

Walking through the woods, I noticed a snag had tipped,
but its fall was arrested by the spreading branches of a birch.
Other spruce had smashed to the ground, roots ripped from
the earth, upturned and clawing at the sky.

No one seemed to remember such a massive insect decimation of these forests. Maybe the north had once offered protection against bark beetles—like an inoculation of latitude.

The forest beside the house had survived a century of settlement. The homesteader, Charles Larson, did not clear that
patch, perhaps because the terrain was hillier than the rest of
his homestead. The LaRoses and subsequent owners must have
had the same opinion, deciding to farm gentler land to the south,
only venturing into the woods to cut firewood or bury trash.

The trees had grown large so I surmised that the soil was similar to the nearby hayfields. I liked the forest because it bristled with wildflowers and highbush cranberries. Wild red currants stretched, seeking leaf-filtered light.

C A B I N • The constellation of bridge spikes embedded in a corner of the living room floor ruined the appearance of the straight-grained wood that looked to be fir, a tree that does not grow in Alaska. I hammered the large nail heads, adding my efforts to that of others who attempted to sink them deeper into the floor. They didn't budge. Still trying to figure out how to camouflage the spikes, I took an electric sander to that patch of floor, further gouging the wood. Sparks shot out as the fast-spinning sandpaper struck metal. Realizing the danger of a stray spark igniting the floor and cabin, I stopped the sander and pulled the plug.

I had the notion that the house could be modernized, but we had a limited budget, much like the penny-pinching circumstances that I suspect previous owners faced. Nevertheless, before we came, a foundation and basement were installed and siding had been fastened onto the logs—twice.

The first layer of siding, shiplap boards, certainly would have changed the character of the house. The bulky garage had not yet been added and the new siding, painted white, gave the cabin the appearance of a cottage—small and inviting with a large lilac hugging one corner. Perhaps the siding was added soon after the basement was installed. The residents moving out while the cabin was jacked up and the digging underway, followed by cement work. With a basement and siding, the cabin astonished everyone, as if someone had switched houses when no one was looking. Yet like the effect of cosmetic surgery, the inside hadn't changed. Breezes still whirled through the cracks between logs. Condensation filmed the single-paned windows with moisture dripping and pooling onto the sills.

We did not re-carpet the living room. Instead, we installed another floor, this time oak, on top of the original floor.

Now I think adding one floor on top of another was an odd solution, and I would be inclined to ignore the spikes. At that time, though, my views had not developed beyond memories of my grandparents' house. I had adopted my grandmother's impossible ideal of a flawless home.

The oak was not from Alaska. In fact, oak trees don't grow in Alaska. The flooring was shipped across the North Pacific from the Lower 48 just as the second layer of siding—grooved cedar shingles—had been. You also won't encounter cedar forests in southcentral Alaska because winters are too severe, at least that's the environment and history that we know.

A few weeks later, Chuck and I bought do-it-yourself flooring. Each box contained oak in a jumble of lengths and hues as if from many trees. The strips were touted as easy to install.

We rented a nail-setting contraption designed to be positioned at the tongue-edge of a board. With a nail inserted into a collar, you swung a sledgehammer at the plunger-head. Done with good aim and sufficient force, the nail would be driven through the tongue of the board, and the next board could be slid into place, unimpeded by a protruding nailhead. (These days you would use a compressor and some sort of nail gun to fasten the floor, or lay a "floating" floor with no nails at all.)

Neither Chuck or I could get the mechanical apparatus to work reliably. Finally, we gave up and predrilled each nail hole. When we finally finished, solid oak covered the original cabin floor, and we forgot about the spikes embedded in the corner.

T I M E • My stories are about the future as well as the past. Consider the past as event and evidence based. Spikes in the floor caused adaptations based on notions I'd acquired beforehand. The future has a different timbre. More tentative, I think, the possibilities not yet secured.

E A R T H • The garden intrigues me. Summer had not quite arrived when I yanked out an overgrown and rambling flower called snow-in-summer and unwove a thatch of bulging iris rhizomes, digging and chopping, and replanting more than before. I clipped broken branches, transplanted a mountain ash seedling, and tied a spindly honeysuckle to a stake, hoping that would help it stand up to the weight of snow.

Gardening, I'm empress and laborer, nanny and tutor. I attempt to direct growth but also find much that's out of control. Is this what I learned from my grandmother? The physical and mental effort required to eradicate and excise but also the patience and imagination to experiment. Each summer I anticipate how the garden's story will unfold, but a new twist always surprises me.

The garden speaks shape, color, sound—motion. And time. The garden is macro and micro. Ideas and plans. The garden is only semi-tamed. This garden appeals to my senses. I breathe scents of flowers. Birds trill. I hear a beguiling whisper of wings.

The trees have leafed by the time I'm on my knees beneath the old lilac, raking dried leaves with my fingers and lifting the detritus into a bucket. The earth leaches dampness through the fabric of my jeans. Prodding for quackgrass roots, I turn up a bird wing and a miniscule skull, bleached white, the beak bone curved like a fingernail. Above me, window glass mirrors clouds and shrubs, conjuring a phantom landscape deadly to birds.

Beside me, lilac branches with the girth of small trees protrude from a gnarled root-knob like a botanical being in a Tolkien landscapes. Beneath the shrub, a carpet of lilac sprouts has even invaded pernicious clots of clover. I blame myself for the seedlings because I neglected to clip the lilac's faded blooms the previous summer. Seeds matured and dropped. Thousands of them.

Hoeing would have offered a quicker way to excise the sprouts, but I felt empathy, for once, for the old lilac's progeny. Digging with a trowel, I lifted out several clumps and packed the seedlings into buckets. After that, and feeling somewhat absolved, I callously yanked the remaining lilac shoots, tossing them along with hunks of clover into the wheelbarrow. Later, I dumped the wheelbarrow at the edge of the woods and carefully placed two little tubs of lilacs on the shady north side of the garage. I intended to transplant the sprouts, perhaps along the edge of the lawn where, in a dozen years, they would form a fragrant hedge.

More than a mere shrub, the lilac has a knack for nudging memories. When I was growing up, every place my family lived had a lilac bush, usually large and overgrown, beside the house. When I was six or seven, Mom showed us how to make May Day baskets by folding and taping heavy paper into little boxes. My sisters and I filled the handmade boxes with fresh lilac blooms and hung them on neighbors' doorknobs.

Seattle has a mild climate, and my memory of lilacs blooming on the first of May strikes me as reasonable. A May Day basket stuffed with lilacs from my Alaska garden would be impossible because the lilac doesn't bloom until June.

A few weeks later, I was pulling vetch that had threaded the columbines in a plot reclaimed from the driveway by the front door. A pickup truck turned off the road and slowly motored toward our house. Expecting the occupants were evange-lists or selling something, I considered various greetings in the vein of "I'm not interested." The truck parked and a mid-dle-aged man climbed unhurriedly out of the cab. He stared at me doubtfully. "My mother is looking for trees and saw your bush," he said.

The trees Chuck and I had planted across the lawn had not yet grown large enough to block the view of our yard. The large lilac with its cloud of lavender blooms was perfectly visible from the road.

An old woman, wearing a cotton dress and head scarf, clambered out of the passenger seat and walked slowly toward me. Her pale eyes met mine and she spoke delib-erately, as if each word was a great effort or of the utmost importance. "Bush," she said and, after a pause, "flower." She swept her hands expansively as if holding a bouquet. Inhaling audibly, she smiled at the notion of a delightful fragrance. I smiled back at her, cradling my own invisible bouquet and breathing the aromatic scent of lilacs.

She beamed, her smile becoming a grin, and blurted, "Home. Like home."

M I G R A T I O N • I shared something fundamental with this woman, something as crucial to identity as memories and stories, and more deep-seated than nostalgia—the longing for a familiar landscape of food, flowers, and trees. I hadn't emi-grated across an ocean to a place where the language, and even the alphabet, was different. I had only migrated from the Pacific Northwest, but that move encompassed a shift, from desert steppe to subarctic.

Uprooted from another life, the old woman grasped at memories like birds to hold and give to her children. Whatever actual circumstances led her to my doorstep, she yearned for lilacs—a shrub that attracts hummingbirds and butterflies, wafts perfume through open windows, and freshens memories.

E A R T H • I motioned toward the gnarled shrub with pale lavender blooms, "Lilac."

"Lilac," she repeated, her eyes crinkling.

The man smiled but didn't say anything.

I walked around the garage and brought back a tub of lilac sprouts.

"Here, take these," I said. "They'll grow. Like home."

"Thank you," she said, smiling even more, "Like home," she said, with utmost satisfaction.

"Thank you," the man repeated.

The two of them climbed into the pickup and drove slowly away.

M I G R A T I O N • I did not see this pair again, and I only surmise that they migrated to Alaska after the Chernobyl nuclear disaster. Even three decades later I find this story oddly unsettling, and I puzzle over the confluence of events that brought the older woman and somewhat younger man to my house where I handed them a bucket of lilac sprouts—which made the old woman very happy. The questions raised are multiple and profound—and may have no answers—except to recognize that in dire situations we adapt, or we migrate and attempt to adapt.

❧

CABIN • The house did not come with an owner's manual, although in the basement cardboard labels dangling from copper pipes indicated which direction to turn the valves in order to switch from the oil furnace to the coal furnace, or vice versa. The oil furnace was situated in the basement. The garage housed the coal-burning furnace. Both furnaces heated and pumped water through a system of baseboard radiators.

The steep-pitched cabin roof transitioned to a nearly flat roof over the garage. Inside the garage the log house wall had been coated with urethane, a sprayed-on chemical intended for insulation. The original insulation, laid along each log as the walls were being erected, would have been oakum—jute-like fibers embedded with a tarry substance—or maybe moss. The urethane hid the logs and any hint of oakum or moss. A layer of gray paint as dingy as river silt did not improve the wall's lumpy appearance.

When we moved in, urethane also blanketed the roof. An uncommon roofing material, the inch-thick foam was painted with a silvery compound that was supposed to be waterproof. The shiny surface attracted magpies that pecked holes in the roofing, exposing crisp and porous foam underneath.

We hired a roofing contractor who replaced the bird-pecked roofing with composite shingles on the steep cabin roof and hot-mopped tar onto the garage roof. The contractors also added six inches of insulation to the cabin roof and installed a layer of plywood over the garage roof boards "to increase stability," he said. At the time, we did not notice any-thing structurally amiss in the garage.

E A R T H • Someone else created the raspberry patch, but that time of planting is long forgotten. It's as if this is the right place for raspberries but tension exists between our desires and nature. Raspberries don't care about my efforts and puny tools, and I'm not the first caretaker who has tried to beat back meadow and forest.

In the spring, I raked dried leaves and vaguely sensed blisters blooming inside the gloves on my winter-soft palms. My movements acquired a tempo like Gertrude Stein's writ-ing. With rhythm and a bit of ridiculosity, she starts with "A Light in the Moon" and ends with a "magnificent asparagus, and also a fountain," as if the connection is perfectly obvi-ous. As if the sound and rhythm of language is enough to create meaning.

What I'm after is taste, and quantity. Even from one end of the raspberry patch to the other, a distance of only fifty feet, the berries differ. The canes at the northern end are weaker and the raspberries smaller and more astringent than nearer the house, nearer the slope where the log crib version of a septic tank was buried.

At the north end of the raspberries, the shovel sliced mud and loosened grass, but the next time I stomped it, the blade clunked against ice—not permafrost but a remnant of winter.

Frozen earth blocks drainage of meltwater, and each spring a pool forms in the adjacent hayfield. The shallow pond lingers long enough to attract a few migrating ducks and geese. As the ground thaws, the water percolates downward and the pond vanishes.

Weeding raspberries is triage, not surgery. Unlike currants or strawberries, raspberries appear on two-year-old canes. During their first year, canes grow tall and willowy, spawning a jungle of leaves that hide stickery stems. Two-year-old raspberry canes are branched and easily break, cracking like dry sticks—but they have berries. Canes older than two years are faded bones, speckled with orange dots that might be lichen or fungus, in any event aiding decomposition. Canes supported by their younger sisters, like siblings, emerge from the same roots.

T I M E • During my later teen years, I pruned trees in my parents' orchard, walking between rows, stepping over chopped-off branches half buried in snow, deciding which limbs to cut. I tried to envision a scaffolding of branches suited to producing fruit, like a sculptor chipping off unnecessary stone to create form. With misty breath, cold feet, and a degree of ennui, I hacked at a loosely woven basket holding the sky. Time crept. Day by day. Week by week. Bound by a universe of branches, weather, and tools—loppers, clippers, a pruning saw, and sharpening stone. By March the sun had climbed higher and fruit buds swelled with possibilities. Pruning trees in my parents' orchard was a mercenary endeavor. At the time, I didn't realize that I was beginning to develop my relationship with plants.

E A R T H • By midsummer, the raspberry patch is a lush jungle that proves the ineffectiveness of my weeding. In August, when the berries ripen, I wear rain pants and rubber boots and shove through drenched tangles of bluebells, wild geraniums, cow parsnip, wild celery, and quackgrass. Vetch entwines raspberry canes as vexingly but less painfully than stinging nettles.

I try to avoid touching the nettles while fishing among leaves for a plump raspberry, one so ripe that the lightest touch will send it plummeting. Like cherries or apricots, raspberries foster a craving rewarded by memories. Even one berry, segmented into minute pouches of flesh purpled by sugar and sun, plucked and popped onto the tongue, riffles recollections.

I brushed the crustacean back of a wasp, immobile yet desiccating a sugary berry, one Lilliputian lobe at a time. I yanked my hand away without getting stung. Again, I pushed aside leaves. Spying another purple berry that bulged like an overinflated balloon, I plucked it. In my mouth, the flavors lingered, ferrying me back to my youth and my grandfather's garden. "Look under the leaves," he'd say, "that's where you'll find the ripest berries."

❦

T I M E • In September 1979, Chuck and I packed our belongings—all except for a few boxes of books that we mailed—into an aged Camaro. We drove north from Washington and west across British Columbia. After several days, we reached Prince Rupert, British Columbia, where we planned to board a ferry bound for Haines, Alaska. The next morning, at the ferry dock, we learned the ferry was cancelled and the next sailing wouldn't be for two or three more days.

Alaska seemed very far away. Chuck assured me that we would gain no advantage by backtracking to the ALCAN Highway and driving to Alaska. I didn't have a sense of the time it would take to journey across 15 degrees of latitude. Before that, I had flown to Alaska once. By plane from Seattle, it was a quick flight, barely over three hours.

While we waited for the ferry, time stalled. We tried to avoid driving around the town because uneven pavement along the highway had knocked the muffler off, and the car roared obnoxiously.

"How long will it take the ferry to sail from Prince Rupert to Haines?" I asked.

"Most of three days," Chuck replied.

Eventually another ferry docked at Prince Rupert, and several days later, in the afternoon, we disembarked at Haines. After passing through Canadian Customs, we drove north toward Haines Junction where we planned to get a motel room for the night. Driving into Haines Junction at twilight, we encountered the effect of hunting season—the motels were fully occupied.

"We might have to drive all night," Chuck said, steering the car west toward Alaska. "Hopefully, we'll find a roadhouse that still has rooms available. Otherwise, Tok is another three hundred miles."

"Tok is the next town?" I asked.

"Yes. It's in Alaska. Maybe there are rooms at Beaver Creek, at the border. I wonder if the border crossing is open at night," Chuck mused.

"I hope we find a place," I said. "It's going to be cold." We'd seen new snow on the mountains, and the air held the crisp smell of autumn—or of impending winter, considering how far north we were, in the Yukon Territory.

As we rounded the southern tip of Kluane Lake, I peered through the car window at darkness, barely discerning the dim form of a person huddled over a tripod near the lakeshore. Chuck drove, focusing on the narrow headlight beam.

Gradually, the sky blossomed from starry black to a canvas of oscillating rainbows.

"Chuck, is that the aurora?" I asked, knowing it had to be but not a sight I had ever seen. The dark glassiness of the vast lake reflected shimmering northern lights, silently but as audaciously as George Gershwin's jazz overture "Rhapsody in Blue."

Chuck knew the aurora from growing up in Alaska, but he was also surprised by the spectacle over Kluane Lake. Exhausted from traveling, we stopped at every roadhouse and inquired about a room. Finally, at one establishment a single vacant room remained. Shivering in the freezing night air, we hurried inside the tiny tourist cabin. A small heater and bed piled with blankets provided refuge from the nighttime highway.

"Do you think the car will start in the morning?" I asked sleepily.

"I hope so," Chuck replied. "I don't think the temperature will drop much below zero."

The next morning, the car engine cranked reluctantly but then started. For the last eight hundred miles, we journeyed along a roller-coaster and potholed highway that meandered between snowcapped peaks and forested hills. Leaves still clung to aspen and birch gleamed startlingly gold.

C A B I N • During our initial walk-through, Mrs. Webb mentioned a time when the place froze. "We had rented the house," she said. "No one was home and wind burst the door open." She paused for effect, giving my imagination time to conjure deep-freeze temperatures and lots of ice. "The pipes froze," she continued.

This story was a little gift bestowed by the owner even though she couldn't be sure that we were the ones who would buy the house. The undercurrent of this caution seemed as important to me as the actual story. Much later, I suspected that she was urging us to take care with the place, that it could be tricky.

Each winter, when the frigid Matanuska wind starts its incessant blustery jiggling, Mrs. Webb's story comes to mind. Perhaps, that was a day the door didn't latch tightly and the entryway footings had canted. Wind shook and shimmied the door frame, and even the whole boxy entryway, until the latch slipped the tiniest bit. Cheerily as a butler, another gust swung the door wide, inviting all the icy blasts inside.

How long does it take a house to freeze? For the heating system to quit? For water to crystallize and pipes break? For well water to gush out of shattered pipes and carouse down the walls and across the floor? I imagined that by the time the renters returned, the situation was out of hand with ice everywhere, and a sad bleakness.

My mind wanders to the ice palace scene in *Doctor Zhivago*; I engage my willingness to believe that one time, in this house, water flowed from burst pipes, and froze, layer upon layer, until the structure was encased in ice and everything was ruined. Yet Chuck and I saw no sign of this damage.

When we moved into the house, my desire was for a comfortable and predictable home, but Mrs. Webb's cautionary tale fused with my concerns, and I worried about the unsettled front door. During summer, the door hung straight, but each winter, when the ground expanded or contracted—depending on soil moisture and freezing—the foundation underneath the entry heaved or settled. I imagined how easily the wind might jostle the door open. Whoever built the arctic entry neglected to dig below the frost line for the foundation. During fall freeze-up and spring breakup, the room bobbed like a vessel on a slow-motion swell.

I suspected the entryway was added in the 1950s or '60s, at about the same time dark paneling became a popular wall covering. The nearly flat roof over the entry merged with the garage roof, suggesting both were constructed at the same time.

Now I think that the small added-on room had adapted to a poor foundation. The walls didn't fall apart nor did the roof leak, but the recalcitrant door latch became an ongoing annoyance for me.

N I G H T • The first northern lights I saw in Alaska were disappointing—muted grayish streamers with no resemblance to the shimmering rainbows we saw above Kluane Lake in 1979. Twenty-two years later that changed. November 2001. Driving home from Anchorage Chuck watched the aurora develop. He parked and hurried into the house, saying, "Quick, come outside. There's a red aurora!"

Standing in the driveway, I slowly spun around. My neck craned back, I gazed up at a sky afire. Red streams glimmered and arched like Mardi Gras clouds or bridges to a fiery world or the afterglow of a war god's rampage. What a sight! Yet that night remains the only time I have seen a totally red aurora. The effect, though, was to change me into a night watcher. On clear and dark nights, I detoured past the front door, glancing wistfully out the only north-facing window, always hoping to see another fiery red aurora.

❧

TERRAIN • Large living room windows framed a lawn that merged with grassy terrain—a plot of hay we had fenced for a pasture plus the neighbor's large hayfield. To the south, beyond the fields and forests, Pioneer Peak dominated the horizon. East of the house, a gravel road and forest bordered our small field. Whenever I glanced out that window, my eyes roamed farther, toward Matanuska Peak, a two-faced summit—one side a vertiginous crag, the other a steep inclined plane. Lazy Mountain, smaller and more rounded, nestled in front of Matanuska Peak.

The expansive view didn't last. Chuck and I changed the landscape surrounding the house. Fencing was our first priority, but I was also worried about how the landscape would change when the neighboring farmer, Leonard Moffit, decided to subdivide his hayfield.

"We need to plant trees," I said out of the blue to Chuck one afternoon.

"Of course, but when they get big, they'll block the view," Chuck commented.

"Right. That's the point," I replied cheerfully. "By the time Leonard subdivides, our trees may be ten or twelve feet tall."

When Mrs. Webb said, "We lived here when it was the best," I wondered why a seller would say that. Maybe she really didn't want to move. Maybe she had recently noticed more houses being constructed and more traffic. Perhaps the area was becoming more suburban. Mrs. Webb's comment, along with what we saw of farms being subdivided and lots sold for housing, worried us.

We started by digging up a small spruce by the driveway and replanting it in the lawn east of the house. I hoped the tree would thrive and grow large enough to screen the house from the road. Transplanting trees—an activity I learned from my parents and grandparents—became a habit and, later, a compulsion. Chuck and I kept planting, stippling the lawn with crabapples, an Amur chokecherry, multiple Colorado spruce, white spruce, and lilacs. (We didn't care whether the trees were native to Alaska. We only cared that they thrived.)

A decade later, when the first transplanted spruce was densely branched and nearly six feet tall, Chuck suggested cutting it for a Christmas tree. "It will make mowing the lawn easier," he said. "One less tree to maneuver around."

I protested. The first spruce we plunked into a sea of lawn had grown large enough to provide some privacy. Instead of cutting the spruce for a Christmas tree, Chuck wound strands of colored lights through its branches, which added festiveness to the bland winter scene. After a couple more years, the tree had grown too tall to fit inside the house and the question of cutting it didn't come up again.

T I M E • Early in the 2000s, on a winter morning, I donned parka, hat, gloves, and boots and picked up my camera. Outside the front door, to avoid trudging through thigh-deep snow, I sidled along a gap of dry ground beneath the eaves where, the previous morning, a spruce hen had hunkered, filling her crop with sand. At the back of the cubic entry, I squeezed between a Chinese golden apple tree and the wall. Indoors, on the windowsill, a webcam perched, its cyclops-eye steadfastly peering over my shoulder. My knit hat bobbed in front of the webcam that recorded and uploaded a picture a few times each hour.

Few momentous events happen on the strip of yard within the webcam's view. At least that's what I thought. Except, with further consideration, I suspect that idea reflects my inattention to detail, or an impertinence toward time.

As if ground-truthing the webcam's observations, I raised my handheld camera and peered through the lens at blurriness. With gloved fingers, I spun the focus ring until the image resolved into a crystalline landscape. Beneath an eggshell sky, rays of sun exploded over the rim of mountains. In the yard, strands of lights leached red, yellow, and blue through the spruce's snow swaddled branches. Happy that we had not chopped that tree, I returned to the warm and fragrant house.

I still smile when I think of that morning, easing along bare earth beneath the eaves and intentionally photographing sunrise and lit-up tree. I could have taken the same picture from indoors, the house cozily infused with a cinnamon aroma of muffins baking while classical music played on the stereo. Bundling up and stepping outdoors offered sensations of crinkly cold and frosted eyelashes, and meditation on a frozen landscape—and not just an anonymous scene but the place where we lived with a yard blanketed in snow and rimed with ice. That morning, exiting the house for just a few minutes, allowed outdoor nuances to lodge among distinctive memories that I might revisit, mucking about to see if I find some noteworthy detail that I hadn't noticed before.

E A R T H • By February Chuck and I were strategizing ways to cheat winter. At first, experimentally, we studied charts listing the number of weeks between starting seeds and transplanting outdoors. After a few years of experience, we just watched the calendar.

In January Chuck set up sawhorses in the living room beside the picture windows and placed old closet doors on top as makeshift tables. On Super Bowl Sunday, Chuck planted Ailsa Craig onion seeds, and in early March, when the Iditarod began, he planted tomato seeds. Sun streamed through the windows and the aroma of moist earth seeped through the house. In a few weeks, the sawhorse tables were blanketed with onion spears and leafy vegetables even as the blustery Matanuska swirled snow off the eaves.

During April I planted broccoli, cauliflower, and cabbage seeds. We thinned and transplanted. When daytime temperatures finally hovered above freezing, each morning we lugged the flats of seedlings out to the greenhouse. At night, we hauled them back into the house so they wouldn't freeze.

Finally, during the first week of May, one of us patted lettuce and bean and cucumber seeds into trays of soil. We still had to wait a month to transplant. Freezing nights could occur even during the first week of June.

✣

C A B I N • The wooden deck west of the house had been painted the same grim gray as the urethane wall inside the garage. A birch grew through a cut-out square in the deck. The tree had been topped, giving it the bushy character of a tall shrub. Even without lofty height, the birch grew. Slowly, over years, its expanding girth and roots lifted and crumpled the deck. Besides that adverse effect, a section of decking had been installed against the ground and moisture seeped into the wood. Especially during summer, we noticed uneven footing as wood flaked off, and after a rain, deck boards squished underfoot like a drenched sponge. We pried up the worst boards and nailed in new planks, sometimes finishing the repair, even with new paint, in one afternoon.

We might have continued with annual piecemeal repairs but, after fifteen years of that, feral rabbits moved in under the deck.

"We should replace the whole deck," I commented after my shoes squished into a rotting board and a rabbit chewing grass looked up and skittishly scooted underneath the wooden platform.

From inside the greenhouse, where he was staking up a tomato plant, Chuck asked, "With what?"

"A stone patio would solve both the rot and the rabbit problem.

"That would be quite a summer project," Chuck replied.

Dismantling the deck was not a quick endeavor. We levered out the boards and hauled the rotten ones to the dump. We pulled bent nails and stacked the intact boards beside the barn. I eyed the birch tree that had warped the deck and, also, increasingly shaded the greenhouse.

"Let's take out the birch too," I said. "We can use an umbrella for shade."

Chuck cut down the birch with a chainsaw, then worked on digging out the stump. He shoveled around the roots. The pile of excavated earth grew larger, but the tree stayed staunchly rooted. Even after sawing the large roots, the stump remained bound to the earth. Eventually, Chuck telephoned his friend John Larson. They dug and chopped for an afternoon with the only outcome a larger pile of dirt and more exposed roots. After that, like a strange hobby, whenever he had time, Chuck dug and chopped at the stump.

Finally abandoning the hand labor, Chuck called a neighbor who showed up one afternoon on a backhoe. After positioning the digging machine and lowering the stabilizing feet, the driver jumped down from the high seat. He wrapped a chain around the stump and attached the other end to the machine's shovel. Climbing back onto the seat, he manipulated levers, lifting the shovel until the chain tightened.

Chuck and I stood back and watched, anticipating a battle between backhoe and tree roots, but one mechanical tug popped the stump out of the ground.

"Looks like you had it all loosened up," the neighbor laughed as he climbed down again and snugged the chain tighter around the stump. "Where would you like me to drop it?"

Chuck walked across the lawn to the edge of the woods where I'd been dumping weeds and branches. The stump would be out of view—and would decompose like any fallen tree. Maybe, in time, wild currants would take root there.

F O R E S T • Currants thrive according to some mysterious whim, perhaps where berries fall or a bird defecates gut-scarified seeds. Time is marked by volcanic ash, windblown silt, and each autumn, a thick falling of leaves from birch and alder, willow, highbush cranberry, roses, monkshood, fireweed, larkspur, cow parsnip, and tiny flowers—twinflower, dogwood, violets, and *Pyrola*, also called wintergreen, not because it is a culinary herb but because the leaves remain green all year.

Wild currants colonize moss-covered humps of toppled trees. Hunting for currants, I lift leafy branches, searching for clusters draped like tiny scarlet grapes. Sweat glues my shirt to my skin. Prickly rose thorns nick my arm, the marks blossoming like cat-scratch welts. Mosquitoes hum and whir—spots flitting across my narrowly focused vision.

Picking currants isn't picking flowers, it's whack mosquitoes that drop gangly legged on your arm. It's wipe sweat from your eyelids and listen to your own heart beating. Why pick currants at all? They are a pretty berry but seedy. Good for jelly and wine, and that's about it. But the attractiveness, I think, is that currants have been used for a very long time. Stripping away modern trappings, I imagine concocting currant wine or jelly. The ingredients are simple: berries and sugar.

GREENHOUSE • The greenhouse walls were constructed from old windows and the roof was corrugated fiberglass. When we moved in, the greenhouse was neatly painted and I didn't discern telltale signs of age or decrepitude. I didn't notice the recycled materials, cracked putty, or veil of moisture between the double-paned windows. Outside, at the far end of the greenhouse, Mrs. Webb had shown us a wedge of soil held in place by loose rocks. She said delphiniums would sprout there when the weather warmed up. Later, the leafy stalks and lithesome blooms hid the pile of stones that served as foundation for the end of the greenhouse perched at the crest of a hill.

Inside, hip-high planting beds flanked a narrow aisle. Mrs. Webb had explained that the earth-filled boxes created a heat sink that helped keep the greenhouse warm at night. She also pointed out a thermostat and copper pipes connected to an industrial-looking heater bolted above the door. When nights approached freezing, the thermostat would call for hot water from the coal furnace in the garage. The piped-in heat saved her young vegetables from freezing.

CABIN • I wondered about the circumstances that caused Mrs. Webb to double the heating systems. An oil furnace in the basement heated a mixture of water and glycol that was pumped in a loop through baseboard radiators. Every month or so during the winter, a truck delivered heating oil. Perhaps it was 1973 when Mrs. Webb became more concerned about reliably heating the house. That was the year that the Organization of Petroleum Exporting Countries

(OPEC) blocked oil shipments to the United States. The price of fuel skyrocketed, and shortages ensued. I speculate that, worried about a reliable supply of furnace oil, Mrs. Webb bought a coal-fired furnace and had it unloaded at the back of the garage. Mac McCartney, a local plumber, hooked the secondhand furnace into the existing heating system, creating a dual system that, by turning certain valves, you could switch back and forth between the oil and coal furnaces.

T I M E • How was Cabin 135 heated in earlier times? Before there was a basement, garage, and multiple furnaces, surely there was a freestanding stove fueled by wood. Or coal. During World War I, in order to acquire coal to power battleships, the U.S. Navy helped construct a rail line from the deepwater port of Seward to Chickaloon, a place with coal deposits upriver toward the Matanuska Glacier. By 1918 trains were hauling coal along the route that passed through land that would later become Palmer.

C A B I N • When we moved in, the coal furnace and a long narrow coal bin occupied the back of the garage. At the front, two car doors had horizontal panels with an upper section of glass, all hooked together with hinges, springs, and pulleys so that when you yanked a handle, the door heaved upward, clattering along steel tracks. Wind rattled the doors and swept through the cracks, shifting coal dust along with a perpetuity of glacial silt. Having a backup furnace that burned coal must have seemed a good idea during the oil crisis of the early 1970s.

In the basement, Chuck and I puzzled over pipes and cryptically labeled valves attached to the ceiling.

Chuck spun a tag, voicing the neatly printed word: *Coal.*

I read another label, *Oil.*

Repetition of the words *coal* and *oil* confirmed two heating methods that seemed to be mutually exclusive. They both existed but wouldn't be operating at the same time. So it was one or the other. Both fuels burned, and both originated from ancient peat. When combusted, both emitted carbon into the atmosphere, but in the early 1980s that was not something we recognized or thought about.

For us, coal proved to be the messier fuel.

"Which direction should I turn this valve? Clockwise or counterclockwise?" I wondered.

"The plan for connecting the furnaces must have been in Mac McCartney's head," Chuck commented wryly.

As if we had gotten ourselves onto a spaceship without an operator's manual, we kept asking, "What does this (or that) valve do?" Neither of us knew the answers, and we moved from questioning to experimenting.

"A boilermaker's delight," I commented, sitting down on the bottom stair. "Why didn't they just install a woodstove?"

"That sounds simpler, but it wouldn't automatically have heated the house when no one was home," Chuck said as he experimentally twisted a valve that caused a swoosh of fluid inside a pipe.

During our first winter, we started the coal furnace. In the garage, a mechanical stoker churned powdery fuel into the firebox. Coal dust drifted upward. Once was enough. With the oil crisis resolved a decade earlier, burning coal seemed unnecessary, and unclean. In fact, that's what Mr. Webb said, "I don't know about coal. It's unsanitary."

The next summer, I gave away the coal furnace and sold the ton of coal in the back of the garage. The buyer came with a truck towing a trailer and carted it all away.

❧

F O R E S T • On the lookout for spring, I prowled the woods behind the house, intent on finding the orchids as soon as they erupted—like pale winter legs—through dry leaves.

Orchids were a new occupant. There hadn't been any in this scrap of forest until I spied some at a nursery. Like the inclination to rescue a puppy from a shelter, I bought a pot of fairy slippers (*calypso bulbosa*), hoping to find a suitable site for them in the forest north of the house. Birch and spruce had been growing and falling—and rotting—there for a very long time. Centuries, probably. Or millennia. I knew, though, that grass, wildflowers, and shrubs grew more densely than in predominantly spruce forests where colonies of orchids flourished along moss-covered humps of rotted logs.

I lay on my stomach between thorny rose stems and pale shoots of wild geraniums. Sun dappled the forest floor and my back. Mere inches tall, the orchids bristled with brushy yellow centers flanked by pink petals like the wings of a miniature tropical bird. An orange-butted bumblebee buzzed past my face and plunked onto a tiny orchid that swayed beneath her weight. The bee wallowed in pollen, then leaned, reaching and clambering onto another bloom where she lost her grip and slid down the stem. Instead of climbing, she whirred upward. Alighting on another orchid, the bumblebee, her legs already thickly coated with pollen, resumed her labor.

I had a front row seat, so to speak, lying on my belly in dry leaves, contemplating bumblebee and orchid. This view of nature was small and quiet and personal. The scene felt almost invisible, and it would have been for anyone who never ventures into the forest, or who doesn't look down. I was watching an enduring ritual—yet my actions were part of the story. I had purchased the orchid. I had planted it there. I hoped it would thrive. Although I wondered about the origin of that orchid. What rotting tree had it been lifted from for a mercenary endeavor? I hoped the orchid had been raised specifically for the plant nursery, but I had my doubts.

E A R T H • In the vegetable garden, seeds we planted sprouted profusely, as did weeds. I pulled rain pants over my jeans and slid my feet into rubber boots. Tiny seedlings crammed the rows as if every seed had sprouted. Some shoots threaded out of the same teensy hole. With beets and chard, what looks like a single seed is actually a clump of seeds, so it's easy to overplant. On my knees and elbows, my face close to the ground, I picked apart clusters, pulling the outliers first, then those closer in, working toward the center of each miniature clump until the remaining sprouts were spaced evenly and each beet root had room to grow.

Next, I crawled along a row of lettuce, the plants already developed into dense bundles several inches high. Tugging gently, I slid small lettuces out of the soil until each remaining plant could grow without competition. I saved the lettuce thinnings for a salad.

Mosquitoes landed on my arms. I brushed them away, and they seemed to evaporate, along with the nighttime dampness, when sunshine broke through the clouds.

Later in the afternoon, at the end of a row of carrots that I had been heartlessly thinning, black spots, smaller than pinheads, splattered across the back of my hand. Erratically shifting, the dots clung to my skin. I squinted at my hand. Insects. Not specks of dust. Flies or midges tiny enough to pass through a fine sieve. I was disconcerted by the bugs creeping across my skin, but I had disturbed them as I crawled along, thinning vegetables and pulling weeds. I brushed the insects off and nothing happened. No bites, stings, or twinges. No excuse to quit before finishing.

Close to earth, glued to the earth, fussing with food plants, the word *husbandry*, a decidedly male-sounding word, came to mind. As far back as the fourteenth century, *husbandry* meant "raising plants or animals for food." Like flicking through a stack of flash cards, the next word I thought of was *gardening*. As if the flipside of husbandry, *gardening* suggests a genderless enterprise with all sorts of possibilities.

T I M E • As a child, I watched my grandmother and grandfather pursue different gardening interests. Grandpa cared for vegetables in a plot near the edge of the bluff. He planted and watered, weeded and harvested.

Grandma's domain was the perennials. Scattered about the broad lawn (which Grandpa mowed) were islands of flowers and shrubbery, heather, rhododendrons, dogwood, roses, large and small trees, and a pond with lilies and flashy goldfish. Grandma planned the planting and transplanting; she mixed fertilizer to match the needs of each plant and monitored watering.

I'm fairly certain that memories of my grandparents' gardens propelled me toward an affinity toward plants, and yet there's more to my inclination than that. Gardens provide rewards, aesthetic and edible, but also frustrations and problems to be solved. A gardener acts more as guide than emperor. Her partner, nature, has a wild temperament never tamed, only provisionally cultivated.

T E R R A I N • Mrs. Webb proudly showed us the rock garden that she developed on a slope beside the driveway. She explained that by June the hillside would be festooned with strawberries, columbines, and lupines.

Creating that garden required labor. Clearing forest— chopping cottonwoods and birch, digging out roots, loosening soil. Large rocks were hauled in and positioned for a pleasing effect, and a stone path curved up the rise.

I neglected Mrs. Webb's rock garden. After several years, the strawberries had mostly disappeared. A few columbines survived in crevices between rocks, although the short purple-flowered lupines, nudged against the forest, were flourishing. From across the driveway, the rock garden appeared as a tangle of grasses, and wildflowers had colonized the slope—fireweed, cranesbill (a pale purple flower also called wild geranium), and bluebells. I didn't mind that Mrs. Webb's rock garden returned to wildness, although I imagine she would have been disappointed if she knew. I had not expected any benefits from that garden, unlike the raspberry patch where Chuck and I both periodically pulled weeds and hacked out tree sprouts.

E A R T H • In my sleep, I relive the sensation of digging sod (a motor memory transferred to my dreams?). I stomp the spade, bend, and tug another chunk of turf. After a garden is planted, more digging and weeding is needed just to keep the plot neat. My grandmother was good at designing and implementing (with Grandpa's assistance) interesting plantings. She also excelled at pruning, weeding, and fertilizing. I oscillate between a compulsion for getting the job done and neglecting the plants.

The backhoe that filled in the hand-dug well also destroyed the lawn. Rather than replanting lawn, I visualized a garden where wind ruffled exuberant blooms. Sweet-scented annuals and perennials would add a cheeriness never dispensed by blandly shorn grass.

Planting a new garden requires arranging and rearranging, adding and subtracting, plus doses of diligence, patience, and time. Without a thought to the work required, I pounded stakes to mark each corner of a rectangle between the seemingly ancient Siberian crabapple and the lofty white spruce. String tied between the stakes marked straight lines around the uneven perimeter left behind when the backhoe filled in the hand-dug well.

Spading rootbound turf, I stopped when the shovel became dull and honed the blade with a rasp. I had watched my grandfather sharpen blades—knives and even shovels—with a grindstone bolted to a workbench. He angled the steel against the whetstone and turned a crank. The stone spun and sparks flew.

My unmechanized rasping only flaked grime and rust off the shovel blade—no showers of sparks. Eventually, the shovel felt sharper and sliced more easily through the rootbound grass mat.

Several years later, delphiniums, scarlet-blooming lychnis, short-spurred red-and-yellow columbines, and two home-grown apple trees flourished in the plot where colonists dug the first well (that we know of). This spot felt like a time warp to me, a moment to ponder all the doing and undoing. The old well, a squarish pit revealed itself four decades after it was abandoned. Should anyone ever dig in that spot, the shoring-up planks might still be there, preserved for a while longer by the subarctic soil.

T I M E • When I was thirteen, my family moved to a small house on twenty acres. The first summer my parents planted twenty apple trees. A couple years later, they ordered seven thousand young pear trees.

Expanding their orchard, my parents learned to graft—a technique used to create new trees by merging varieties of desirable eating apples with strong and winter-hardy rootstocks. Like an apprentice, I also learned to wield a grafting knife (small, like a paring knife) to meticulously slice scion wood into a wedged tip that fit into a slit cleaved in the rootstock. The trick was to precisely align the cambium, that ultrathin region of growth cells, in both scion wood and rootstock and secure the graft by meticulously taping the joint. With luck, after several weeks, the wound would heal and the rootstock and treetop would fuse and thrive.

Years later, while visiting my parents, I asked my mom about the grafting tools. "Try the cupboard in the hall," she replied.

I rummaged through small cans of grafting paint with black goo congealed on the rims, rolls of dried and cracked masking tape, and orange surveyor tape until I found a box of knives. The budding knives had blades with curved tips for shallowly incising bark; the grafting knives had longer, straight blades. Mine was pushed farther back on the shelf, still inside its cardboard sleeve. Gingerly, I touched the blade with my thumb and found, after so many years, it was still sharp. Carefully, I slid the knife back into the cardboard and packed it in my suitcase.

E A R T H • Planting any tree occurs with a nod to patience and hope, but starting a tree from seed and, several years later, grafting on a top suggests extreme optimism and an unhurried affinity to time. One autumn, I plucked tiny crabapples, no bigger than the tip of my little finger, from the Siberian crab-apple near the house. I also collected golf-ball-sized crab-apples from a tree in Chuck's parents' yard, south of Palmer.

I planned to create my own trees by grafting hardy eating apples onto the seedling crabapples. It didn't occur to me to buy apple trees at a nursery because I assumed that most would have been grown outside Alaska—with rootstocks poorly suited to subarctic planting.

In our cramped kitchen, I chopped crabapples and picked seeds out of the crumbled fruit. Arranging the seeds on paper towels, I left them to dry.

Apple seeds require periods of freezing and thawing, which scarifies the hard seed coat and allows sprouting. An Alaska winter offers plenty of freezing and thawing.

On an autumn afternoon without rain, I scattered the crab-apple seeds in a plot beside the raspberries. After patting soil on top of the seeds, and with a feeling of accomplishment and optimism, I climbed the hill to the house.

Eight months later and with the snow melted, a few crab-apple sprouts poked up through the wet earth. Soon these were followed by fifty, a hundred, or more. Such luck! Nearly every seed had sprouted. I replanted some with more space in between. After that, I ignored the seedlings for a couple years, until they were waist-high with stems large enough to graft.

T I M E • Visiting and helping my mom prepare apples for sauce, I slid the peeler around each apple like it was a miniature planet to be examined, layer by layer. Strips of peel dangled over the sink. The apples had been stored in Mom's cold room for months, and the skin dried and puckered due to the low humidity of the desert steppe, where everything desiccates. Food left uncovered shrivels rather than molds. With apples it's a gradual process, crispness leaching into the air and crunchiness changing to sponginess in a slow course of mummification, yet the fruit remains tasty enough for applesauce.

I discarded fruit with an ashen hue, skins stretched too tightly over rotting flesh. I don't know what the difference was except perhaps the putrid apples suffered a freeze while the desiccated fruit had not.

Each apple that I peeled, Mom sliced in half, paring out the core and stem and blossom ends. She chopped the halves into eighths and dropped them into a water-and-lemon juice solution intended to prevent browning. With enough apple slices to fill the big kettle, we scooped them out of the lemon water and started the pot heating on the stove.

Simmering, apples waft a fruity aroma, and I recall my grandfather stirring a batch of applesauce on top of Mom's stove. He had driven a hundred miles, across the mountains, and after arriving, he peeled, cored, and sliced apples for a batch of sauce. The apples burbled, adding humidity to the kitchen and a warm fruit-sugar fragrance. Mom sterilized quart jars, and when the applesauce was ready, she canned it.

E A R T H • I wanted to coax apple trees to grow in my Alaska yard, and not just tiny crabapples but apples large enough to slice for pie or cook into applesauce. I wanted apples substantial enough to hold in my hand and munch. Looking back, I suspect homesickness as a subtle influence. Nostalgia, not even fully formed or thought out, provides powerful motivation and reminds me of the old woman whose memories of lilacs somehow brought her to my house—as if she mirrored my own intentions. I had not moved to another country, but remembering my parents enthusiastically planting orchards left me with a feeling perhaps even stronger than nostalgia—a craving for what I associated with my youth. (Years later, this sentiment strikes me as strange—but I can't discount it so I'll let it be.)

When the crabapple seedlings were large enough to graft, I collected scion wood from several varieties of apple trees in Chuck's parents' garden. For a couple afternoons, I whittled and sliced, painted and taped, connecting crabapple roots with apple scion that, I hoped, would eventually produce tasty apples of varieties that included Norland and Chinese Golden. Norland apples mature in late summer, a pale red color with a slightly elongated shape. Chinese Golden apples are round and yellowish and larger than a crabapple.

A month later, some grafted trees had sprouted healthy leaves, but other tops had shriveled. Perhaps the scion wood had prematurely dried out, or I had not accurately aligned the cambium layers, or the paint I applied to seal the union had gaps and the grafts dried out. Even weather might have been a factor.

For several years, I paid scant attention to the new apple trees. Summer rains made watering unnecessary. Once or twice each summer, Chuck rototilled between the rows to discourage weeds. When the trees loomed six feet tall and crowded each other, we traipsed around the yard, considering where to transplant them. Eventually, we moved three Norlands to a strip of lawn north of the vegetable garden and transplanted two into the flowerbed where the hand-dug well had been. One Chinese Golden tree ended up next to the house, planted in the niche between the back of the arctic entry and the east-facing picture window. I hoped the house would act as a heat sink and prove favorable for springtime growth, but during winter, the Matanuska blasted that wall, creating a harsh environment.

❧

C A B I N • More than once the front door's unpredictable latch, loosening hinges, or capricious threshold set me off on a course of tweaking, hoping that new hardware, longer screws, or a new threshold would prove a remedy. The trouble, I finally realized, was not the threshold but the whole doorway. Rubber weather stripping that hooked into grooves on top of the threshold had cracked, but the disintegration may have been hastened by the pressure of the door. I unscrewed and pried out the oak threshold and installed a lower profile metal threshold. Working in the doorway, I adjusted the new threshold by tiny degrees, testing the effect of each change by opening and closing the door, trying to find the position where the threshold fit snugly enough to block drafts but didn't impede the door opening and closing.

Despite my efforts, the door still fit too tightly. Chuck agreed that trimming a small amount off the bottom might help. We pulled the pins from the hinges and eased the heavy wood-and-glass door out of the frame, carrying it as gingerly as a tea set. With the door balanced across two sawhorses, I measured and marked a line along the bottom. Chuck revved the power saw and trimmed off a narrow strip. After we wrestled the door back onto the hinges, it swung too easily. I had not measured accurately enough. When closed, the door stayed shut and latched, but underneath, there was a gap.

My obsession with the front door arose from hearing Mrs. Webb's story of the house freezing because the wind blew the door open when no one was home. What I didn't consider were all the stories I didn't know that would have added to my worries—like poor electrical wiring, diminishing aquifers, and exploding stoves. Anticipation may be a helpful trait if you act to forestall problems, but whether due to lack of knowledge or imagination, some situations prove impossible to foresee.

C O L D • Living in Alaska, I grew accustomed to large fluctuations between summer and winter—of daylength, temperature, and precipitation. I acquired a suitable wardrobe with rain gear for summer and warm jackets and boots for winter. But clothing does not ensure readiness. At subzero temperatures both machines and animals require extra attention. Mechanical things break—batteries fail, tires deflate, metal fractures. Horses need water (not buckets of ice), more calories, and unless they have the thick coat of an Icelandic pony, a warm blanket.

In February 1989 a massive weather system eased out of Siberia across the Bering Sea and stalled above Alaska. Overnight the temperature plummeted to forty below zero. Weather forecasters, perhaps taking a cue from the practice of naming hurricanes, dubbed the mass of Arctic cold the Omega Block.

At first the extreme frigidity offered the novelty of one postcard-perfect day after another. Chimney smoke drifted upward in tight columns and sunshine glinted through hoar-rimed branches like kaleidoscope glitter. New snow sparkled across the pasture, but sublime scenery did not counter the bone-chilling cold. Every trek outdoors required planning. After several days of deep freeze, I felt as if I'd been consigned to the high Arctic, although I still didn't appreciate how quickly circumstances may go awry.

Twice a day, morning and evening, I bundled into long underwear, insulated coveralls, parka, hat, mittens, and felt-lined boots and wrapped a scarf around my face up to my eyes. Tromping along the snowy path to the barn, frost formed on my eyelashes. The bucket of warm water I carried pulled me off-kilter. I tried not to slosh the water on my clothing where it would quickly freeze.

The small barn, constructed from cottonwood planks and timbers, had two box stalls that opened onto a short aisle. At the end of the aisle a third, and smaller, stall contained a stack of hay. At the wide barn doorway, I set down the bucket and reached to pat Sham who, hearing me coming, had leaned over the chest-high door and nickered a burbly greeting. A loud snort and scrambling noise stopped me in mid-motion. "Tanya," I said and hurried toward the other stall. The mare slammed the Dutch door with her chest. Thrusting her head over the top of the door, she snorted and flicked her ears. White showed at the edge of her dark eyes. "Tanya," I repeated. The mare jerked back and spun frantically in a tight circle. Steam rose from her blanket and neck. I groaned.

Looking back at my experience with horses, easily half a life-time, I thought every horse that came into my life would be a "dream horse." One that would be a solid companion with a good attitude on trails and in arenas and never be frightening. Later, I realized that Sham really was a dream horse, "the best horse ever," I tell people now.

Tanya had the breeding and movement to progress as a dressage horse, and I assumed she would be okay on the trails. I was wrong about that. The previous owner hadn't mentioned the mare was terrified of moose. Or had her fear arisen after she arrived here, at my small barn surrounded by forest?

Snatching a halter and lead rope from a hook, I cautiously opened the door. Mustering calmness, I murmured, "Was it a moose? Moose can't get you." The mare eyed me warily as if I was a menacing stranger, not the one who cared for her every day. "Be still," I whispered, easing toward her. Her wet skin quivered at my touch, but with some unfathomable effort, she stood while I slid the halter over her head and buckled the strap. But agitation trumped stillness, and she jerked her head higher than I could reach and tensed like a racehorse boxed in a starting gate. Gripping the lead rope, I sidled out the stall door, the mare tramping at my heels. In the aisle, her hooves drummed the floor.

Better lighting illuminated the predicament. Tanya looked as if she had just run a hard race. Sweat soaked her blanket and steam rose from hair damply plastered to her neck.

The rule, going back centuries, is never put a hot horse back in the stable. Improbably, I had found this horse overheated inside her stall and at ultracold temperatures. I did not have a large heated space or a horse-sized hairdryer. A dry blanket would have to do.

"Tanya, hold still," I said, heeding her boogying hooves. Like a circus performer dodging cannonballs while juggling awkward objects, I unhooked the straps and pulled off the wet blanket. Another blanket and a horse-sized hood hung over the low wall by the hay. Keeping hold of the lead rope and an eye on her jigging hooves, I grabbed the dry blanket and managed to shove it across her back and hook the straps. With more coaxing, Tanya lowered her head, allowing me to add the wool-lined hood (a horse-sized combination of neck blanket and face mask with holes for eyes and ears) to her trappings.

Over the top of his stall door, Sham watched this rigmarole as if baffled.

Still gripping Tanya's lead rope, I tossed hay to Sham and glanced at his bucket, assuring myself that the little heater was functioning and he still had water from the previous night.

Tromping out of the barn, the mare fidgeted nervously beside me. My vague plan was to walk her and swap wet blankets for dry ones. I hoped that would be good enough to prevent her perishing from hypothermia.

After circling the parked car and wading through knee-deep snow, I stood in front of the living room window, shouting and waving. Beside me, the horse quivered underneath the blanket and hood, accoutrements that suggested a charger readied to haul a knight into battle—not a horse in danger of hypothermia.

Chuck noticed the commotion. He leaned out the front door and asked, "Moose?"

"I guess. Will you please set out a bucket of warm water? And another blanket? I have to walk her."

The sun had not yet cleared the eastern shoulder of Pioneer Peak when, holding the lead rope like a lifeline, I trudged along the driveway. The horse's agitation expressed itself as constant motion. She took three or four little steps where one would have covered the same ground, but she didn't trample me or break away. I wiggled my chilled fingers inside the mittens and switched hands between lead rope and pocket. At the road, I turned and plodded back toward the house.

Each circuit, from house to road and back, was a tenth of a mile. Ten trips made a mile. Twenty loops amounted to two miles. The idea was that by walking—even at forty below zero—the horse would generate enough body heat to stay warm and the blankets would soak up sweat and help hold in heat.

After several more transits of the driveway, sweat again soaked the horse blanket. I swapped the wet blanket for a dry one, but that didn't seem to be enough. Chuck brought out a sleeping bag that I layered underneath the mare's blanket for extra warmth. (All of this buckling and unbuckling was awkwardly accomplished because of my thick mittens. I felt like an astronaut who doesn't dare remove her gloves no matter how much easier manipulations would be with bare fingers.)

I don't recall the duration of that frightening march. An hour? Two? Long enough that the air temperature rose a barely perceptible ten degrees, from forty below to thirty below, and finally, Tanya dropped her head level with my shoulder and walked without jittery jigging or fearfully eyeing the trees. Her gait mirrored my pace, and the lead rope hung loosely over my arm. I buried both hands in my pockets.

Beside the house, I stopped and pulled off a mitten. Pushing my hand underneath the hood I rubbed Tanya's neck. Her skin felt warm and dry. Satisfied she was finally out of danger, I let her loose in the snowy pasture. Calmly, she watched me.

Immeasurably relieved, I tromped to the barn and led Sham out of his stall. At the pasture, as soon as I unbuckled his halter, he dropped to the ground and rolled with utmost abandon in the sun-flecked snow.

Inside the house, while peeling off my jacket and boots, I glanced out the window. Both heavily-blanketed horses picked at a pile of hay—as if nothing frightening had just happened.

C A B I N • Eventually, my worries about keeping the house heated shifted toward the possibility of an extended power outage rather than wind blowing the door open.

After getting rid of the coal furnace, we installed a woodstove in the corner of the living room where the stairs in Mrs. Webb's story had been. By changing the staircase, Mrs. Webb gained space for more furniture. The woodstove we installed again shrank the sitting area, but we also desired backup heat. A double-walled metal chimney rose through a hole in the ceiling and a ledge beside the staircase and exited near the peak of the roof. The small woodstove was a model designed to burn efficiently without emitting huge amounts of contaminants, but creosote quickly accumulated in the chimney. After a couple winters, I would gladly have exchanged it for a stove like the one at my parents' cabin, of rusted iron and sheet metal with a tiny isinglass window and the name "Wanda No. 22" in raised letters across the front.

When we had the first chimney fire, Chuck calmly closed the damper, smothering the fire. A year or so later, another chimney fire occurred but during the afternoon. The fire roared like a beast inside the double-walled metal chimney.

I called Chuck who was at work.

"I'm going to call the fire department," I told him.

"Close the damper," he replied calmly, from his office in Anchorage. "The fire will go out."

"I already shut the damper and the chimney is still roaring," I said and abruptly hung up the phone.

Running outside, I stared at the roof. Sparks shot out from underneath the chimney cap, but snow hadn't blown away yet so the roof wasn't in immediate danger. I realized I had to get up on the roof. Like fast-forwarding a movie, I raced to the barn and hauled the awkward extension ladder up the hill to the house and leaned it against the eaves. Grabbing a short-handled sledge hammer from inside the garage, I scrambled up the ladder. A running start across the garage roof propelled me up the steep cabin roof. Balancing awkwardly, I swung the hammer upward at the chimney cap. The metal cover flew off and rolled down the roof. Dropping the hammer, I threw a handful of snow down the chimney. Encouraged by sizzling, I tossed more snow into the chimney until the smoke changed to steam and the hissing stopped. Retrieving the hammer, I slowly climbed down the ladder. Inside the house, the chimney was quiet. A puddle of melted snow had formed on the tiles under the stove.

I dialed Chuck's number. "The fire is out."

"What did you do?" he asked.

"I'll tell you later. But I'm getting rid of that stove."

As if I was trying to get even with the woodstove, I placed an advertisement in the newspaper. A man showed up in a pickup truck and bought the stove for his cabin. He seemed genuinely delighted and not a bit worried about the recalcitrant damper. After that we put furniture back in that corner of the room. Years later, after natural gas was piped to the neighborhood, we installed a gas stove where the woodstove had been. The gas stove had a thermostat and vented through a smaller chimney inserted into the woodstove chimney.

C O L D • The effects of the 1989 Omega Block multiplied. Some were foreseeable, others not. A few days into the epic cold spell, the battery in the pickup died. Chuck got his commuting car started and drove to Palmer where he bought a new battery. That night I wasn't worried about getting stranded when I started the pickup and drove to the community college for a night class I was taking. In the parking lot, most of the cars were cloaked with frost—windows, roofs, mirrors, body panels all furred as if the vehicles had been marooned in a meat locker.

By the time the class let out, the mercury had again dipped to forty below zero. Leaving the building, I walked alone across the icy and dimly lit parking lot, wondering whether the other students had exited more quickly. Or had they parked somewhere else? An automobile starter clicked forlornly. Changing course toward the vehicle making the clicking sound, I tapped lightly on the icy window. The door opened a crack. Angela, another student in the class, sat glumly in her frozen car.

"I can give you a jump," I offered.

She looked at me skeptically, "You're not a guy."

"I have jumper cables. I'll get my truck," I said, shivering. The thermal difference between the classroom and the parking lot was a startling 110 degrees.

With the strong new battery, the pickup started easily, but during the couple hours I attended class, burly ice invaded the windshield. The defroster blew warm air across the inside of the glass and I shoved the plastic scraper back and forth across the outside. With the windshield mostly cleared, I maneuvered the truck next to Angela's car where she had propped open the hood. With mittened hands, I clumsily hitched jumper cable clamps onto battery terminals. The truck engine dogged down like a great weight had been added. After a few minutes, Angela turned her key but the engine barely hiccupped. We waited without talking. The next time she tried the ignition, the car started and kept running. I unhooked the jumper cables and closed the hood.

"Thanks," Angela said as she started scraping ice off her windshield.

"No problem," I replied matter-of-factly, "see you next week. Hope it warms up."

W I N D • After five weeks of extreme subzero temperatures, when the Omega Block finally disintegrated, it seemed
as if we had survived a whole season, or an epoch, of forbidding cold—and that Arctic weather system didn't just seep
away like desert rain. No. The Matanuska roared to life. As
if in a battle of titans, the wind caterwauled and bludgeoned
and finally vanquished the most excruciating and prolonged
cold I have ever experienced.

While the Matanuska blasted the house, Chuck and
I watched a television map that showed the bitter weather
rampaging across Canada and extending into the Lower 48.
For once I was happy with the Matanuska's howl. Stepping
outside, the ten-below-zero wind chill felt practically balmy.
During that windstorm, we didn't mind the blizzard whiteout
or snow drifts filling the driveway. Even when a gust rattled
the house and the windows shivered like transparent mem-
branes, we didn't complain.

❀

C A B I N • Surely February is the least likely month to sell a house in Alaska. Inconveniences abound. Freezing weather precludes outdoor painting; wind and storms forestall chores like shuffling excess belongings to another location. Someone house-hunting in February would need to look beyond dirty snowdrifts, drafty doorways, frosted windows, and drearily lit rooms. To buy an Alaska house in winter, you would have to be attuned only to potentialities—anticipating summer, imagining abundant daylight and profusions of greenery.

By the time we bought Cabin 135, it had changed ownership four times—including twice in February. After nearly twenty years, the first owners, the LaRoses, sold to a fellow named Yadon in April (often still winter). Three years later, in February 1957, Yadon sold to Hugh Adams; and five years after that, again in February, the Webbs bought the colony-era cabin from Adams.

Chuck and I bought the house in May, but judging from the faded For Sale sign, the house had been on the market all winter. May begins with lawns like dried buckskin and trees a network of twigs, catkins aquiver. A week or two later, verdure drifts across forest and garden.

February, though, is the heart of winter with warm days still several months off. I suspect the house of complicity in an owner's desire to sell during winter, and I marvel that any buyer came forth. Perhaps the house wished to shake off inhabitants like a dog flings water after a swim. Maybe the house played little jokes with heat or electricity or was in cahoots with the wind, loosening the door latch, welcoming Arctic blasts, and chortling like an uncle who devises a prank that no one else finds hilarious.

Selling in winter probably had a logical explanation related to the owners' personal circumstances—a change of job or health; although I would never discount the influence of blowing snow, subzero chill, incessant chattering of the Matanuska, and even the house's antics.

More than once I suspiciously eyed the refrigerator tucked tightly into the cramped kitchen. The angular appliance, perkily labeled Harvest Gold by the manufacturer, had the off-putting color of an overripe avocado. Stylistically, the fridge fit with the rest of the kitchen's mid-twentieth century décor—turquoise-hued Formica countertops and dark cabinetry, the cupboard doors having panels of nubbly amber-hued plastic overlaid with metal grillwork.

When we moved in, a freestanding dishwasher occupied most of the kitchen. Walking from sink to stove required a roundabout route. The so-called portable dishwasher was intended to be stored out of the way, yet the kitchen was so small and the passage so narrow that there was no other place to park it. Within a few weeks, we dismantled the dishwasher enough to ease it out of the kitchen and the house.

We coasted nearly twenty years before an appliance failed. On a summer morning as I was about to slide a pan of muffins into the oven, smoke burst from around the control knobs at the front of the stove. An acrid smell of burning plastic filled the kitchen.

"Chuck! Help!" I cried, dropping the pan on the counter and grabbing the fire extinguisher. Chuck rushed down the basement stairs to the electrical panel and shut off power to the electric range. Brandishing the extinguisher, I watched but nothing else happened—no more smoke. No flames.

Chuck hurried up the stairs and looked at the stove. "We could turn the power back on and see if the stove still works," he joked.

"Seems like an electrical problem," I said. "The stove has to go." A few years earlier, we replaced the oven element and a couple of burners in order to avoid redoing the kitchen.

The cut-out space in the cabinetry where the stove sat would not accommodate a free-standing range. Eventually, an appliance shop found an appropriately sized electric range, left over from a contractor's over-ordering. Delivery men installed the new stove and carted off the old one, lifting it up and over the kitchen counter peninsula as if that was perfectly normal. Chuck and I were relieved to have avoided launching a kitchen remodel because of a failed appliance.

The refrigerator quit in early December 2008, its last throes denoted by an off-kilter humming. I opened the door and turned the dials to off. The compressor hum stopped but a Hopalong Cassidy, three-legged race, waltz-with-an-extra-beat clamor continued.

Tromping to the basement, I peered at the electrical panel, deciphering cryptic jottings made over the years by various electricians. Flipping off breaker number 6 caused the carbon monoxide detector to screech a no-power warning and the basement freezer motor to stop.

Chuck's voice drifted down from the kitchen. "That's it," he called. "The refrigerator is off."

In the kitchen, we perused the scene like there might be another solution besides the obvious one of replacing the refrigerator.

"We're still not in a position to remodel the kitchen?" I asked.

"I don't think so," Chuck said gloomily, tugging the silent fridge until it budged an inch or two from the wall. I leaned across the counter and reached behind it, pulling the plug so we could turn the breaker back on for the freezer and carbon monoxide detector.

Wind buffeted the car as we drove to Wasilla. Sears had a couple of refrigerators that would fit if the top cabinet was removed. The sales guy said one could be delivered before Christmas.

"Is it in Anchorage?"

"No, it's shipped from Outside."

Fast delivery of an appliance transported halfway across the United States and transiting the North Pacific in December seemed unlikely.

"Do you have any this size in stock here? Or in Anchorage?"

The salesman searched his database, finding a similar refrigerator stored in an Anchorage warehouse. For another ten dollars, he said, the deliverymen would haul the old one away, but we didn't read the fine print. Like the derelict electric range, the refrigerator would have to be lifted and tipped over the countertop.

T I M E • I have come to a stage of life where, like a mysterious sixth sense, nostalgia conjures memories as lively concocted scenes, as if from a movie or a snippet of dream. Sometimes a word triggers this wistfulness. When the avocado-colored refrigerator quit, I felt annoyance, not nostalgia. Then the word icebox popped into my head.

My grandmother caller her modern electric refrigerator an icebox, as if her mind had never left the time when blocks of ice were cut from a frozen river or lake; ice that was used in insulated compartments—iceboxes—to keep food chilled during the warm months.

One house, an old farmhouse, where my family lived for a few years when I was young, was situated near a creek—and had an ice house. The building for storing blocks of stream-cut ice was about the size of a garage with double walls, the space between the walls insulated with sawdust. My family didn't cut and store ice because we lived there after electrification.

The ice house proved useful (at least in my memory) as a tangential story—a scrap of visual history, another reminder that living wasn't always so easy.

C A B I N • The refrigerator was wedged so tightly between cabinets that we could barely budge it. With a crowbar, Chuck pried the top cabinet off the wall and tugged the dead appliance into the middle of the kitchen. Behind it, the wall was plywood, painted a nondescript yellow and appearing as if it hadn't been cleaned since the 1970s. I scrubbed the newly exposed wall and optimistically painted it a pristine white.

PALMER • Fresh snow, not yet dirtied by traffic and silt, heightened a holiday festiveness that, I imagine, resembles one of the old Christmas market towns in Germany or Switzerland. The air was crisp, the mercury barely above zero. Parka-clad people tromped across a snowy intersection, causing drivers to brake and wait. Flecks of ice drifted and glinted like the inside of a snow globe. The airborne ice magnified the mountains so they loomed enchantingly larger and seemingly nearer than usual—as if the North Pole might actually be a town in an alpine valley rather than drifting coordinates in the Arctic Ocean.

I met my sister Barbara at the coffee shop Vagabond Blues. We settled at a table next to the windows with a clear view of everyone entering and leaving the old train depot. After lunch, we bundled into coats, hats, and mittens and trudged along the snow-packed sidewalk to a boutique where Barbara's flute ensemble would be playing holiday music. Aromas of coffee and hot chocolate drifted from the back of the shop. While waiting for the music to begin, I browsed dresses, glancing up just as a stylish mannequin blinked disconcertingly and the shop door swung open. My neighbor Helen entered along with a blast of freezing air. Like me, Helen planned to shop for gifts at the boutiques and bazaars. Neither of us had any interest in other events—like the winter triathlon—although Chuck and I planned to watch the evening fireworks that would be launched from the library parking lot.

The flutists finished setting up and began to play. The music added to the magical ambience that made me want to linger, but after several songs, I yielded to my intention to shop and went next door to Fireside Books. A few minutes later, the door swung open with a cheery tinkle of bells and Helen entered.

"Has the train arrived?" I asked.

"No," she answered, "but it must be close."

In a moment, a whistle blared, followed by deep rumbling. We turned and watched the huge engine—iconic midnight blue with a yellow stripe—and several passenger cars lumber toward the depot. Last was another engine, hitched on backward.

T I M E • Up close, trains appear larger than I expect, probably because I rarely travel by rail. The imagery of trains comes to my mind as distant scenery, like a movie where smoke-belching engines haul a line of carriages across a vast landscape. A train rumbling into Palmer fits my notion of the town—in an abstract historical fashion.

In 1935 Matanuska colonists arrived by train. There was no other transportation; although a year later that changed. Coinciding with the first Matanuska Valley Fair, on September 4, 1936, a new highway and bridge across the Knik River opened. For the first time it was possible to drive between Anchorage and Palmer.

P A L M E R • I suspect my nostalgia for train service to Palmer is misguided. I asked Chuck what he remembers about passenger trains in the 1950s and 1960s.

"There weren't scheduled trains to Palmer," Chuck said, "although unscheduled 'special' trains brought high school basketball players for tournaments and visitors to the state fair."

T I M E • The railroad monopoly on transportation between Anchorage and Palmer ended in 1936, but this was not the first big shift in transport in southcentral Alaska. Nearly twenty years earlier, in 1917, the rail line constructed from Anchorage to the valley had eliminated the need for small vessels that lightered passengers, goods, and livestock across Cook Inlet. The newly constructed rail line shifted the paradigm, offering transportation independent of ocean tides and unhampered by winter ice. The railroad eliminated the economic reason for the town of Knik, where (thirty years earlier) George Palmer transplanted his store to take advantage of vessel transport across Knik Arm.

P A L M E R • The ponderous train stopped in front of the depot, a wood-framed structure that had quickly become a historical footnote. In the late twentieth century, the building was repurposed as a community center and rented for parties or events—like this holiday shopping bazaar. Outside the bookstore, I crossed the street and joined train passengers straggling toward another bazaar at the borough gymnasium.

Inside the high-ceilinged gym, I stood for a moment, pulling off my jacket and mittens and waiting for fog to clear off my glasses. A maze of tables and stands displayed hand-made items—hats and scarves, jellies and honey, potholders and aprons, welded iron hooks, birdhouses and birdfeeders, framed photographs, and paintings of stupendous landscapes and wildlife. I wandered through the labyrinth seeking gifts for Chuck and the boys. The gym smelled of sugar-infused popcorn chortling in a large glass-sided popper. Cheery holiday music mixed with a babble of conversations.

Veering from my intention to buy gifts, I paused to peruse a painting of a bloody beach. The artist, Ken Lisbourne, watched me from a chair on the other side of the table. The scene was not of a whaling crew butchering a recent kill. No, the painting depicted catastrophic destruction. An Armageddon. Corpses of people and sea animals lined a beach as if a mixed-species platoon had all died at once.

"What is this scene?" I asked.

Lisbourne explained that he was a child when Edward Teller and the U.S. Atomic Energy Commission launched a plan to use nuclear bombs to excavate a harbor at Cape Thompson, on Alaska's northwestern coast.

My memories of that time are of duck-and-cover drills at an elementary school in Seattle. I cannot fathom how school-children would survive a nuclear attack by huddling under classroom desks flanked by windows up to the ceiling.

The artist continued, "I never forgot that close call. I painted this scene to keep the memory alive, so others would see what might have happened."

Besides killing people and wildlife, nuclear explosions would have poisoned air, polluted waterways, and besieged ecosystems. Cape Thompson is also very close to Russia. Detonating enough nukes to blast a harbor-sized pit would have caused unimaginable tensions between the nuclear-armed neighboring superpowers.

I bought the print, not because I would give it as a gift but because of its cautionary message. Alaska escaped that particular peril, but other places did not.

Outside the borough gym, with the end-of-the-world print under my arm, I trudged toward the Colony House Museum. The old house was well-heated and cozy. Volunteers had set out plates of cookies on a table in the living room. I felt as if I had stepped into another era, a time when lace doilies graced chair arms, electricity was sparingly doled out, and wood or coal was used for heating and cooking. Besides offering a nostalgic glimpse of the past, the Colony House Museum is rooted in a time of economic and environmental catastrophe, when the Great Plains became known as the Dust Bowl and economic hardships abounded. Families, including my father's, uprooted and migrated west because of loss of livelihood. Some families participated in New Deal programs, like the Matanuska Colony, and ended up in Alaska.

By three o'clock, long shadows cleaved the pink glow that precedes twilight. I didn't see my sister again that afternoon but ran into Helen two more times. We laughed at how so many choices at the gift bazaars made deciding what to buy more difficult rather than easier.

Driving home in waning light, as I turned on Fishhook Road, I glanced across the valley toward Cook Inlet. Fog had settled like an ephemeral landscape. Visitors returning to Anchorage on the train would have a more relaxing trip than those who drove the icy and cloud-shrouded highway.

C A B I N • A week later, deliverymen hauled a new refrigerator through the front door and around the corner into the dining area. When I pointed to where the appliance needed to go, in the kitchen on the other side of the stove peninsula, they balked. One of the men said caustically, "Sorry ma'am. We don't lift appliances over obstructions."

Sure enough, the fine print listed banisters and railings as obstructions. Countertops with electric ranges weren't specified but clearly presented a similar obstacle. The men parked the new refrigerator—big, white, and blocky—near the dining table and a dozen steps from the kitchen. They also mentioned that the cardboard appliance box could be used to help slide the old refrigerator across the stovetop.

When the boys came home for the holidays, they muscled the old fridge out of the kitchen and carried it outside, shoving it into the back of the pickup. Later, they hauled the defunct refrigerator to the borough landfill, unloading it beside a battalion of cast-off appliances.

In the cramped kitchen, you only needed to take a couple steps to shift between stove, fridge, and sink. Having the new refrigerator beside the dining room table changed that arrangement. I walked back and forth, traversing the narrow aisle, to retrieve food from the refrigerator. In spite of the inconvenience, this awkward configuration required less effort than trekking to the basement to collect a food item from the cold room.

"Chuck," I commented, "this situation, with the fridge by the table, is temporary. We have to remodel the kitchen."

"I know," he said.

"I'll call Jim and see if he has time." Jim was the contractor who had redone the bathroom and the staircase. "Maybe we can also enlarge the kitchen."

"I agree," Chuck said.

Unspoken, though, was that we both worried about the cost and the possibility of finding something untoward that would further complicate the renovation.

"We can add a built-in dishwasher," I said, already imagining a kitchen so different that it belonged in another house. For twenty-five years, we had washed every dish, pot, and pan by hand. Guests sometimes offered to help with the cleanup.

"No thank you," I usually replied. "We'll wash up in the morning."

T I M E • When we bought Cabin 135, we didn't consider that we were buying into the experience of an old house that began as a cabin. All the rooms were undersized. At some point, a big garage had been added rather than more living space.

Stacked over time, the remodels and renovations revealed decisions of former residents as well as changes we wrought. Our decisions reflected our experiences. Our expectation of normalcy seemed different from inclinations just a few decades earlier. If—and when—we remodeled the kitchen, we would make sure there were many electrical outlets, good lighting, and plentiful countertops. Plus a built-in dishwasher and a gas stove. Cost would also play a role in our decisions.

ECOLOGIES

T E R R A I N • Still winter, February can go either way—bone-chilling frigidness where you barely venture outside, or temperatures above zero with perfectly skiable snow.

The absence of snow was notable on a gloomily overcast afternoon in February. Chuck and I drove to Palmer. We parked on a side street at the northern edge of the town and walked north along the old rail line, toward the Matanuska River. The path cut between a subdivision and a hayfield, the shorn grass encrusted with icy rime.

T I M E • By 1917 railroad builders had carved a route along the bluff above the Matanuska River to reach coal mines near Chickaloon and Sutton. Engineers must have considered geology and hydrology and how the bluff might collapse or the river change its course. I imagine the planners also focused on cost. They knew the least expensive line would follow the river, not cross a mountain range.

The first train loaded with Chickaloon coal arrived in Anchorage during October 1917. Coal continued to be hauled along this route until the 1960s when development of natural gas in Cook Inlet doomed large-scale coal mining in the Matanuska Valley. Natural gas proved to be a more economical and cleaner fuel. The railroad abandoned the coal train route northeast of Palmer.

TERRAIN • Beyond the hayfield, we tromped beneath a basket-weave of alder branches and stepped awkwardly between blocky railroad ties that had not decomposed or been carted away. A few steel spikes remained embedded in the timbers, but most of the rails were gone. The partially deconstructed tracks suggested disorganized industry—or thievery.

After another quarter hour of walking, we sauntered out of the alders toward a flat place overlooking the river. Partway down the slope, a tangle of old vehicles and household appliances piled against the steel bones of a railcar. Weather had stripped much of the paint, and bullet holes pocked the metal carcasses. A few spots of brightness remained—shiny chrome outlined the yawning windows of one rusted auto; I Miss U, in purple and blue spray paint, gaudily adorned another.

TIME • The hodgepodge may have accumulated piece-meal, decades before steel recycling became an industry. Perhaps the discarding began with one railcar pushed, or levered, over the bank so that it tumbled down the slope and splashed into the river. A non-motorized railcar in the river suggests institutional intention rather than rogues with a spur-of-the-moment impulse. Perhaps railroad managers, desperate to prevent further erosion below the precarious tracks, shoved another boxcar over the bank, but this one stalled before splashing into the river.

I imagine more dumping—of autos and appliances—occurred during early summer, accompanied by a festive spring-cleaning attitude. Pickup trucks arrived towing a broken-down vehicle or hauling a defunct washing machine. There'd have been a bonfire and plenty of insect repellant. And men laughing and working together with chains and winches—or a backhoe—lifting and shoving each unwanted hunk of metal over the edge, watching it tumble, perhaps with cheers, or bets on which would fall farthest. The first relic smacked against the railcar and after that everything piled up. The jumble appears to me as an impulse gone awry. If I met someone who participated in this dumping, they would probably rather hotly inform me that I wouldn't understand. I was too young. I might ask whether they had drained the toxic liquids from the vehicles? "Why?" one of them may have asked. "That stuff is long gone. Washed away down the river."

"Polluting the river and the ocean," I'd reply. "I don't think you understand our concerns."

The problem with interrogating people from the past in your own mind: it's a one-sided conversation. You think they're wrong, and they're not around to explain. And all the mores of then and now exist beneath an umbrella of culture, society, and what's accepted as generally reasonable. I worry about how people of the future will puzzle over our decisions and doings that have increased carbon in the atmosphere and acidity of the ocean, melted glaciers and pushed species to extinction.

T E R R A I N • Chuck and I continued along the abandoned railroad bed. Without snow, shades of gray and tan rendered a melancholic landscape, except for the river, which flowed a clear and beguiling green-blue between ledges of opaque ice. During summer, leafy foliage and pink fireweed blooms swathe the riverbank, but that's also the melting season when glaciers release loads of silt and the river flows furiously and steely gray.

Having traipsed beyond the trees, above us small caverns—perhaps summertime swallow nests—pitted the bluffs. Higher up, pebbles cascaded like jittery maracas.

The railroad—rails and ties—had vanished, whether removed or sloughed into the river, I couldn't guess. At the next slide area, we tramped across fist-sized stones. I glanced guardedly upward, watching for tumbling rocks. For a while after that, the trail improved but another bluff presented even more deeply eroded grooves. The path vanished and more stones clattered above us. Chuck climbed upward a short distance, searching for a route. All I could see was a deep cleft and more rocks, but I heard him shout that he'd found a trail although he returned a few minutes later saying that path also disappeared.

When a trail vanishes, you can retrace your steps or continue onward, hoping to rejoin that trail or find another leading in the same direction. The question of which direction to go relates to motivation, and risk. That winter afternoon, hiking along the old railroad route above the Matanuska River, we were not intent on reaching a destination. In fact, we didn't even know if there was anything noteworthy farther upstream. Instead, we were enjoying the terrain from a different vantage than on top of the bluff, although my imagination became snared in a peculiar weaving of time. The eroding bluff pushed my notion regarding the rhythm of geologic change. The pile of cast-off appliances and the abandoned rail route was more troubling because it suggested a casual acceptance of deterioration, disintegration, and obsolescence—and no apparent plan.

Losing a trail is not the same as being lost. When Chuck and I lost the old railroad trail, we turned around and hiked back to our car. Driving home, we stopped at the bluff-top viewpoint and climbed up the short silt-drifted path. I wanted to ascertain if we had made it that far upriver along the railroad trail. I couldn't tell, though. The weak bluff edge made it unwise to lean out far enough to see below.

C A B I N • Cabin 135 was built before electrical service, the interior wiring added later in a piecemeal fashion. Even a half century later, when we arrived, the house had minimal wiring connected to a fuse box in the bathroom and a small breaker box fastened to the basement ceiling. We didn't notice the electrical limitations until we acquired more appliances, particularly a microwave oven. Simultaneous use of microwave and hair dryer proved too much for the electric circuit shared by kitchen and bathroom. A fuse would blow, cutting off power to both devices and extinguishing the lights. While getting ready to go to work on a dark morning, this was annoying.

Chuck and I knew nothing about electrical service. The 1950s-era house we'd lived in in Anchorage had sufficiently modern wiring, so we hadn't faced a parade of blown fuses. Basic questions such as "what's modern?" or "what's obsolete?" mystified us.

Electric wires were draped between poles alongside the driveway and slung above the garage to a tall pole beside the greenhouse.

Exasperated after yet another blown fuse, I called the electric company. The representative looked at records for our house and, with a note of surprise, said, "You only have fifty amps of electrical service."

"What does that mean?" I asked.

She explained that new houses routinely have two hundred amps—four times as much—as if that explained everything.

When we moved in, we realized the poor state of the roof and the septic, but we didn't consider that the wiring also needed to be upgraded.

I called the electric company back and asked if the old fifty-amp wires might be a safety hazard. Surprisingly, they agreed to upgrade the lines along the driveway as long as we hired an electrician to install a new meter base. We also had the electrician add a modern electric panel in the basement and decommission the fuse box in the bathroom. We didn't rewire the whole house, though. Not then. That took much longer. One room at a time. And when later I found a wad of mouse-chewed wires behind an attic wall, I wished we had a quicker timeframe.

T R A I N • The first Saturday in January 2011, Michael drove us to Wasilla to catch the train to Fairbanks. As recommended, we arrived twenty minutes before the departure time. Climbing out of the car, Chuck and I stepped across the rails and set our small packs on a raised platform at the back of the hip-roofed building that had once been the Wasilla train station but now housed the Chamber of Commerce. A small red car with frosty windows raced into the Chamber of Commerce parking lot, which was posted with signs forbidding parking by train passengers.

Even with a warm jacket, I shivered in the cold. Across the street, an electronic billboard switched between a video of snowmobiles hurtling across a snowy landscape and displaying the temperature: 8 degrees Fahrenheit. A breeze swirled frozen mist and the wind chill made the air feel even colder. Our destination, Fairbanks, three hundred miles to the north, would be even colder.

Traveling by train to Fairbanks in January was an on-a-lark trip to see Alaska differently. I imagined the winter train would offer a degree of civility very different from a quick jet flight or steering an automobile along the highway's endless curves. I felt as if the train was an anomaly or anachronistic, from an earlier era, and that there was something to be learned from this trip.

I asked Chuck about his previous travel by train to Fairbanks. He said he'd ridden the train twice, both times in the late 1960s before the Parks Highway was built. At that time, the driving route was longer, via the Glenn and Richardson Highways, roads that wound through mountain ranges—the Talkeetnas and Chugach, Wrangells and Alaska Range.

Catching the train in Wasilla proved to be an improvisation. After a quarter hour of chilly waiting, I heard the train whistle intermittently warning of each street crossing. Finally, the engine's single headlight pierced the frozen fog. The ground trembled as the blue-and-yellow engine rumbled past us, stopping on Knik–Goose Bay Road where warning lights flashed, claxons clanged, and signal arms blocked traffic.

People who had boarded in Anchorage peered out the windows, looking down at us. At the back of the passenger car, a door popped open and the conductor, dressed in black like an undertaker, leaned down and placed a small step stool on the icy pavement. He cheerfully asked whether we were the "party of three" or "party of two" and after verifying our names handed us an envelope with our tickets.

Chuck and I climbed several steep steps into the passenger car and walked along the narrow aisle, finding the row designated on our tickets. After shoving our packs onto an overhead rack, we settled into the seats. Through the windows, I noticed the driver of the red car was stymied in his effort to maneuver out of the prohibited parking lot and around the corner to the designated railroad parking. The man had let off his wife and mother-in-law beside the old station building so they could board without stepping across the rails. The women boarded when we did, the conductor stowing the grandmother's wheelchair in the baggage car.

Slowly, the engine reversed, backing off the street, the signal arms rising. Traffic gradually advanced until, finally, the red car crossed the tracks and turned into the railroad parking lot. Again, the train lumbered forward accompanied by signal clamor, warning lights, and barricades, and stopped on Knik–Goose Bay Road. This seemed a strange odyssey—like a video caught in a repeating loop—initiated because the train station had been switched to another use.

The conductor opened the door on the other side of the train, facing the railroad parking lot. The driver of the red car hurriedly boarded and the conductor secured the door.

Now the train advanced, crossing Knik–Goose Bay Road and rumbling west, parallel to the Parks Highway. I looked down at cars jockeying for lanes and, across the highway, at a strip of low-slung commercial and government buildings that grimly faced parking lots heaped with dirty snow. The whistle blared as the train approached each side street. Nearing the western edge of Wasilla, I anticipated we would accelerate and zip past highway-bound vehicles, but the train slowed and stopped beside a parked pickup. The conductor hurried along the aisle, murmuring, "We're picking up groceries for his dad." Outside, a man clad in a bulky parka hefted tubs and coolers out of the truck and shoved them into the baggage car.

We had boarded a version of a work train, a lifeline for people living remotely. Finally, we were underway, the train rolling faster with a slight rocking motion along tracks that curved northward. The passenger car was the middle of three carriages, behind the snack car and in front of the baggage car. With no caboose, the baggage car comprised the end of the train.

Midmorning, only a couple weeks past winter solstice, the sun grazed the southeastern horizon, glinting through hoar-encrusted birch. Periodically, snowy expanses of lakes and bogs opened to a wider view.

The conductor paused beside our row and mentioned that we were allowed go into the baggage car. He said that the view through the large side doors was especially fetching and, as an afterthought, added that the smoking section was a platform at the end of the train. (You would have to be bundled up to sit outside for very long traveling across Alaska in winter, no matter how great your need for nicotine or desire for wondrous vistas.)

An hour later, approaching Talkeetna, the conductor announced the train would slow for a view of Denali. Along with most of the other passengers, we trooped through the narrow passage between the cars, stepping gingerly across a wobbling hinge in the floor. The conductor slid open the wide door, and frigid air surged inside. The train slowed to a crawl, and we crowded around the opening with only a drooping chain between us and the snowy woods. At a break in the forest, overlooking the frozen Susitna River, the train stopped. Beyond the river and across a hundred miles of forested ridges, loomed Denali, the tallest peak on the continent, a frozen massif seeming undiminished by distance.

T I M E • My first encounter with Denali occurred only a few months after moving to Alaska. In February 1980 one of Chuck's friends invited us to a cabin-finishing party. The remote cabin was situated in the Susitna Valley. Chuck and I drove north on the Parks Highway past Talkeetna, then followed the Petersville Road until it diminished into a snowy track. When we couldn't drive farther, we switched to skis and followed a snowmobile trail. Most of the other people rode snowmobiles that towed sleds carrying building supplies. Several hours later, we skied into a small clearing where a plywood-sided cabin nestled beside a frozen lake. One couple arrived by plane, landing a ski-equipped Super Cub on the lake ice.

That afternoon the couple with the plane invited me to go sightseeing with them. Wearing every layer of clothing I'd brought—down jacket, mittens, knit hat, felt-lined boots—I squeezed into the third seat of the plane. The motor revved and the single nose propeller spun until it revolved too fast to see. We lurched forward, sliding then bouncing across the ice, finally climbing above the shadowy forest and into pink sunshine.

I left Chuck behind that afternoon and sailed into the sky with people I had just met—that's how curious I was about Alaska. How would the land look from above? Forests and lakes? Rivers? Mountains? Inside the small aircraft with a heater so weak that breath froze on the windows, I rubbed off the ice with my mittens, clearing a porthole-sized view. I'm certain that I saw a bird-sized shadow of the plane drifting across the face of Denali—although now I wonder if that could have been true. In any event, the mountain was near and unbelievably massive.

Having glimpsed a remote vastness that pinched my soul, I shivered, even with all my warm clothes. The plane veered away from Denali, and we made an unplanned stop along the frozen Yentna River to walk around and then bounced back into the sky. The sun had set but twilight lingered as we landed on the frozen lake beside the unfinished cabin.

TERRAIN • Still a hundred miles south of Denali, outside the baggage car door, foreground and mountain merged into a stupendous tableau. Could it be that Denali defies logic? Is it possible for distant terrain be visible at all?

Standing on a treeless plain, you can only see about three miles in the distance before the ground vanishes beyond the curvature of the earth. Climb a hundred-foot tower and the vista expands to twenty-two miles. Distant mountains also compensate for the earth's curvature. A hundred miles away, Denali still dominated the landscape.

TRAIN • An icy breeze wafted through the baggage car. We hurried back to the heated passenger carriage as the train heaved forward, gaining momentum but not speed. A few minutes later, without any hoopla, the train pulled into Talkeetna. The station was an open-air stop beside a parking lot and in sight of the Fairview Inn, a boxy two-story building with a famous bar. Winter muffled the town—every roof, porch, sidewalk, street, and automobile was coated with snow. Even between heaps of snow there was more snow. Smoke drifted straight up from every chimney.

The conductor opened the carriage door, letting a wave of cold roll along the aisle. A few people boarded while several passengers departed. A man with a gray beard and large glasses, who was wearing a bulky jacket with reflective tape and heavy boots, disembarked. He'd been sitting across the aisle from Chuck, and they had been discussing mountain climbing—apropos since Talkeetna is the usual departure point for climbers tackling Denali.

We stayed in Talkeetna for only a few minutes. Ahead of us was the flag stop route that diverges from the highway. Yet really it's the other way around. The railroad predates construction of the Parks Highway by fifty years so it's the highway that veers away from the tracks. Before the Parks Highway was completed, the flag stop route extended a long ways, not just fifty-five miles north of Talkeetna.

A quarter hour later, the train slowed. A fabric-draped birch branch marked an ad hoc stop where three people clad in bulky jackets waited on a patch of packed snow. A trail disappeared between the trees.

The conductor marched through the passenger car asking, as he went, if anyone wanted to help lift boxes off the train. Several passengers got up and followed him to the baggage car. Outside, plastic tubs and coolers were handed down and loaded onto trailers hitched behind snowmobiles.

With the train again underway, I settled into the tall-backed seat and gazed out the window at snow-laden birch and spruce. Watching the monotonous scenery, I felt vaguely adrift as if I might be traveling any one of various routes across the circumpolar north, or as if I had glided into another time entirely.

T I M E • Before the Parks Highway was constructed, the railroad provided access to Mount McKinley National Park. Travel from Anchorage or Seward took two days by train and included an overnight stay at Curry. An old photo shows the Curry Hotel as a two-story, rectangular structure squeezed between the tracks and a sparsely forested hillside. The flat-roofed building had little architectural interest: a bumped-out room at one end topped with a glass cupola and two bay windows that flanked an awning-covered porch. The porch merged seamlessly with a train-length platform. Passengers could stay at Curry without ever stepping onto the land. After spending a night at the isolated hotel, travelers boarded the train and continued onward to the McKinley station.

The routine of overnighting at Curry ended in 1957 when a fire destroyed the hotel. Rather than rebuilding, the railroad razed the ruins and everything else. After that, trains passed without stopping. (Interestingly, the first road to the national park entrance was constructed in 1957.) I suspect the railroad's routine of overnighting passengers at Curry was customary and profitable—but not essential.

T R A I N • A half century after Curry vanished, I did not see towns or stations along the rail route north of Talkeetna, just forest and an occasional flag or kite that initiated a stop. If a sign or plaque memorializing Curry had been installed alongside the tracks, I missed it.

Disrupting the monotony, the conductor announced "Sherman City Hall." A few minutes later, an opening in the forest revealed a modest building set well back from the tracks. The blue-painted structure looked out of place, lending a surreal aspect to the treeless swatch as if a suburban house had been plunked into the wilderness or we had encountered a darkly ironic movie set. A narrow path sliced through the snow and directly to the front door.

Farther along, another flag-draped branch prompted the train to stop. A man and a woman, clad in bulky jackets and carrying skis, clambered aboard, stomping snow off their boots. The train lurched forward. Soon, the rails veered toward the Parks Highway. We stopped near a parking lot and the skiers clomped off the carriage.

Again, the train heaved forward. I leaned back in my seat with the idea that little would happen for several hours. Gaining momentum, the conveyance settled into an earnest rocking rhythm. I contemplated a map showing names attached to sections of track—Chase, Deadhorse, Gold Creek, Canyon, Curry, Sherman, Hurricane—like one-word synopses of dreams that drift away, leaving behind stories only for as long as anyone remembers.

To travel by train is to undertake a linear expedition. The train is tied to the rails and to a schedule. If I write "north of the flag stop route, we came to Hurricane Gulch and after that to Summit Lake, and still later to Denali National Park," ennui sets in, but that wasn't the nature of this trip. As we approached Hurricane Gulch, the conductor spoke into a handheld device, talking to the engineer, requesting to take "the bridge . . . at walking speed."

The train slowed until it was barely moving, just creeping across the nine-hundred-foot-long steel arch spanning Hurricane Gulch. The bridge high above the canyon was built in 1921 at a cost of $1.2 million. This was a very expensive bridge, and for eight years it was the tallest bridge in the United States.

Curious, I walked to the baggage car. The loading door framed a vista—unlike the curtailed view you see zooming along the highway. We were also above the highway, and while on the bridge, nothing impeded our view. I walked to the far end of the baggage car and stepped outside onto the little porch. Standing at the back of the train, I was the last one on the bridge. As the engine and forward cars chugged onto solid ground, I watched the rails converge in the distance, my gaze drawn toward snow-laden hills and forested terraces as blanched as the cloudless sky.

Somewhere north of Hurricane Gulch, the conductor announced another unscheduled stop. "For the view," he said, and he might as well have added "in the middle of nowhere" as if the train might momentarily have separated from its staunchly linear and chronological course. He opened the passenger car and lowered the step stool onto packed snow.

We stepped down into a broad openness. Except for the train, there was no sign of human habitation. No electric wires. No roads. No trails. What artists like. What travelers to Alaska have long sought. We stood on hard-packed snow, heeding the conductor's warning not to wander farther after he mentioned that a passenger, who ventured away from the track, floundered in the deep snow and had to be rescued.

The sun was without warmth. Between misty breaths, I clicked photos of snowy terrain fringed by shadowy spruce and stretching across frozen wetlands and meadows, but the real prize was the unimpeded view of the angular jumble of ridges and precipices—crowned by Denali.

Without an obsequious narrator, the Alaska Railroad had brought us to the edge of wilderness—as if that was perfectly normal. I handed my camera to another passenger who snapped a picture of Chuck and me with Denali behind us and a sliver of the blue-and-yellow train.

Cut-jewel facets crisscrossed the face of Denali, edges alternately highlighted and shadowed by the low-angle sun. After taking a few more pictures, I reverted to just looking, searching the terrain for ideas to keep as invisible souvenirs.

A few minutes later, the conductor ushered us onboard, and the train eased ahead, again embracing a slight rocking of steel wheels on steel rails.

Chuck and I walked forward to the dining car where we bought beer and chips. We sat on hard plastic benches with a plastic table between us and unwrapped sandwiches that we brought from home. The landscape changed from canyons and forest to the white expanse of Summit Lake. Again, the train slowed and stopped.

We peered toward the east, straining to see, in the monotone flat whiteness, specks at the far side of the frozen lake.

"Caribou," someone said. Through binoculars, Chuck spotted the caribou. He handed the binoculars to a young woman at another table who had been conversing in Japanese and English. She looked through the binoculars, smiled, and nodded affirmation of the distant herd.

The train pressed onward. At three o'clock, the slopes above Broad Pass were tinged pink by the setting sun. We crossed the eastern edge of Denali National Park in diminishing daylight.

T I M E • Established in 1917, Denali National Park was originally named Mount McKinley National Park to honor President William McKinley. Six years later, completion of the railroad made visiting the park easier. Tracks constructed south from Fairbanks connected (at Nenana) with rails built north from Anchorage. President Warren G. Harding arrived in a private railcar and ceremoniously pounded a golden spike at the juncture. Subsequently, the president traveled to San Francisco where he died, at age fifty-seven, of a cerebral hemorrhage. The golden spike disappeared and its whereabouts remain unknown.

A photo, taken at the McKinley station, shows men in suits and hats and women wearing dresses and long coats. The fashionable couples wait to board buses. The buses look like stretched station wagons with rows of windows and seats. By 1937 a road had been constructed through the park to the Kantishna mining district. Perhaps the people in that photo were about to embark on a bus tour, hoping to see bears and moose, wolves and Dall sheep, and especially, wishing to glimpse Mount McKinley. Or maybe they weren't tourists at all, and their plan was to check out mining claims at Kantishna.

Even in black and white, I see the picture was taken in summer. Shrubs and wildflowers grow beside the rails, and puffy clouds populate the sky. With plentiful daylight, no one would have been in a hurry.

T R A I N • Beyond the deserted Denali depot, the train continued north into the Nenana River gorge where the conductor announced a slow speed. "Treacherous track," I believe he said. The possibility (if not probability) of danger adds to the adventure. I was glad for the leisurely locomotion because it allowed more time to peruse the scenery as daylight dwindled.

From the highway on the other side of the Nenana River, the rail route appears pasted onto a talus slope where, periodically, trestles span chasms.

"Glitter Gulch," the conductor announced enigmatically, indicating a collection of hotels and condominiums on the other side of the river and near the entrance to the national park. Did the name refer to a large amount of money invested? Or ironically infer past times when prospectors toiled, hoping to find a motherlode of gold? Or might Glitter Gulch simply refer to electric lights festooning visitor facilities, although lights would barely be noticeable during midsummer when most tourists visit and twilight lingers all night.

Driving along the Parks Highway during winter, there is no reason to stop at so-called Glitter Gulch. Even in late October, the place resembles a ghost town, not a holiday resort. Cheerless winds drifting dry snow around boarded-up buildings evoke an abandoned border town where even the streetlights seem superfluous.

The train crept around curves, tracing a contour of slope. In the dim light, I was convinced that the trestles were timber. On one high bridge, I pressed my forehead to the window, peering downward, but I could see neither land nor trestle parts and so had the sensation of flying. In the gathering darkness, I inhabited the dreaminess of a place with a long and difficult-to-fathom history. Or I was the child journeying on a mysterious train that rattled through the night, but logic interceded. How anchored and documented the railroad is. And in a few hours, we would arrive in Fairbanks where we would stay in a hotel and eat dinner in a restaurant—and we would not contemplate routes never built, rails never laid, and towns and train stops that never existed.

Beyond the Nenana River canyon, the train hastened. Chuck alternately dozed or read. For a time, I imagined an Alaska with even more rail routes, as if the nexus of investment and transportation occurred earlier and differently, before air travel became the norm. I would happily ride a train west to the Bering Sea or north to the Arctic Ocean or east to Canada. But opinions about the desirability of new routes vary, and the track I imagined as providing an interesting trip could also inundate communities with unwanted tourists.

Fully engulfed in darkness, we rumbled through the coal mining town of Healy. After that, the only sparkling lights were at Nenana where the train slowed but didn't stop. I hoped to glimpse the aurora but the carriage lighting reflected against the window. Shielding my eyes with my hands, I peered out but only saw a few scintillating stars.

An hour south of Fairbanks and still out of mobile phone range, the conductor sauntered through the carriage asking who needed a taxi or hotel shuttle. He jotted notes and names.

The rail route into Fairbanks is different from the highway. The rails follow a circuitous route, navigating around hilly terrain that the highway confronts straight-on. At eight o'clock and exactly on schedule, the train lumbered to a stop at the Fairbanks station.

Chuck and I zipped our jackets, grabbed our small packs, and stepped down into subzero cold. At the door into the depot, a young man with an Eastern European accent asked, "Eberhart?"

"Yes," I replied. "Princess Hotel?"

"Yes," he said, "Where's your baggage?"

"Just these packs," Chuck said.

"OK," the man replied. We trooped through the station and out the opposite doors to a hotel van that whisked us to a large tourist hotel, which, in January, was eerily empty. After checking in, we traipsed across poorly lit parking lots and empty streets, searching for a restaurant that was still open. I shivered and wished I'd also worn long underwear. We found a bar still serving dinner and, later, returning to the hotel took a more beeline route, only veering around huge piles of plowed snow.

T I M E • The next morning, a hotel van shuttled us to the airport where we boarded an Alaska Airlines flight bound for Anchorage and, forty-five minutes later, approached a city shrouded in clouds. Only steam from the power plant jutted above the drab matting. The plane leveled and rumbled toward the mountains as if the pilots were searching for a gap in the clouds. I wondered whether we would overfly Anchorage and find ourselves unexpectedly in Seattle, but an opening appeared. The plane landed, and Michael was waiting to drive us home.

Our winter jaunt to Fairbanks had taken just over twenty-four hours. We had traversed three hundred miles of Alaska by train—stunning landscapes that appeared even more magnificent because of the clear weather.

I was tempted to think we had encountered a section of the "real" Alaska. The entanglement of human occupation and nature seemed both starkly obvious and subtle. Places like Curry, along the flag stop route, had disappeared. Caribou roamed the far side of Summit Lake. The industrial railroad bridge across Hurricane Gulch was only ten years shy of a century.

Telling our stories, there's a tendency to make them about ourselves, yet the challenge is to recognize the arc and course of time. We had crossed a nuanced landscape where the cycle of settlement and abandonment was well underway.

CABIN • What if a house comes with intention? Or are connotations solely due to whims of the residents? Colors and curtains? Furniture and floors? The structure?

After Mrs. Webb dismantled the bottom stairs, her husband had to assemble a half dozen new stairs before he could go to bed. He would have measured the stairwell, scribbled notes with a stubby pencil, scrounged some boards. Perhaps Mrs. Webb helped him, or maybe she stayed out of the way, washing dishes or watching television. After a couple hours, he finished nailing supports and began sawing boards for treads. The new steps were semi-triangular—wider at one end than the other. The shapes created a curved staircase that connected the back hall to the rectangular upper stairs.

Journeying up and down that staircase required mastering a certain pattern of footfalls to navigate the bottom treads—two narrow, two wider, one much wider, and a couple more. But I was unaware I had learned anything new; I didn't realize that I was adapting to the house.

The first carpet I pulled off the stairs was a mottled green shag. Twenty years later neither Chuck nor I recalled what defect caused us to quickly have new carpet installed. My inclination would have been to sand and varnish the treads, eliminating carpet fibers entirely.

Day after day, year after year, we trod the stairs. The slate-gray carpet we installed harbored history of our footsteps along with dust and silt—a micro-geology filtered between fibers that resisted vacuuming.

I pounded the hammer, driving the crowbar through a seam in the carpet, prying and ripping and tossing hunks of carpet down the stairs. The short-handled crowbar was embossed with the words *Wonder Bar*. I wondered at the manufacturer's obliviousness to absurdity, or were the words part of a preposterous marketing campaign?

My arms ached and one of the flimsy latex gloves ripped. I switched to leather gloves and kept at it, inhaling dank air trapped inside the paper mask, my breath raspy like Darth Vader's.

Sitting on a step, surrounded by detritus—carpet and carpet pad, nails and tack strips—I closed my eyes. Downstairs, the fish-tank aerator whirred, and in the basement, the furnace pump started with a little whoosh followed by faint clicking inside the wall where copper pipes expanded as hot water flowed through them. The stairwell certainly was the heart of the house, and for a moment, it may have been the center of the universe.

I am intrigued by the idea that one spot might be the center of the universe, but as a poetic matter rather than a scientific question. Perhaps the center of the universe is akin to the pole of inaccessibility, which is the most inaccessible place, measured as the farthest point from a shoreline in any direction. Likely, our self-centered nature allows us to imagine we occupy a point that feels like the center of the universe when we encounter a sublime scene. Of course, this evocative moment—a point in time and place—cannot be the stairwell of my house no matter how many stories orbit there, yet I still like the idea.

T E R R A I N • Inside a windowless room, walls mutate—
gold blending through gray to mountain blue agate. From hidden speakers, melodic flute, elfin whistle, and bells lilt as thin
as mist drifting along a far shore. When I paid my admission
to the Museum of the North, the attendant said, "This morning the room glowed red."

A day earlier, I drove to Fairbanks to attend the Beringia
Conference and listen to researchers' presentations about
Alaska and Siberia, regions only fifty miles apart but practically
impossible to travel between due to geopolitical fractiousness.
At the conference, presenters discussed settlements, whaling,
and ways that animals and plants migrate and adapt to the
changing environment. Most presentations were in English,
but some were in Russian. The Russian speakers received
headsets with simultaneous translation into Russian, but
Russian researchers' presentations came to us (the English
speakers) in a more disjointed fashion. Every few sentences,
the presenter paused while a translator relayed what he (or
she) said into English.

The Russian researchers and scientists arrived a day or
so after the conference began because of issues with their
chartered plane or government regulators. Traveling between
Siberia and Alaska wasn't a routine matter—but it isn't always
like that.

Even though national borders may impede journeys,
national boundaries cannot barricade weather systems or
ocean currents, wildlife migrations and changes wrought by
a warming planet.

At the Museum of the North, a room called *The Place Where You Go to Listen* offers a side trip to nonverbal terrain. I sit on a bench, letting my mind drift and hoping for insights regarding how we interact with Earth. Other people come in but quickly depart, chased out, I guess, by the room's baffling pulse.

My mind wanders and my heart pounds. Was the sound coming from inside my head? Aspects of Earth and the heavens swirled like wisps of fog or eddies in a stream. The room, situated at the core of the museum, replaces the sensory stimulus of the outdoors with an enveloping improvisation concocted by computer algorithms using real-time data from sunrises, sunsets, the aurora, moon phases, and earthquakes.

T I M E • What is cause and effect?

A seismic event occurs and data is collected, transported, converted to tones and colors, and piped into the enclosed space. The room offers a very different experience compared to being outdoors, observantly watching and listening. External stimuli are absent. No distant sounds or far-off views. No glint of sunlight on automobiles. No electric lights, blaring car alarms, sirens, or strobes. No conversations or food. The wind doesn't muss your hair, melt snow, spray fire from treetops, or shift seeds. Absolutely no silt in *The Place Where You Go to Listen*. The room is a sanitized art-space, unlike Earth, and yet I am immersed in the inscrutable throb of the planet.

T E R R A I N • After nearly an hour, I depart to attend to the chore of washing my car, which, after three days parked in Fairbanks, still toted a shell of dirty ice. Driving from Palmer, I'd encountered rain, snow, slush, and freezing slush. North of Denali the temperature plummeted and ice lumpily accumulated on my car—like it was the nucleus of a dirty comet.

Even in late October, the afternoon sun barely cleared peaks of the Alaska Range. Waiting in line at the car wash, I asked the attendant which level would remove the ice. "Premium," he replied without hesitation.

After my car was thawed, cleaned, and dried, I returned to the museum. This time, I stopped to read the explanation. The composer, John Luther Adams, wrote that the music (inside the room) has "no beginning, middle or end." Unlike an orchestral composition that either ends quickly or drags on but still eventually gets wrapped up with big chords or lyrical sweetness, the music inside *The Place Where You Go to Listen* "changes at the tempo of nature." This interests me because most indoor places exist parallel to nature, not entwined with nature. I'm tantalized by a real-time musical interpretation of Earth and the heavens, yet the complexity is daunting.

What if the anciently hypothesized music of the spheres could be represented by a technology-enabled translation of the natural world? Unlike a musical composition that begins and must eventually end, nature proceeds timelessly—like tidal ebbs and flows—but at a sedate pace of sunrises and sunsets, although sometimes punctuated by the ground-ripping outburst of an earthquake. I wonder, how would I write rules to musically convey earthly and celestial occurrences? Would my computer code be gnarly? Or elegant? Either way, my interpretation would likely be overly complex. I would descend into minuteness, needing a magnifying glass or macro lens to decode the details.

Inside, the room has changed—again. A band of lavender shades the floor while the wall has acquired a blond hue like dawn, or dusk. Gold bleeds upward, morphing to shades of amber. Near the ceiling, blue merges into lavender like a collision between noon and night, and bands of turquoise arch upward like cathedral windows.

This place, for indeed it is a place, situated inside the Museum of the North, has no expectations of me. I find myself entertaining the idea of staying longer, just to see—if I really camped out here—what else I might learn. Of course, this interpretation of Earth and sky is wrapped in museum structure. Rules. Hours. Institutional control of access. I look at my watch. Outside, the sun sinks below the Alaska Range, disappearing beyond the curvature of the earth.

Driving home a couple days later, I am still thinking about the museum room, digitally linked to segments of the natural world unaffected by humans. Staying inside the room longer than a few minutes changed the experience from casually interesting to eerily disquieting. Mutating colors hinted at a rainbow gone amok.

That room would render a very different experience if data inputs were switched to circumstances like traffic, unemployment, and housing, although economic data would likely prove to be tedious entertainment. Tonal and visual displays concocted from data on deforestation, urban expansion, loss of biodiversity, and extinctions would offer an edginess but also an admonishment for mindfulness. I imagine an installation that is redesigned numerous times and eventually ends up as an ad hoc biodiversity simulator. There would be a switch allowing visitors to select data streams from an array of postindustrial accelerations—biologic, geographic, atmospheric, oceanic. Like the original, the place I imagine would function in real time but with a focus on human-wrought change. As time passes, the effects would prove increasingly restless and troubling, the tonal landscape devolving into a thunderous entanglement as if between Tchaikovsky and Holst—*1812 Overture* colliding with *The Planets*. How could these composers from the past have figured out our times?

C A B I N • When we moved in, the stairway walls were wallpapered with a pattern of tiny fleurs-de-lis, in brown and white, like you might expect on men's pajamas. Eventually, the drab walls bothered me enough that, using a stepladder and planks, I assembled scaffolding above the stairs. Balanced on this platform, I sponged and scrubbed, attempting to wash the dreary paper off the wall. Getting nowhere, I tried gouging with a metal scraper, but only thin shreds peeled off. Several hours of tedious labor revealed only a few patches of plaster and plywood. I gave up on removing the wallpaper and instead spackled holes and cracks, and sanded it smooth.

The hardware store had flyers with instructions on how to paint a sponged—and mottled—wall. Photos of the finished sponge-painting showed how well it obscured badly plastered walls. I rolled on a coat of cream-colored paint, then daubed and swirled a layer of green. Not perfect, but good enough, which may have been what Mr. Webb said after he nailed in the last oddly shaped stair tread before climbing the new stairs to bed.

C A B I N • Our well was not the first in the neighborhood to quit. The year before, we heard rumors of other wells drying up. Sometimes I noticed a drill rig parked in someone's yard, punching a new hole into the earth. When we mentioned our well's reduced flow to our neighbor, Ralph Hulbert, he mused that the beaver population had declined in the Talkeetna Mountains and speculated that subterranean flow feeding valley aquifers had been affected. Water backed up behind beaver dams would percolate into the soil slowly rather than coursing downhill along a streambed.

Water records show the well in the corner of the basement was drilled in 1949. Not long after we moved in, water stopped flowing from the faucets. A plumber diagnosed the problem as the pump, a squat mechanism that sat on the basement floor with a pipe threaded down the well and an electric cord plugged into a ceiling outlet. After finishing the repairs, the plumber said, "No guarantees. Your pump may last a month, or another ten years."

A decade later, in early spring with birch still bare of leaves and the ground partially frozen, the well quit. The pump whined and air spit from the faucets. Chuck lowered a weighted string down the pipe. When he pulled it up, only the very end of the line was damp. I doubted a plumber would be able to coax water from the well this time.

To the west, beyond a hayfield, sunlight glistened on a small lake. Rainfall and snowmelt and springs or other subterranean flow fed that pool. Some years the water level dropped. As if a tipping point had been reached, would the lake become a wetland, too shallow and grassy to even launch a canoe? A few years later, the water level rebounded. Apparently, this hydrologic ebb-and-flow also occurred underground.

I called several well drillers listed in the phone book and asked whether they could deepen our existing well. This strategy struck me as more efficient and probably less costly than drilling a new well. When I mentioned that the well had four-inch casing, one of the men remarked that he'd seen an old drill rig with a four-inch bit in a junkyard.

"We use six-inch casing now," he laughed. "No one has an antique rig that could deepen your well."

Not only was our well dry but the small-diameter well pipe was obsolete. Even if that hadn't been a problem, local well drillers were scheduled for months drilling new wells or deepening existing wells.

Without water, Chuck or I drove to Palmer every day and filled several five-gallon containers from a hose behind a gas station. Sometimes I waited while someone else filled their containers. The lack of running water proved an annoyance, and we stingily conserved water as if we were camping inside our house.

Although the state did not declare an emergency, there was enough work that well drillers came from outside Alaska. We hired one of those well drillers. A few weeks later a big drill truck slowly backed past the caragana hedge and spruce and maneuvered around the front of the house, between the Siberian crabapple and the old lilac. A truck hauling well-casing pipes followed. The drill rig parked in the backyard near the kitchen window. Slowly, men splayed the rig's stabilizing feet and raised the drill tower.

After a couple days of nearly continuous pounding, silty water flowed from the deeper well. A backhoe dug a trench to the corner of the house beside the bumped-out basement room with the obsolete and dry well. A submersible pump was lowered into the new well. Electric wires and pipes were laid in the trench, and the trench was filled in. After that, the trucks lumbered away, leaving deep grooves in the half-thawed lawn.

The new well pumped from a strata fifty feet deeper than the well drilled in 1949. Once again, water flowed from faucets and filled the toilet tank. Water from the deeper well tasted different—sharper and less sweet, but not objectionable.

T E R R A I N • The new well solved our lack of water but did nothing to address a diminished aquifer. My inclination was to quickly fix the problem by drilling deeper—as if we were the only ones who faced this situation. Causes of the lower water table were likely multiple, including less precipitation and more houses (with wells) tapping into the same aquifer. The role of beaver ponds in aquifer stability was a tantalizing idea. I wondered whether the aquifer would recover to what I assumed were normal levels. Or was the climate becoming drier? More desert-like? Palmer averages sixteen inches of precipitation annually. A desert generally receives less than ten inches of precipitation in a year.

The valley would look considerably different as a desert. Less rain and snowfall accompanied by warmer, or colder, temperatures would likely change the plant communities. Farmers would irrigate more. Perhaps irrigation canals would be constructed like in dry valleys across the western United States. Maybe farmers would request permission to drill high-volume wells for irrigation. After that, every summer, sprinklers would roll back-and-forth or pivot in large circles, soaking fields of vegetables, barley, and hay.

T I M E • The question "What is normal?" nags me. I'm inclined to assume that what I experience, whether snowfall or droughts, is the norm and not that I live in an anomalous time. The difficulty with perception as a guide is that there are too many situations competing for our attention. Like looking across a landscape, from the flowering meadow you're standing in to distant mountain peaks, the vista appears as one vast scene rather than myriad details.

E A R T H • I planted a few flowers and a clematis vine to camouflage the new well pipe sticking up in the backyard.

W A T E R • "There," Ralph said, "eggs that will never hatch."

"Why?" I scanned the shallow pool for anything other than pebbles. Ruth quickly spotted the eggs and finally I, too, spied them—tiny orbs, purple and translucent like beads scattered from a broken necklace.

Ralph explained that in order to hatch, salmon eggs must be buried, but these were plainly visible.

It was early October. I had accompanied Ralph and his daughter, Ruth, to count salmon in Spring Creek, a slow-flowing stream that starts near Palmer and meanders across the hay flats to Cook Inlet. We parked one vehicle near the interchange and drove the other, with a canoe on top, toward Old Matanuska, one of the original valley settlements but now with too few relics to even hint at a ghost town. Ralph parked near a pool between the gravel road and the railroad berm where a few spawned-out salmon swam listlessly and several dead salmon wedged along the shallow edge.

After a few minutes we abandoned our examination of the pool and launched the canoe. I climbed into the front and Ruth settled on waterproof cushions in the middle. Ralph gave the vessel a final push and quickly stepped into the stern. We paddled easily along the channel, helped by the lazy streamflow.

Cottonwoods, willows, and alders hemmed Spring Creek. A fin rippled the water. I counted the first fish.

Beneath a flat gray sky, raindrops whispered against the stream. Now and then, a ruddy-hued salmon split the surface, then sank out of sight. We had counted twenty-eight salmon by the time that a mass of submerged plants slowed our progress. Ralph announced he would stand and look for a better course. I braced my hands against the sides of the canoe and glanced back. Ralph was standing but then he sat again and we continued on the same course, shoving our paddles into wads of *Hippuris*—mare's tail—that looked like pond weeds to me. The plants were rooted in the streambed with narrow leafy whorls breaking the water's surface. Finally, we were beyond the paddle-grabbing vegetation, but then—as in a story where characters must overcome obstacles—the watercourse became shallower and cluttered with clumps of grass as stiff as brooms. We pushed hard with the paddles, poling like gondoliers along the grass-choked waterway. (Viewed from the sky, the canoe would be a red needle darning holes in the stream.) Ruth leaned out and aimed her camera at algae that formed a submerged structure like crushed geodesic domes—surely more barricade than thoroughfare for fish. Indeed, how do salmon navigate a vegetation-clogged stream? By tunneling? Or leaping? But fish have one view, and we have another. In fact, we have many views, even from space.

S K Y • Above the slate-colored clouds, satellites and the International Space Station orbit. The space station has humans aboard, the satellites do not, and both carry data collection devices and cameras. Onboard the Space Station, an astronaut angles a camera through a porthole framing a swath of Earth with an intriguing habitation pattern or unusual weather systems. On the dark side of the planet, astronauts photograph brazen lights marking the spiderweb-creep of civilization.

I see these photos as remarkable—at night our settlements are reduced to electrical networks that appear like phosphorescing dendrites. We know how to interpret these images—as cities and streets, highways and towns—spread across continents.

Daytime views highlight visual geography—oceans, rivers, mountain ranges—and clouds.

T I M E • If astronauts could have photographed the Matanuska Valley in the mid-twentieth century, they might have focused a lens on southcentral Alaska, photographing the western edge of the Matanuska River where steel sheet piling was installed in an attempt to stop erosion. Chuck remembers family picnics and a good swimming hole at "the dikes." Now forest has overgrown the rusted metal walls and the river is nowhere in sight.

W A T E R • We paddled onward, eventually emerging from the grass-strangled channel into deeper water with an assemblage of lilies. At the height of summer, the glossy leaves float like giant saucers cradling tea-cup-sized yellow blooms, but now, in autumn, the lilies' tubular stems have bleached, the leaves as pale as faded gingham.

Ruth pointed toward a bald eagle hunched on the top branch of a cottonwood tree, and I noticed electric poles, faded silver and leaning, with insulators but no wires. As we paddled, our angle of view changed. The poles formed a line, like a giant fence, along a swath chopped through brush and trees straight toward Pioneer Peak. Ralph commented that the poles had once supported lines conducting electricity from the Eklutna power plant. The cleared strip beneath the disused poles suggests that the electric company still views the right-of-way as an asset.

Water dripped off my paddle as I rested it on the side of the canoe. "The stream has changed again," I commented.

Ralph replied, "The land itself has changed. In fact, everywhere we've been today has changed."

T I M E • The topic of a changing landscape had come up earlier that day. Before we launched the canoe, we drove west of the Glenn Highway along Nelson Road where we stopped beside every culvert to assess the possibility of salmon passage. Rain pelted us each time we got out of the vehicles to check for flowing water, free-swimming salmon, and a canoeable channel.

"Of course, everything has changed," Ralph said.

"Like what?" I asked, standing on the gravel road that stretched straight as a tightened string between an upland subdivision and the freeway. After the overpass and interchange were built, the highway became limited-access, ending Nelson Road's usefulness as a shortcut for commuters. Glancing back the way we'd come, the view was dismal—of rain-slicked and puddle-pocked gravel hemmed by thickets. In the distance, a speck gradually became larger, materializing into a white car splashing through potholes, with two large hounds bounding alongside. Approaching us, the driver seemed to change her mind, slowing and reversing direction so that both car and galloping hounds receded. We continued our search for culverts with enough flow for salmon passage.

"The land used to be drier here," Ralph commented, "and homesteaded."

Small landlocked lakes or ponds may become shallower over many decades, filling with fallen leaves and silt, transformed into bogs and, after much time, meadows. But what does it take for the land to become wetter? A change in hydraulics—of subterranean water flow? More rain? Subsidence? Rising sea level?

During the Great Alaska Earthquake on Good Friday 1964, the hay flats sank by as much as two feet—a lot of falling for terrain already near sea level.

W A T E R • Paddling along Spring Creek, concrete piers of the freeway overpass loomed larger, but perspective plays tricks. The pickup, parked near the bridge and blurred by rain, remained small. Aiming for the truck, the first channel we entered proved impassible. The shallow water was choked with willows that had been flailed to brushy stumps by mechanical choppers maneuvering across ice during winter highway construction.

Searching for another route, we drifted toward the bridge columns, where the stream widened. Ralph reached with his paddle and hooked a bladderish object, a slimy thing that hung like a plastic placenta, water streaming out until it shrank to its real form, a shopping bag. Ralph dropped the flimsy plastic into the canoe. Now distracted from our search for salmon and a route to the parked truck, we crisscrossed the pool beneath the overpass, plucking out trash. Water leaking from the cast-off plastic trash sloshed in the bottom of the canoe.

Paddling toward three small culverts, I noticed that the yawning mouth of one culvert was plugged by a tire, still on its rim, and some boards. Whose job is it to clean the culverts? How do migrating salmon manage to navigate between Cook Inlet and upper Spring Creek? An otter or beaver could climb out of the stream and amble overland, avoiding the constricted channel, but salmon must swim.

Peering into the culverts, I saw nothing but darkness, no pinprick of light at the end, but three live salmon and a dead one lingered nearby. We turned and paddled beneath overhanging willow branches, pausing to untangle another plastic bag from a twig.

Ruth looked at the brushy mound that rose six feet above us. "An abandoned beaver lodge?" she asked.

"Yes," Ralph said, "and not that long ago."

Why no beavers now? Did they abandon their lodge when construction began on the freeway bridges? Before that disruption, the highway had been only a few feet above the stream.

Beavers might survive here now, perhaps finding this lake more peaceful with traffic confined overhead.

After another quarter hour of searching, we located a passable channel and a few minutes later pulled the canoe ashore near the pickup.

I came away from this canoe trek thinking about how complicated ecologies are—and how we constantly interrupt nature. Reengineering the highway intersection improved traffic flow and raised it above the wetland, which seemed like a positive nod to stream ecology, but the blocked culverts and floating trash told a different story.

CABIN • While watching television on a summer evening, I glimpsed a quick scuttle alongside a wall. More shadow, shape, and movement than form and easily dismissed as nothing. A day or two later, a rodent—short legged with fur as dark as mink and smaller than the palm of my hand—dashed across the room. I shouted, and the creature scurried faster. Grabbing a box from the closet shelf, I pushed aside furniture, hoping to drop the container over the mouse. (Or was it a vole?) The creature nudged along the bottom of a bookcase and vanished into a slim crack.

Of course a single mouse in the house does not constitute an invasion, but later that afternoon the rodent raced past my feet in the bathroom. Like the Roadrunner, sensing danger, it spun and dashed the other direction. I wished for shoes on my bare feet as the rodent frantically clawed the bottom of the door. Grabbing a basket from the countertop, I dropped it, intending to trap the mouse. Again my reflexes were too slow. The tiny creature dashed behind the toilet and disappeared, this time beneath the heating register.

Had I seen a mouse? Or a vole? A mouse has a long tail, a vole a short tail, but I hadn't noticed particulars. The difference mattered because a spring-loaded wire trap needs bait, and mice can be lured by peanut butter but voles prefer meat.

The next morning while brewing coffee, I heard agitated scratching inside the wall. I'd been reading a book called *Ice Is Where You Find It,* and it struck me that mice (or voles) are also where you find them. Scrounging in the garage for traps, I found two, unused since the previous winter. Gingerly, I baited the traps and hooked the spring-loaded wires and placed one by the bookcase and the other in the bathroom.

T E R R A I N • Rodents don't usually venture inside the house during summer. Winter is a different story though. When the ground freezes hard without a cover of snow, mice and voles search for avenues into this warmly heated house. Each autumn, with a certain futility, we hunt for possible entry points, cracks between logs or a notch near the foundation, but we never locate all the gaps, and we will never find the ingress underneath the siding. A mouse can leap or scramble up the foundation and slip behind the siding where he climbs, unimpeded, along what may be well-traveled routes, even ramps, in the narrow dark space. At the top of the log wall, the rodents flatten themselves, squeezing into the framed walls and ceiling.

When snow comes early, falling thickly across lawn and garden, mice rarely venture into our living space. Even when the Matanuska sweeps away the snow, drifts form in the lee of trees, offering habitat and protection. In the spring, after the snow melts, winter rodent life manifests as intricate mazes cropped into the lawn.

C A B I N • The first solid evidence of repeated passage by mice or voles appeared as black seed-sized turds underneath the sink. Surmising an off-putting stench (of death, perhaps?)

with the old traps, I smeared peanut butter on a new trap, carefully hooked the wire, and shoved the trap into the cupboard. The next morning, the trap was still empty. I tapped it with a screw driver and the wire sprang with a thwack. Switching bait from peanut butter to meat, I reset the trap. A day later, that bait was gone, licked clean.

"You need a hair trigger trap," Chuck said, and he baited an old one that had been tinkered with to be more easily sprung.

By the time Chuck set the hair-trigger mousetrap underneath the sink, I envisioned the creature that had licked the bait as a survivor. Having cheated death once, I hoped she would return to the garden or forest, and we would just file away the summertime incursion with other anomalous memories.

The next morning, a loud whack sounded underneath the sink. I cautiously opened the cupboard door. The trap's hard-sprung wire had crushed a vole. Glossy brown fur belied its deadness.

T I M E • My grandmother Violet delighted in telling stories about her tough life as a kid during the early 1900s, growing up on a wheat farm on the Saskatchewan prairie. Hearing her stories when I was a child, perhaps the same age she had been, I thought her youth was very adventuresome. For a time, she had been a bounty hunter.

"The government paid for proof that a rodent had been killed," Grandma said, hurrying through a household task. "I trapped mice. Hundreds of them. Proof was a set of ears, so I cut off the ears and turned them in to get paid."

"That sounds disgusting," I said, mesmerized by her story.

"It wasn't that bad," she replied. "They were dead and I had thrown them all on a pile. The funny thing," she mused, "was that the government changed the rules, deciding to take tails instead of ears."

"They probably didn't like counting all those little ears," I said smartly. "What did you do?" I asked even though I had heard the story before.

"I went back to the pile of carcasses and cut off the tails. You couldn't tell, from just the tails, how long they'd been dead. I doubled my bounty-take."

Grandma Violet always dressed impeccably in a straight knee-length skirt and pumps. If she was gardening or cleaning house she wore a smock over her blouse and skirt. No one would have guessed her hard-edged youth.

C A B I N • I don't wish extinction upon mice or voles. I don't mind them encamped underneath snow, but that's where I wished they would remain—outside, roaming forest and fields.

Indoors, I tolerated gray spiders as reclusive as ghosts and practically as invisible, and I barely noticed when a cricket escaped just before being dropped into the terrarium with two hungry lizards. After a few weeks, having reached maturity, the lonely cricket—hiding in the basement ceiling or underneath the refrigerator—began to chirp. With amazing stamina, he carried on his monotonous chant all night, every night, it seemed for weeks. In Asia and other places, crickets are said to be a sign of household luck, and why not? The crickets inside our house had their own good luck of not being eaten by a lizard.

Once a cricket escaped we never found it. I suppose, eventually it died of old age but only after bedeviling us for weeks.

I have no patience, though, for indoor forays by squirrels, birds, and bats. Once, a chickadee found its way into the house. I tried to shoo it out the front door, but instead the tiny black-capped bird swooped around the living room then landed on a curtain rod. He stared at me incredulously. Of all birds, chickadees strike me as the least wild and most inquisitive, as if they might hop onto an outstretched finger like a tame parakeet. With the front door open, and holding a large towel like a portable wall, I again tried to shoo the chickadee outside. He launched from the curtain rod, flew past me, and spotting the open door, escaped.

Very infrequently, a bat slips into the house, perhaps entering through a tiny crack in the wall underneath the eaves. If the bat had only napped in the attic, I would not have noticed, but awakening in the dark hours of a late-summer night, I sensed a slight rustle of air and heard a faint clicking.

"Chuck," I whispered, "I hear a bat."

"What?" he mumbled, sleepily.

"A bat. In the house."

Slightly more awake, he asked, "Did you see it?"

"No. It's too dark."

I got out of bed. At the top of the stairs, I felt a whoosh beside my head as I flicked on the light switch. With the stairwell illuminated, I saw nothing.

Returning to the bedroom, I carefully shut the door and, for good measure, pushed a blanket against the crack underneath.

"I think it flew downstairs," I said, climbing back into bed.

"Good," Chuck replied, already mostly asleep.

"I'll look for it tomorrow," I whispered wide awake and imagining the bat flying through the other rooms. Was he hunting inside our house? Or searching for an exit into the night?

The next morning, eating breakfast with sunshine streaming through the large windows, I scrutinized walls and ceiling for any nook or cranny where a bat might sleep.

Chuck departed for work and I was supposedly working from home that day, but actually I was searching for the bat even though I wasn't totally certain there was one inside the house. In the basement, with overhead lights on, I pointed a flashlight at ceiling joists that were visible between several drop-ceiling panels. The basement resembled a cave. Dark and quiet. And underground. Another time, I had found a bat, upside down and asleep, clutching a beam in the basement ceiling. Despite careful inspection, I did not find a bat in the basement.

The rest of the morning I kept watch, trying to discern where a bat might conceal itself but also wondering if I had imagined it.

At lunchtime, sitting at the table, I looked anew at the window shade. The blind was stitched from thin strips of wood with a flap at the top of the same material. I stood and slowly lifted the edge of the valance. Underneath, gripping the matchstick-sized slats, a bat slept. Very slowly, not wishing to wake the creature, I lowered the valance.

Relating this story, I stop and consider the characters. Chuck was a minor character. He barely woke up in the night and departed for work first thing in the morning. So the story sounds like it's about me. During the night I thought I sensed a bat, and I spent the morning searching for it. But the small brown bat is the main character. If it had only slept in the attic space, always entering and exiting through the same aperture, I would not have noticed it.

I am sympathetic toward bats. Along with dragonflies and swallows, bats devour insects while in flight, which makes the yard more habitable for us. This is my human-centric view of comfort, but more importantly, bats exist within an ecological niche—they eat and get eaten (by owls, for instance) and even provide habitat for other life forms.

I propped open the front door and donned a heavy jacket and leather gloves. Gingerly I pushed a thick towel upward, behind the valance, gently clasping the sleeping bat. The small animal awoke to this affront and struggled, but the swaddling kept it from thrashing about. Like transporting eggs, I carried the terrified bat outside, only then realizing that I had no release plan. As a kid, I had seen bats hanging like odd ornaments from the limbs of fruit trees. The caragana hedge beside the driveway caught my eye and I unfolded the towel among the branches. The shock of capture and the daylight discomfited the bat and I wished that I had released it in the dim interior of the barn. The little bat balanced for a moment in the shrubbery then flopped onto the lawn, its wings splayed wide, its brown fur glossy and very beautiful. With no predators in the vicinity, I left the bat in the shade of the hedge where, I think, it found refuge until dusk.

TERRAIN • The east-facing picture window framed Lazy Mountain, which nestled like a child-peak in front of Matanuska Peak. Unlike the taller mountain, Lazy had sloping flanks and no escarpment, at least that was the view from our living room window, six miles away.

At the Lazy Mountain trailhead, I plucked a pair of trekking poles from the back of my car, zipped my windbreaker, hooked a small pack around my waist, and tramped across asphalt toward a notch in the brush where the trail began. Beyond the first fringe of trees, the path squeezed through a botanic tunnel. Pink spike-blooms of fireweed crowded my shoulders and bluebells hugged my legs. Crossing a thin stream, mud oozed around my shoes. Where nettles draped the trail, I raised my hands to avoid touching the stinging plants. The path steepened and I propelled my legs forward, my arms swinging, the poles rhythmically striking the ground. My breathing came faster. A chickadee called from the scrub, and a raven soared above me, guffawing like an old man. Something rustled in the foliage but no animal appeared. A plank spanning a wet spot squished into the mud as I trod across.

Trudging uphill, I concentrated on my own locomotion and motivating my legs to climb. The humid air bore enticing aromas of rain-drenched vegetation and damp earth. At a grove of whimsically slim aspens, I grabbed tree trunks and pulled myself up over roots that protruded like cockeyed stairs. When the trail leveled off, I breathed more easily but that didn't last.

T I M E • On my first visit to Alaska, Chuck and I climbed Lazy. At the summit, I was euphoric. The wide view was nothing like my previous experiences in the Pacific Northwest, hiking along game trails in pine forests or riding horseback across rangeland. I had not encountered such graceful alpine terrain or such a magnificent vista.

I do not recall my first trek up Lazy as particularly tiring, but I was in my twenties at the time. The trail to the summit gains three thousand feet in two and a half miles, and some sections go straight up the mountainside as if pioneered by hiking anarchists intoxicated by perpetual summer daylight.

T E R R A I N • Glimpsing movement, I stepped off the trail. A gray-haired man wearing running shorts hurtled past with the abandon of a big flightless bird. I continued plodding uphill. Fatigue accumulated, each footfall a measure of muscle burn. After an hour of climbing, the brushy vegetation opened to a vertiginous meadow awash with lavender-hued geraniums and scattered with chocolate lilies. Far below, the Old Glenn Highway meandered through forest. I paused, letting my breathing slow and watching automobiles—tiny as matchbox cars—trundle along the minute ribbon of pavement. Mincing steps like a tightrope walker, I trod a hairline path across the abrupt slope. Reaching a thicket, twiggy limbs offered handholds beside a staircase of thick timbers.

Stepping out of the alders was like slipping through the side door onto an unbounded stage. Squinting in the bright sunlight, I dropped my pack on a hefty picnic table incongruously situated on this roadless ridge dubbed the "first hump" of Lazy.

To the east, gravelly terrain and tundra sloped into McRoberts Valley where a stream sliced the slopes brocaded with aspen. At the far end of the valley, a pencil-scratch trail etched the scree-laden shoulder of Matanuska Peak. To the south, Knik Valley glistened with lakes and wetlands. In the far distance, where the Knik River begins, Knik Glacier gleamed like a marooned ice planet.

Scanning nearby slopes for moose or bear, I saw neither. Nor cattle.

S W I T Z E R L A N D • Chuck's cousin Irene, who has short gray hair and a mischievous smile, lives on a mountainside above the Rhône Valley. One morning, while visiting Irene, we piled into her station wagon. Her old dog, a Belgian Malinois named Salto, jumped into the back of the car. I sat in the backseat and Chuck sat in the front. Irene planned outings without telling us much. "Wait and see," she would say mysteriously. "Bring your jacket." Or, "No, we won't pack a lunch this time." Irene backed the car out of the garage and up a short, steep driveway. We zoomed along narrow roads, winding between patches of forest and astonishingly precipitous—and ancient—terraced vineyards. In early September, weather in the Alps felt like summer, which seemed surprising to me. In the Matanuska Valley, early September offers up decidedly autumn conditions of cool days and freezing nights. By the fall equinox the first snowfall might arrive as an annoyance but not a surprise.

Irene steered into a side valley toward the mouth of a tunnel. Inside the one-lane tunnel, black rock walls muted the headlights. Irene drove deftly and fast, the curving darkness only periodically illuminated by daylight streaming through alcove windows.

"Listen for honking," Irene said casually. I checked my seatbelt as she blasted the horn and spun through a blind corner.

The tunnel straightened. A horn-blaring crescendo accompanied the gleam of oncoming headlights. Irene yanked the steering wheel and slammed the brakes, pivoting the car into an alcove. Realizing that I'd been holding my breath, I exhaled. A vehicle whizzed past but we lingered. Outside the car, we leaned over a low stone wall with a bird's-nest view. Across a chasm, trees and shrubs laced a precipitous stack of rock ledges—like a wildland tableau or the ancient Hanging Gardens of Babylon.

We scanned the cliffs through binoculars, searching for birds and wildlife. Seeing none, we squeezed back into the car and continued through the tunnel in the same disjointed manner as before. Honking. Zooming. Waiting. I was relieved when we finally exited into a narrow valley surrounded by steep slopes and pinnacles as dramatic as the fabled Shangri-la.

"Le Derborence," Irene announced as she parked under trees beside a couple of other vehicles. "I'm glad we didn't meet the PostBus in the tunnel," she commented as if the thought had just occurred to her. The pristine morning combined with being free of the tunnel contributed to a lightness of mood. Salto bounded about excitedly.

Irene pointed toward a trail high up the slope where, years before, she hiked over the mountains to the next valley. Peering through binoculars, I finally discerned a trail traversing a meadow so green the grass appeared painted on.

Above the meadow, the footpath vanished amid scree slopes and cliff faces. Continuing my magnified perusal, I noticed animals scattered across the abrupt and incessantly green meadow. "Irene, are those cows?" I asked.

"They're battle cows," she replied matter-of-factly, "raised for meat not milk, and the cows—not the bulls—fight. They head-butt, and there are tournaments to decide which cow is the best."

The cows weren't fighting and didn't appear hostile through my distant binocular view.

Walking, my feet generated locomotion while my mind acclimated to the slower pace and sensations of nature that are so different from being inside a fast-moving vehicle. Salto ran ahead and splashed through streams while we balanced on log bridges and later soaked our shoes jumping between rocks near a footbridge ironically stranded in a dry channel. While hiking through woods and meadows and around a small lake, our changing perspective did not affect the grandeur. We stepped over a low electric fence and strolled past chalets that, Irene said, had once been inhabited by shepherds and farmers but now were vacation homes. The chalets looked like houses to me, unlike the rustic homesteader's cabin where my family spent weekends when I was a child.

After more traipsing, we came upon a café where, at midday, diners already crowded the outdoor deck. Sliding onto benches, we ordered cold drinks. Salto hunkered in the shade under the table.

I thought we had chanced upon the eatery, but later I realized that Irene had planned, and intentionally guided us, on a

meandering route through the mountain-and-meadow landscape. We fancied ourselves in the wilds, but we were actually pupils that day. Irene was teaching us about Switzerland
as a long-inhabited place, and we were learning the lesson of
not taking landscape at face value.

T I M E • When Irene visited Alaska, she was not interested
in cities, culture, or human settlement. She wanted to see
what she wouldn't encounter where she lived—large wildlife, especially bears. She signed up for a bear viewing tour
on the west side of Lower Cook Inlet. When she stayed with
us, we hiked in the Talkeetna Mountains. On a September
afternoon, Irene and I drove to Hatcher Pass. We parked and
trekked up the rocky slope to Hatch Peak, a mountaintop that
resembles a hogback ridge rather than a crag. I mentioned
that we might see a whistling marmot and birds. From the
summit, the vista to the south encompassed the Matanuska
Valley, spread like a green handprint, the fingers interlaced
with silvery threads of the Knik and Matanuska Rivers. Smoky
haze from a forest fire festooned Pioneer Peak and obscured
the distant Chugach summits. If the atmosphere had been
spectacularly clear, Denali would have peeped over the jag-
ged ridges to the north. A raw breeze betokened autumn.

Irene and I settled in the lee of an outcrop and munched
snacks. Overhead, movement caused us both to glance up.
An owl soared low and soundlessly and, for an instant, stared
down at us, the sedentary ones. As if my whole lifetime was
encapsulated in the owl's dismissive gaze, I felt gravity pulling
at my skin, wrinkles forming, my joints stiffening. Even with

the trekking poles, hiking down the long rock-strewn pitch proved more vexing than the ascent.

T E R R A I N • On the first hump of Lazy Mountain, I grabbed my pack off the picnic table and continued uphill along the worn footpath. The summit appeared near—beyond just one more hill—but the voice in my head that relies on memories insisted the peak was farther than I thought.

For another hour, I trudged uphill across tundra, period- ically navigating through thickets of stunted alders. Several times the path zigzagged up a bulky knoll that appeared to be the summit, but topping the rise, I realized that the trail still meandered upward. After yet another false summit, the pitch became steeper and littered with scree.

A storybook character climbing a mountain would need to collect a token at each waypoint—or each false summit. But this wasn't fantasy, my tired leg muscles attested to that. Finally, where the trail detoured beside a bony backbone of rocks, I was certain the summit was near. Summoning cour- age, I gripped the outcrop and sidled across. Below me the slope descended vertiginously and the hairline path I'd been following dead-ended at a rock face.

My determination faltered. No one else was around. Nobody would know whether I stood precisely on the sum- mit of Lazy, likewise no one would immediately realize if I tumbled over the edge. Nobody would hear me shout.

Leaning the trekking poles against the scarp, I gingerly stepped sideways along a ledge. With the greatest care—and not glancing down—I lifted and placed a foot then reached, feeling for another handhold. Eventually, this crablike passage brought me to a dip in the rocks. I pulled myself over the brim onto a broad patch of nearly flat ground. Alone on the summit of Lazy, I spun around, enthralled by the vista of mountains, rivers, and valleys.

For a few moments, I felt a magical vastness far more profound than encountered during a quick stop at a highway viewpoint. This was the sort of sublime solitude that drew monks and sages to mountaintops long before I sought reprieve from my technology-laden life. Without a smartphone, the summit of Lazy had no technological distractions. Only terrain. Wind. Temperature. Cloudiness. Feelings.

I looked across the Matanuska Valley, hugged by Cook Inlet and flanked by mountain ranges. Farther west, the elongated hump of Mount Susitna—Sleeping Lady—protruded from the seemingly flat Susitna Valley. The perpetually snow-covered Alaska Range embraced the farthest horizon, hooking Alaska into the Ring of Fire—a string of volcanoes rimming the Pacific Basin from Alaska to Asia, New Zealand, and the Americas.

C A B I N • Nearly ten years after replacing the urethane roofing, Chuck and I turned our attention to the wall in the garage, not because we were eager to remove the urethane coating the logs but because we needed more space. With two young children, the cabin-sized house had become exceptionally cramped.

I contacted a contractor who came over to assess the project we envisioned: merging half of the garage with the house. The contractor arrived to size up the project and discuss strategies for building a wall across the middle of the garage, replacing an automobile door with a wall and windows, and raising the floor. Flipping open a steel tape, he began measuring and jotting notes. Looking up, he studied the ceiling.

"That beam is sagging," he said, pausing thoughtfully, "and it isn't really a beam."

I had never considered the ceiling in the garage, but now I diligently looked up at it. Exposed between sections of drywall, what ought to have been a hefty timber was actually an agglomeration of overlapping boards, and none were long enough to span the thirty feet between the walls.

"I'll put a post there to support the ceiling until I build the new wall," the contractor said as he was leaving.

Later I asked Chuck, "How many times has the snow been deep enough to risk the garage roof collapsing?"

"I shoveled it a couple times," Chuck replied, shaking his head. "Probably more than one close call."

A close call suggests unexpected and dire circumstances with an inadequate contingency plan, or no contingency plan. Having a plan for an unlikely event explains life vests on boats and oxygen masks on jets. Yet creating a contingency plan requires recognition of risk. As far as I knew, the garage was okay—not structurally unsound and inadequately supported by a weak span that chanced collapse, especially with a heavy snow load. The timeline of possibilities—garage stands, garage falls—was unpredictable, unknown, and unthought of.

If I had been an engineer, architect, or builder, I would have noticed the weak span in the garage, but I was oblivious. I assumed that the garage would continue standing because it was standing. Eventually, the contractor constructed a wall that split the garage into two sections. In the absence of any other structural intervention, the new wall likely saved the structure.

During most of November and December, plastic sheeting hung across the back hall, isolating the construction mess from the rest of the house.

When we moved in, the living room walls were covered with dark paneling. A bookcase and a gun rack—both made from mahogany—had been installed on one wall, and mahogany baseboard and ceiling molding edged the room. Finding the dark paneling oppressive, I painted the walls white, taking care not to slop paint on the mahogany. At the time I felt an appreciation for the straight-grained beauty of the tropical wood. Now I wonder how mahogany ended up in a cabin-built house in Alaska at all.

Preparing to cut a doorway between the new living room and the original one, the contractor dismantled the gun rack and a section of the bookcase.

On the garage side, in the still unfinished room, one section of the urethane-coated log wall was not as lumpy.

"Could that be a window?" I asked.

The contractor studied the wall. "Yes, there was a window there." He tapped the wall with his hammer, knocking off a chunk of urethane and revealing plywood underneath. "The window was boarded up. Probably they took the glass out first, but we'll see."

Later, he pried off the plywood and, underneath, there was no glass or insulation. The contractor powered up a chainsaw and noisily sliced through the house logs below the abandoned window, creating a doorway connecting the original cabin with the partially renovated garage.

"What about the stability of this wall?" I asked, after the doorway was roughly cut.

"I'll brace the doorframe with steel," the contractor said matter-of-factly. He measured the distance between logs and drew a schematic for a bar that would stabilize the doorway. A couple weeks later, I picked up two customized steel bars at a metal fabrication shop. After the steel was bolted into a channel sawn into the log ends, that doorway became the place where I took shelter during earthquakes because I knew for certain it was well-anchored.

Inside the garage, the urethane-coated wall had been easy to ignore. As the remodel proceeded, that unappealing wall became an interior wall, and we needed a log recovery plan. The contractor mentioned that the quickest solution would be to install drywall over the urethaned logs. Chuck and I briefly mulled and then rejected that approach. Our inclination was toward rehabilitation.

"How long will it take to clean the wall?" I asked. Chuck and I were standing in the half-finished room. With the heating system connected, the space, still awaiting the drywall crew, was comfortably warm.

Chuck tapped a crowbar against the urethane and experimentally pried off a chunk. "It will certainly take much longer to peel it off than to spray it on," he said.

"Varnished logs would look nice," I said, imagining the surface of the logs thoroughly cleaned and polished and displaying the house's log cabin heritage.

T I M E • One time I levered off a corner of paneling in order to see the side of the logs that faced into the house. If they had been natural—gorgeously rounded—I would have yanked off all the paneling, but they weren't. Underneath the paneling, the logs had been slabbed off, not smoothly planed but gouged and feathered as if the tool used had been an adze, or a dull axe.

C A B I N • The urethane-coated wall rose nine feet to the ceiling and stretched nearly thirty feet—the length of the cabin. Cleaning the logs became an extended project. On weekends, Chuck put on old clothes and a dust mask and pried and pounded off clumps of urethane, clearing one small patch at a time. After a couple months of sporadic work, he had knocked the largest chunks off the entire wall.

The logs were more visible but not clean. Clots and nubbins of urethane remained. The logs felt rough to touch, as if coated with sand and pebbles. I helped. We switched to smaller tools—paint scrapers and rough sandpaper, and eventually fine-grit sandpaper like what my grandmother used to refinish furniture. Unmasking the logs boosted our enthusiasm as if we were archaeologists excavating evidence of prior lives, or an art restorer uncovering an original painting underneath more recently applied layers. We discerned beauty in the irregular shapes—stubs where a branch had been chopped, long angular cracks that formed as the logs dried, even a protruding steel spike had a mysterious charm.

C A B I N • The cut end of a house log is akin to a stump. Growth rings in the wood tell a story of wet and dry years, cooler or warmer temperatures, even insect infestations and stress. The logs in Cabin 135 contained an accounting of events from before our time, and from before homesteaders and colonists arrived in the valley. These logs had been trees when Russia owned Alaska—when communities in the valley were Dena'ina, and when the Ahtna people traveled across the mountains, from the Copper River valley, to trade with Cook Inlet people.

T I M E • Later in the nineteenth century, George Palmer, a trader and merchant, built a store near the village of Niteh on the delta of the Matanuska and Knik Rivers. During that same period, a staging point for shipping supplies to miners and prospectors was developing across Upper Cook Inlet. By the late 1880s, George Palmer had moved his store to New Knik on the western shore of Knik Arm, where goods could more easily be transported on small vessels from the port that eventually became known as Anchorage.

The history of Upper Cook Inlet shows a tangle of names—Old Knik, New Knik, Knik, Knik Anchorage, Niteh—some well-established, others forgotten. The urge to name is strong; we name our children, cities, streets, mountains, and rivers.

Naming adds familiarity and is how places get tagged, often by newcomers inclined to memorialize their own culture, reminding themselves of their former homes. I'm troubled by the inclination to import names. I wish to understand the history of a place—and geographic names can help realize, or at least ask, "What happened here?"

New Knik was a bustling town, but that changed in 1917 when the railroad was completed fifteen miles to the north where Wasilla was developing. Rail transport offered advantages over lightering, where small vessels depended on favorable tides and might be stymied by ice. After the railroad was built, New Knik declined.

A century-old postcard of New Knik displays a shoreline with docks and houses nestled between grassy hills. The scene looks romantic, with gardens and fences, like a place designed for a movie, or a hamlet on a foreign shore. A hundred years later, in the early twenty-first century, the shoreline where New Knik had been was a gravel pit, and adjacent areas were being investigated by the Matanuska-Susitna Borough for archaeological evidence.

A R C H A E O L O G Y • During the summer of 2008, I volunteered at the Knik archaeology site. The drive from my house took forty minutes. South of Wasilla, I turned onto a gravel pit road, my car trailing a cloud of dust and heaving through hollows and humps like a tired beast. Pulling off the track and parking in a weedy patch, I got out of the car and balanced on one foot then the other, swapping sandals for lace-up leather boots. Renée, another volunteer, arrived, her vehicle also shadowed by a plume of dust. Renée and I dawdled along the track toward the borough storage shed where archaeologist Dan Stone was stacking tools and supplies into a wheelbarrow.

The morning was pleasantly sunny. Dan greeted us cheerfully. As usual, he wore a dingy orange surveyor's vest and a wide-brimmed hat that gave him the appearance of an older Indiana Jones.

Renée and I traipsed after Dan, who pushed the wheelbarrow. Where the dirt track curved around the gravel pit, we veered left between scrubby trees. Beyond that, brush had been scraped away and a neat row of old cars suggested a hopefulness regarding repair or reuse. Dan maneuvered the wheelbarrow along a footpath into the forest. In a few more minutes, we reached the dig site, several thigh-deep pits clustered amid fully leafed birch and gangly wild roses. This excavation was not at New Knik, rather it was where Dena'ina were thought to have lived in earlier times.

For recordkeeping, archaeologists identify each site with a numeric code. Dan added names to these numbers, so we knew the pits descriptively, as Shore House and Rose House. Renée and I measured a one-meter square at the edge of Shore House and pounded spikes at the corners.

Kneeling in dappled shade, I used a diamond-shaped trowel to scrape thin layers of soil. Near my shoulders, stubs of chopped-off birch roots protruded from the earth. Cool dampness seeped through the fabric of my jeans. Being below ground level, at the bottom of the shallow excavation, offered a different perspective—trees stretching taller than normal, gravity seeming to grip me more fiercely.

Gurgling minced the air. Startled and curious, I climbed out of the hole and shoved through undergrowth to the top of the bluff. Far below and beyond a narrow beach, water surged north along Knik Arm. From the bluff, I watched the first coursing of the incoming tide that flowed like a river, but in reverse, toward the glaciers not out to sea.

Even though I lived near Cook Inlet and knew about the tidal fluctuation of thirty feet or more, the scene was new to me. Returning to the dig, I mentioned the forceful incoming tide.

Dan explained that the Dena'ina word for Cook Inlet, *tikahtnu*, means "big-water river." The name perfectly described the tidal flow.

Returning to the shallow pit, I scraped thin layers of soil into a dustpan and dumped the dirt into a bucket. When the bucket was full, I lugged it a dozen feet to the sifter—a metal screen attached to wheelbarrow handles, the handles fastened with hinges to a pair of wooden legs. Tipping earth from the bucket onto the screen, I repeatedly yanked the handles, shaking the screen back and forth. If something unusual appeared on top of the screen, even a flake of stone or a blackened rock, Dan would advise how to proceed.

Fine soil fell through the mesh. The agitation aerated particles and released an earthy aroma reminiscent of my grandparents' moist garden. Scrutinizing the tangle of rootlets and pebbles that remained on top of the screen, I frequently asked "What's this?" As a new volunteer, I had much to learn. What was truly of interest? A tightly curled piece of birch bark? A flat flake of stone? A smidgen of charcoal? The next day, a corner of Shore House yielded a cluster of stones that might have been collected for making tools, and Renée unearthed a board that was too fragile to remove intact.

T I M E • Like a fact of life or an aspect of history infrequently discussed, I consider how people come to reside in certain places and then don't. How one change may steamroll into many—but what causes people to leave a place? The draw of other opportunities? Loss of livelihood? Escape from unfavorable situations? Famine? War? Disease?

I consider my family. During the Great Depression, my dad's parents loaded a car with their two children and belongings and drove from Nebraska to Washington State. Nearly a half century earlier, in Manitoba, a black frost wiped out the wheat crop and, consequently, my mother's grandfather lost his hardware business. Family lore tells that after the farmers couldn't pay what they owed for seed and supplies, my great-grandfather sold what he could and moved with his family to the Puget Sound region.

My grandmother Violet spent her youth scheming how to escape the prairie wheat country. Her greatest desire was to live by the ocean. When she was in her late teens, perhaps it was 1919, she scraped together enough money to attend business school in Regina, Saskatchewan. After that, she worked in a law office but remained determined to move to a coast. She'd smile when she mentioned that she didn't care which coast, Pacific or Atlantic. I would comment, "I'm glad you chose the Pacific not the Atlantic."

In 1920 or 1921 Violet traveled by train to Vancouver, British Columbia, then to Seattle. She rented a room in a women's boarding house and found a secretarial position with a law firm.

I entertain the impossible idea of contingency plans for bygone times—yet there's nothing to be done about past decisions. Some were helpful—like those that allowed parents to meet. Some were not. Many are forgotten. All are tangled.

A R C H A E O L O G Y • Digging, I see beneath the earth's skin. Black humus transitions to volcanic ash that might have been from Mount Katmai's 1912 eruption. A small area of charcoal suggests a fire for cooking and warmth. Where the blackened layer extends farther, I think of forest fires that, along with volcanic eruptions, do not seem particularly far-fetched.

V O L C A N O • On May 18, 1980, Chuck and I boarded an Alaska Airlines flight for Seattle. Approaching SeaTac, the pilot announced matter-of-factly that Mount St. Helens was erupting. The flight attendants rushed to the cockpit to view the billowing ash. A few minutes later, we landed. Chuck and I deplaned and picked up a rental car. We planned to visit my parents on our way to Washington State University at Pullman, in the far southeastern corner of the state. Chuck and I both had final exams scheduled for the following day, and we had a come-hell-or-high-water intention to be there.

Ninety miles east of Seattle, we encountered the first roadblock. A state patrolman leaned down to the car window and informed us that the interstate was closed to the east. I asked about other routes. He vaguely replied that traveling north on Highway 97 was still permitted.

The cutoff road from Cle Elum to Highway 97 meanders through the bucolic Teanaway Valley—a patchwork of pastures, dude ranches, and pine forests with no hint of volcanic fallout. At the intersection with Highway 97, instead of turning north to Wenatchee, I turned the car south, still with the idea that we would visit my parents. Climbing through forest, the highway was strangely devoid of traffic. A few minutes later we began the long downhill grade through dry scrub—sagebrush, greasewood, and bunchgrass—toward the Kittitas Valley. A thin haze surrounded the car.

Change happens fast at sixty miles per hour. Suddenly, a cloud thicker than fog engulfed the vehicle. Like being blindfolded, or having a blanket dropped across the windshield, the highway completely vanished.

I stomped the brakes. "Chuck, I can't see anything."

"Can you turn around?" he asked.

"I'll try."

The east side of the highway had a gravelly ditch; the west side a steep drop-off, maybe with a guardrail. Or maybe not. I fervently hoped no one else had this same bad idea. Feeling through the steering wheel for the edge of the pavement, I jockeyed the car back and forth on the enigmatic road. Reversed, as if driving by Braille, we crept uphill and back the way we had come. Gingerly, I corrected course each time a tire lurched off the pavement. After a quarter hour of painstaking steering, the airborne ash thinned enough to glimpse the highway and faint outlines of fences and trees.

Already, Chuck and I had learned that driving through thick volcanic ash was impossible—and scary—and that the ash cloud was drifting more toward the east than the north. Having now definitely abandoned the plan to visit my parents, we continued north, hoping to circumnavigate the ash cloud and find a more roundabout route to WSU. We were still optimistic that we would reach Pullman later that day.

At Wenatchee, sixty miles to the north, the haze was no worse than on a smoky day. About twenty miles farther, we turned on Highway 2, a two-lane route that connects a string of towns with names like Douglas, Farmer, Hartline, and Wilbur. As we drove east, farmland gradually gave way to rangeland and sagebrush, and we again encountered ash.

Automobiles trailed gritty plumes and an AM radio station switched from music to broadcasting ash-fall survival tips, like a suggestion to wrap pantyhose around the car's air filter and to avoid Interstate 90 because of the numerous roadblocks.

At one of the small towns, we stopped and bought a six-pack of beer at a bar where patrons happily passed on rumors that rocks were falling out of the sky to the south.

At a gas station near Grand Coulee Dam, gritty ash drizzled from the sky. People dawdling in the grimy parking lot could have been cast as extras in a post-apocalyptic film. A State Patrol car was parked, the windshield wipers robotically scraping ash back and forth, the patrolman just sitting in his vehicle, as if stunned or catatonic. Everyone had cloths wrapped over their faces. A hefty woman frantically pummeled the ladies' room door, and I changed my mind about waiting to use that restroom.

We drove onward. I studied a map, trying to pick a route to Pullman that avoided I-90. At the far side of each town, we noticed sheriff cars rushing into town. At the eastern edge of Wilbur, we were the third car stopped at a hastily established blockade. Suspecting that we would eventually be snared by a roadblock, I had been watching for places to stay.

"Chuck, we passed an old camper park when we came into this town. Maybe we can get there before all the rooms are rented."

Chuck maneuvered out of the lineup, doing a U-turn just as the word NO flashed in front of VACANCY at two motels next to the roadblock. Backtracking for the second time that day, we secured a room in a partially renovated cabin.

Later that evening, through the thin wall, we overheard women discussing departing because the highway had reopened.

"We should go if the highway is open," Chuck said.

"We're lucky to have this room," I argued, happy to not be stranded at an emergency shelter or along the highway.

Chuck drove to where the roadblock had been to see if the rumor was true. At the Billy Burger, he asked if the highway had reopened. Someone guffawed, saying the food had run out so the roadblock was taken down. Refugees drove onward, to the next town where, presumably, they were stopped again.

Early the next morning, May 19, 1980, Chuck and I quietly departed from the half-renovated tourist cabin in Wilbur, Washington. We drove east into an eerie orange sunrise, still hoping to arrive at WSU in time for exams that were scheduled that morning.

Ash transformed the landscape. Everything—houses, barns, trees, equipment, fields—was blanketed gray like a sepia photo of the morning after a battle, except with no evidence of mayhem. Using a road map to navigate the unfamiliar terrain, we crossed over I-90, creeping past a barricade manned by a policeman who was asleep in his patrol car. Proceeding south, the ash got deeper, the volcanic particles rattling noisily against the undercarriage. In the next hundred miles, we encountered only a half dozen vehicles. Each time we met a car along the ash-laden road, both slowed to a crawl to minimize lofting ash into a persistent sight-defying cloud.

Nearing Pullman, we dialed in a local radio station and heard an announcement that the university remained open. At 8:00 a.m., we parked and traipsed into the Agricultural Economics Department. Our shoes left a trail of ashy footprints on the polished floor, and the office staff stared at us like we were ghosts.

Later that morning, the university announced that it was officially closed because of the ash. Our exams went on as scheduled, except Chuck's was moved to a professor's house because one of his committee members had emphysema. After that, Chuck and I found ourselves adrift in Pullman because Highway 26 to the west was closed due to blowing ash.

T I M E • Considering our journey across Washington in the aftermath of the eruption of Mount St. Helens, I believe that we should have turned around and gone back to Seattle when we encountered the first roadblock, but that is like second-guessing ourselves—who we were—in 1980. We believed that if we didn't arrive at WSU in time for the exams, we would have wasted years studying. Chuck and I assumed WSU would remain open because we knew of no time in the past when the school had suddenly shut down. Even considering the circuitous route we had driven and the accumulation of ash, we were sure there would be no school closure. Coming from Alaska, we also had the attitude of "how bad could it be?" Which of course is incorrect, but that's how it was. I suppose what I should be learning from contemplating the situation we found ourselves in after Mount St. Helens erupted, is to have more empathy toward people of the past. However, attempting to play devil's advocate to myself, I switch sides again, in favor of our journey through the volcanic fallout because I can't change the past.

A R C H A E O L O G Y • Rootlets feathered the earth inside my string-bordered square. Despite attentive scraping, I had not come across anything unusual. At noon, we traipsed back to the parked vehicles. Retrieving our lunches, we ate while sitting on the berm overlooking the gravel pit. Our feet hung over the edge and even a slight kick sent pebbles skittering downward. The terrain was nothing like the bucolic century-old postcard of New Knik. Beyond the gravel pit, a mountain of sand loomed beside steel trusses and conveyors—like a scaled-up erector set—poised to funnel product onto barges destined for Anchorage, to fill in low-lying land in preparation for more development.

The panoramic view was both distant and near. Ducks flapped north above the inlet and large planes roared, descending toward one or another of Anchorage's airports.

Dan mentioned that the gravel pit would eventually envelop our small excavations. Such expansion would erase evidence of prior communities and added an urgency to the archaeological investigation.

Below, on the floor of the pit, a front-end loader, tiny as a toy, waltzed—biting at the slope then rolling backward, cagily avoiding burial when an overhang collapsed. The loader scooped rocks, lifting and tipping the articulated bucket over a dump truck. The rattle of rocks reached my ears more slowly, like a movie where lip movement and words have drifted apart.

After lunch, we walked back to our small excavations in the forest. A thick root blocked my digging. I retrieved an axe from the wheelbarrow, took aim, and swung. The axe struck the root with a satisfying thunk. The motion reminded me of camping and campfires. With some sadness for the tree, I chopped until the root severed.

"This birch is especially large," I said loudly like I was speaking to someone across an empty concert hall.

Dan glanced over from another pit where he was meticulously scraping soil. "Abandoned fire pits offer more nutrients. A hospitable place for trees to grow," he commented.

The substantial birch, its trunk dappled with lichens, sprouted from a seed smaller than a grain of wheat. The seed had settled into charcoal-laced soil a week or month—or years—after the last human-lit fire. No one lived here anymore. Leaves drifted into the vacant house. Ash fell, perhaps from the Katmai eruption. Winds swirled silt. Or, maybe, fire devoured the forest, reducing the house to charcoal, but the old fireplace still had the most nurturing minerals.

C A B I N • If I had documented the house, Cabin 135, photographing or sketching ceilings, walls, floors, and every edge and corner and had done this repeatedly for years, would I have noticed the house changing? Would I have observed the basement walls becoming dingier? The stairway carpet flattening? The basement stair treads abrading? Some things I noticed sooner, like moisture that crept between double-paned windows, finger smudges on a doorframe, a ceiling tile askew after the glue failed.

I thought of myself as an instigator of change with remodels, renovations, and stopgap interventions, but later I realized that I had a tolerance—or obliviousness—to the constant deterioration. After twenty years, my attention turned to the living room ceiling—acoustical tiles comprised of some mysterious manufactured material with sound-dampening perforations. During dark winter nights, the ceiling seemed lower and the room gloomier than I recalled, but perhaps the dimness was only due to poor lighting.

A clean white ceiling makes a room lighter and cheerier. The color white varies from a squinty brightness like fresh snow to the lusterless white of eggshells, fuliginous clamshells, or the achromatic hue of chimney smoke drifting upward on a windless afternoon.

If I had been documenting the house like an archivist, perhaps I could have pinpointed the precise moment when the ceiling shifted from a decent white to pale gray.

I spread drop cloths over the floor and furniture. The paint-spattered sheeting had been curtains my mom helped sew when she visited after our first child was born. Mom and I stitched muslin lining to burgundy-colored panels. The new curtains added a sweet country-cottage ambience, but after a few years, sunlight faded the dark fabric to a sickly pink. The next curtains were an unfadeable white, and the old ones were repurposed as painting drop cloths.

Prying the lid off a half-used can of paint, I stirred with a wooden stick, mixing streaks of gray into the overarching white pigment. After pouring paint into a steel tray, I screwed an extension handle onto the paint roller. Soaking the furred cylinder in paint, I lifted it above my head and pushed the roller back and forth against the ceiling. The startlingly bright swaths of new paint proved my suspicion of accumulated drabness, like living beneath a pouty cloud. I was as pleased with the new brightness as if I had discovered a secret method for turning back the calendar.

A R C H A E O L O G Y • At the Knik dig, my trowel scraped against a solid surface. I brushed enough soil aside to see a sliver of something dark, smooth, and charred.

"Is it a post?" I asked.

Dan reached across from another quadrant and pushed at the soil with his trowel. "Clear around it," he said.

With utmost care, I excavated the thinnest layers. By the end of the day, most of a wooden post was exposed and we covered the pit with a tarp to protect it overnight. After sifting my last bucket of earth and picking through residue on the screen, I saw nothing but sticks, roots, and pebbles. "Am I missing something?" I asked.

Dan prodded fragments on top of the mesh. Carefully, he plucked out a pale-white circular object. Balanced on the tip of his finger was a seed-sized coil. A snail shell with a Fibonacci spiral. After that, while holding the shape of the miniscule shell in my mind, I stared hard at the detritus on the screen. Yes. There! Another! Just as tiny, but this coil stretched into a helical spiral. When did snails live here?

What changed? Were there ponds or streams here when the shells were occupied?

E A R T H • A slug crawled out of the crisp romaine lettuce. Like a snail without a shell, its body was pale and moist,
with a pair of antenna eyes. The slug crept across the white
ceramic plate. I stopped chewing and examined the last bite
of sandwich even though I had no strange twinges, tangs, or
flavors in my mouth. The tiny plant-eating creature had survived two days in the refrigerator and, inside the sandwich,
experienced the sharp stab of mustard, greasy pall of may-
onnaise, and charred meat that had once been a bison. The
slug paused at the lip of the plate then plunged over the edge,
disappearing beneath the rim.

"Kill it," my family said.

"I've killed two little ones already in the garden," I said,
getting up from the table, my appetite destroyed.

By midsummer slugs had devoured a row of lettuce. The
cabbages, with holes drilled straight into the heads, looked
like green Swiss cheese. Slugs also munched brussels sprouts,
but after I broke off the lower leaves and plucked the lowest
sprouts, they migrated to a row of beans, chewing until the
fabric of the leaves vanished and only ghostly veins remained.

What don't slugs like? They sampled the red cabbage
more lackadaisically, riddling only the less pigmented lower
leaves. Pea plants and leeks were apparently too tough, or
otherwise loathsome. The herbs—parsley, thyme, oregano,
sage, dill, and caraway—were, perhaps, overly aromatic. The
beet leaves had a light scattering of perforations but the roots
remained unscathed.

MIGRATION • Slugs first arrived in our garden in the mid-1990s. At least that's what we thought. We also assumed the slugs (and their eggs) would perish during the winter, but we were wrong. Slugs—and slug eggs—survived a desiccating snowless frigidity when, for months, our garden was deeply frozen, freeze-dried earth.

For several years, as the slug problem worsened, Chuck and I puzzled over where the slugs came from (of theoretical interest) and (more importantly) how to rid the garden of them, or at least reduce their numbers. Most of our guesses included a mode of transportation. We speculated that slugs hitchhiked in soil shipped to a nearby greenhouse. Or that we brought a batch of slugs, or slug eggs, home in the soil of plants we purchased at a nursery. Although perhaps, all along, slugs were eking out lives in adjacent hayfields and, inevitably, migrated and colonized our vegetable garden.

Whatever the correct explanation of how slugs arrived, we began to suspect our composting efforts contributed to the proliferation.

EARTH • The first large compost pile was experimental. Would plant material even decompose during a subarctic winter? I pulled and piled gangly seeded-out radishes, moose-gnawed chard, carrot tops, tomato plants, broccoli stems, and large leaves trimmed from brussels sprouts. The mound grew as I added layers of soil and old compost—which I hoped would contribute microbes to kick-start decomposition. I finished by heaping leaves on top of the pile to hold in warmth as the weather cooled and the ground froze. Ideally, snowfall would further insulate the pile but I had no control over that.

Eight months later Chuck raked the mostly decomposed compost and rototilled it into the garden. Plants in areas with the thinnest soil grew better, but over several summers, slug predation escalated. We began to focus on killing the slugs, wishing to avoid destruction of entire rows of vegetables by creatures better seen with a magnifying glass.

M I G R A T I O N • The annoyance I feel toward slugs and their untoward trek to our garden evaporates when I consider the remarkable journeys of birds—south to north, north to south—in patterns of flight repeated for millennia. One spring Chuck and I traveled, by ferry across Prince William Sound, to Cordova. There, we witnessed some seventy thousand sandpipers pausing during their migration to Arctic nesting sites. The tiny long-legged shorebirds hurriedly fed along the edge of the surf. Startled, the flock launched en masse. As if choreographed, tens of thousands of sandpipers coalesced—an undulating wave, seeming of one mind or utterly adept at foresight—each bird knowing its neighbors' continuously changing position as well as its own.

Plants migrate, too, sometimes with avian help. When a bird eats a seed, acids in its gut scarify the hard seed coat, breaking through the seed's protection and increasing the chance the defecated seed will sprout. We also help plants migrate, sometimes inadvertently. Seeds stuck in the tread of a tire or the sole of a shoe may lodge in another patch of earth, perhaps even in another state or country.

Through a newspaper article, I learned that the National Park Service was attempting to turn back the clock on an invasion—of dandelions. Curious about the effort and success of reclaiming an ecological niche, in 2008 I volunteered for the Denali National Park dandelion-deveg crew.

D E N A L I • One morning in June, I packed a cooler with enough food for a week, cramming in as much ice as possible and loading it into the car along with my camping gear. Four hours later I pulled into the Riley Creek overflow lot near the entrance to the park. Chuck had been asleep when I left the house. I called him to say goodbye for the week. He wished me luck, and after our brief conversation, I stashed my cell phone in the glove compartment because my destination would be beyond the reach of mobile phone networks.

Two women approached, walking between rows of parked cars, a Park Service SUV trailing behind them.

"Are you Katie?" one asked.

Wendy, the invasive species coordinator for Denali National Park, was driving the SUV. She introduced herself and the other volunteers: Patricia, Rashita, and another woman named Katie.

I shoved my camping gear and cooler into the back of the SUV along with everyone else's. Wendy handed me a sturdy bag with a heavy shoulder strap, filled with more supplies, including a bug shirt, insect repellent, a safety vest, dandelion digger, foam kneeling pad, and prepackaged snacks. Besides my tent, sleeping bag, and food, I also brought sunblock, bug spray, leather gloves, and rain gear. After a quick stop at the visitor center, Wendy steered the vehicle toward the Wonder Lake Campground, ninety miles and a six-hour drive to the west.

Sixteen miles beyond the park entrance, at Savage River, we stopped at a roadblock where only buses, official vehicles, and autos with special permits were allowed to pass. Private automobiles and motor homes (except those with a camping permit) had to turn back. After that, traffic lessened and the view changed. Now and then we encountered a bus and, more rarely, another vehicle. The landscape also changed. Spruce and birch gave way to shrubby willow and ground-hugging alpine plants. At Polychrome Pass, the frighteningly narrow road was hitched against precipices streaked with a rainbow of earthen hues, and nothing impeded our view. Far below, the Toklat River threaded gray strands across a raw channel.

Whenever we met a bus, Wendy pulled over. After the bus passed, she continued. Along the roadside, movement caught our attention. Wendy stopped the rig and shut off the engine. A tawny-and-black fox trotted between bushes, her jaws clamped on a bit of white fluff. Several times, she traversed the same route. The last time, she emerged from the undergrowth with the lifeless form of an adult ptarmigan, still with winter-white plumage, clamped in her jaws. The fox proceeded with a keen calmness, intent on feeding her pups and heedless of our vehicle.

Witnessing wild nature does not come with the breathless voiceover of a nature program on television. Watching the fox tote each dead ptarmigan chick, there was no germane commentary.

Later that afternoon, we arrived at Wonder Lake Campground. Wendy parked and we lugged our packs over a small rise to where tents spread across a slope. I walked along a dirt track above the tents, finally spotting an unoccupied site beside a clump of alders but also quite near one of the cooking shelters. I dropped my gear on the patch of sand.

Thick clouds rendered Denali invisible.

Wonder Lake Campground fosters the notion of a busy station but with an erratic schedule. Camper buses mostly run on time but no timetable exists for when clouds dissipate and Denali appears. Nearly everyone arrives by bus, lugging coolers, boxes, and packs. One man pulled a red wagon loaded with his family's camping gear. Without motor homes or camping trailers, only tent fabric separates you from your neighbors. The campground resembles an open-air hall where winners of a Grand Vista Lottery are sporadically announced amid electric excitement and twenty-four-hour daylight. If even a sliver of North America's highest peak emerges, someone shouts, "Look! Do you see it?" The question, an exclamation, resonates across the slopes, and everyone adds the massive alp to their cabinet of memories.

If the clouds dissolve, I'll find myself compulsively studying the peak's geometry of slopes and angles. The lure, or allure, of rugged promontories is difficult to pin down. Perhaps it is an invocation that recognizes the vast permanence of the landscape compared to our transient flesh-and-blood selves.

Peaks in the Talkeetna and Chugach ranges are far smaller than Denali but still with thousands of hikers gouging trails. In the Talkeetnas, we trek uphill, our hearts pounding, hurrying to ascend a bracingly breezy ridge where we anticipate the seductively majestic panorama.

In Japan, four hundred thousand pilgrims climb Mount Fuji each year, and high in the Himalayas, Mount Everest attracts serious climbers, some who are checking off each of the Seven Summits, of which Denali is one. But that's a very different view from a ground-based situation, myopically digging dandelions.

The next morning we loaded supplies into the SUV, and Wendy motored slowly around Wonder Lake, which—when the air is calm—sublimely reflects the alpine landscape.

Wind riffled the lake so that even if Denali had peeked through the clouds, no reflection would have materialized. Wendy parked beside a gravel airstrip at Kantishna, a community just beyond the national park boundary that once centered on mining but now caters to tourists who prefer luxurious lodging to tent camping.

M I G R A T I O N • Places where people and vehicles— boots and tires—enter the park prove to be ground zero for invasive dandelions. Even though outside the park, the Kantishna airstrip was no exception. Clumps of dandelions dappled the edge of the runway.

We each donned a neon-hued safety vest over our bug jacket and lugged a bucket of tools. Kneeling on a foam pad, I selected a digger with a serrated blade and shoved it into the ground beside a leafy dandelion crown. Rocking the handle worked the blade deeper and loosened the gravelly earth. Tentatively, I tugged the dandelion, assessing whether it would disengage without roots breaking. The weed popped out and I brandished it like a trophy, the long roots dangling from my hand to my elbow. Others on the crew nodded appreciatively. I dropped the plant into a trash bag and reached toward another dandelion.

A wrinkle in the endeavor to eradicate dandelions in Denali National Park is that there are two similar plants: the invasive weed of lawns and roadsides and a native dandelion that grows sparsely in the park. The indigenous dandelion can be confused with the invasive variety, and Wendy coached us on how to examine each plant, to notice whether the bracts (tiny leaf-like structures that enclose the flower bud) point up or down. If the bracts orient skyward, the dandelion is the native plant and we leave it. If the bracts bend downward, the plant is a weed to extirpate. But identification is not always clear. Dandelion growth habits differ because of microclimate, soil, and even previous digging attempts. If a root breaks when extricating a plant, the fragment that remains may sprout a new top, even capable of producing seeds—and reproduce another generation of dandelions, perhaps also characterized by easy-breaking roots.

Digging with hand tools is attitude and altitude—kneeling or sitting, standing and walking, and glancing about for the next target. I stand and the forest becomes a topology of color, texture, and structure. An open area of scrubby grass and brush appears enticingly worth exploring—or else just a distraction. I rein in my inclination to investigate and focus on a few square inches, kneeling and digging but also pausing to scrutinize tiny leaf-like bracts that splay inconclusively. No longer certain whether the plant is a weed, I leave it and switch to another, more obviously invasive, dandelion.

A squall pelts rain and I zip my raincoat. After the shower, the air warms and mosquitoes hum thickly. I swap my raincoat for the fine-meshed bug jacket, zipping the face-screen shut to deflect the insects. Always, the bright orange safety vest is my outermost layer. When the sun beats hotly, I ditch the bug jacket and layer the neon vest over my T-shirt, smearing sunblock and an odiferous sheen of insect repellant onto my arms.

D E N A L I • After the first day digging dandelions, I sat in the doorway of my tent and wriggled my feet out of my boots. Collapsing backward, I stretched out, my body as immobile as if in a coma except my mind kept on, assiduously inventorying each ache—every muscle, tendon, ligament, even the undersides of my kneecaps. Mosquitoes murmured in the arched space between tent mesh and rainfly and a white-crowned sparrow lilted from a nearby alder. Cloud shadows bustled across the foothills, but Denali remained stubbornly shrouded. I hoped my weeklong stay at Wonder Lake would prove to be enough time for the clouds to disperse, so I might glimpse the play of light and shadow across the north face of the massif.

I slept, awaking to rain thrumming the tent and a sparrow trilling. Scattered phrases reached my ears from the nearby cooking shelter, an open-sided structure with picnic tables and a secure room where campers stored food to avoid attracting bears.

We prepared our dinners in another one of the cooking shelters. After eating and visiting, I returned to my tent, intent on sleeping, except each time I drifted off, exuberantly loud voices ratcheted me back to wakefulness. Finally, giving up on sleep, I put on my jeans and sweatshirt, crawled out of the tent, and walked toward the nearby shelter. The energetic conversation stopped, and everyone watched me approach. An hour before midnight, the sky was still as bright as early evening anywhere else.

Feeling like a party crasher, I attempted a smile that probably resembled a tired grimace. "I couldn't sleep. You guys are loud."

A rotund man who spoke the loudest, as if all his words were of the utmost importance, replied, "We wondered who was in that tent." He could have modeled trekking clothing for an outfitter except the gaiters he wore pinched so that his pants ballooned above the knees like old-fashioned jodhpurs. A red bandanna knotted pirate-style around his head seemed to substantiate his cocksureness.

A quieter, thin man dressed in subtle blues said he'd come from England and had just spent a year and a half in Canada. A tall woman with dark hair braided into a ponytail, cooking a packet of food on a tiny stove, didn't say much. A young couple, the man wearing army fatigue pants and a droopy knit hat, the woman dressed in an over-bleached skirt and heavy lace-up boots, played cards at another table. Periodically, one of them offered a congenial comment, mostly about food.

Perched on the end of the picnic table bench, I listened to a conversation that repeatedly returned to the topic of the best gear for photographing sublime scenery. The pirate man was particularly obsessed with bagging a trophy photograph of the uncooperative mountain. Eventually, I drifted back to my tent. This time, feeling more compassion than annoyance, sleep came.

MIGRATION • The next morning, the deveg crew loaded tools and lunches and again drove toward Kantishna, but this time we parked short of the settlement, where dandelions had colonized the roadside. Sitting on the gravelly verge, I extracted one dandelion after another, until tires rasping against gravel interrupted my meditative task. Two bicyclists slowly pedaled toward me. They stopped. The man, darkly tanned, with silver hair jutting from under his baseball cap, asked, "What are you digging?"

Unfolding myself to a standing position, "Dandelions. They're invasive here, in the park."

"Oh," he replied thoughtfully, "we have invasive species in Texas except they're trees and we chop them with chainsaws." He paused, as if considering the distance between Texas and Alaska. "Good luck," he said as he and his partner, a woman past middle age, continued pedaling along the flat road.

The bicyclist's comment echoed in my head. The war on weeds is tough to win. Who adapts best? Or first? Why even care about dandelions, the prodigious occupants of lawns and city lots? After all, we overlook much, from trash to crime, to insipid meals. Dandelions are easy to ignore, like a footnote, and surely someone else's responsibility.

Digging so many dandelions, I gained an awareness that caused me to notice every dandelion, whether one or thousands. At the end of the week, having packed our gear and, once more, ridden six hours in the government SUV, as we neared the park entrance, I noticed masses of dandelions alongside the same stretch of road we had previously traveled. Tackling that miles-long swath of plants, blooming yellow like a monoculture meadow, would prove discouraging for a few volunteers with hand tools.

Geographically, Denali National Park, in central Alaska, may appear out of the way, but a half million people visit each year. I doubt that most visitors recognize the profusion of roadside dandelions as an invasive species. Even if someone suspects an ecological awryness, I imagine complacency. Ironically, Denali National Park is both a protected place and a place impossible to protect.

E A R T H • Most of my adult life, rules have banned littering and with penalties that helped change attitudes. Of course, litter ought not to spawn more litter, but plants transported to a new place may reseed and fan out, migrating farther. Seeds sprouting even a few feet from a parent plant constitute migration.

Along the roadside near my house, sweet clover, a lanky hay fever–inducing weed, flourishes. What native plants did this interloper displace? Cow parsnip? Fireweed? Grasses?

Vetch twining through my garden also came from somewhere else. I never succeeded in exterminating it by hand digging, and I refused to use herbicides because the chemicals would also kill plants I loved. (In the language of war, a collateral damage that I was unwilling to risk.) I hoped for at least a stalemate but expected the vetch to triumph if I failed to pay attention.

Too bad slugs don't favor vetch.

CABIN • Chuck and I shouldn't have been surprised when the septic failed. Mrs. Webb had mentioned that wastewater was piped into a log crib, not a septic tank. "We knocked $3,000 off our asking price," she said as if that would help when we had to come up with the money to install a bona fide septic system.

A year after we moved in, wastewater backed up into the basement. Chuck and I were both at work, but we had visitors, a young couple from the Netherlands who were touring Alaska. They had been washing their clothes and called me at work. I rushed home. The immediate solution was to stop running water, clean up the mess, and call the septic company to pump out the wood-lined tank. The real answer, though, was to install a modern septic system.

When the contractor arrived to assess the job, he measured distances from the well, checked elevations and depth of the water table, and suggested a location for the new septic. A few weeks later, he returned with a truck full of gravel, a backhoe, a large perforated steel tank, and a pile of pipe.

After lowering the tank into the newly dug pit, the contractor excavated a trench to the corner of the house where he planned to connect new pipe to the existing outflow. After a few minutes of digging beside the house, the backhoe shovel clanged against metal. Another mechanical tap broke a pipe.

The contractor, who appeared too young to own an excavation business, climbed off the backhoe and regarded the broken pipe. "That should be it," he said cheerfully.

I balanced at the edge of the ditch, my pregnant belly over the trench, and very glad the ordeal of a non-functioning septic system was being resolved.

"I'll run some water," I said, already having acquired a cynicism toward the house and how the obvious was not always what it seemed. I hurried inside and cranked the bathtub faucet on full blast. When I walked back outside, the contractor was still staring at the broken pipe. Nothing happened. A couple minutes later, we heard water flowing below the hill.

"The water is running in the crib?" the contractor asked, raising an eyebrow.

"Not surprising, actually," I replied.

We tramped down the sloping lawn to what remained of the log crib. After the septic truck had pumped it out, the contractor maneuvered his backhoe around the hill and dug up the lawn, revealing a slimy log-sided chamber. Water from the bathtub faucet gushed out of a pipe into that pit.

After trudging back up the hill, the contractor climbed back onto the backhoe. Again, manipulating the giant shovel with the care of a surgical tool, he prodded the earth, widening the trench until the digger clanked metal for a second time. Another thump with the large shovel crushed this section of pipe. Immediately, water flowing from the bathtub splashed into the trench. The contractor leaned out of the cab and, over the roar of the engine, shouted, "Now I'll hook up the new system."

"Good," I yelled and went inside to turn off the bathtub faucet.

T I M E • Digging a nine-foot-deep trench for the new septic system, the backhoe did not encounter stones or cobbles, bedrock or boulders. Except for a few tree roots, the soil hardly challenged the powerful shovel.

The absence of buried rocks confirmed eons of wind-deposited silt that manifested, incrementally, as thin lines on windowsills and other surfaces, perhaps finding entry into the house through cracks between logs and edges of old windows. Eons ago, this wind-shifted silt was rocks and boulders embedded in different terrain—before ice scoured the land.

The insidious accumulation of silt indoors proved a housecleaning annoyance, but in the garden, as long as the wind courses along the glacial rivers, topsoil is being replenished and renewed, like an hourglass constantly filling.

E A R T H • A gardener knows the origins of most of her plants, and she mentally groups them according to which were there when she arrived and which she planted. Once in a long while, the opportunity arises to gather new plants— even from just a few miles away.

In the spring of 1999, Chuck's parents mentioned that their friends, Mr. and Mrs. Linn, had asked if we would like plants from their garden. Yes, I said, without hesitation, hoping to acquire some exotic plants perfectly suited to our microclimate.

On the scheduled day, Chuck and I loaded shovels and pots into the pickup. When we arrived at their house, Mr. and Mrs. Linn greeted us pleasantly. As retirees, they wished to spend less time gardening, but they also wanted their plants to thrive—just under someone else's care.

Mr. Linn led us around the house to where a mostly bare springtime garden flanked the lawn. Along the way, he pointed out places where we might find bulbs barely sprouting in the cold soil. He said, "Dig anything except the moss campion. We'd like to keep that."

Moss campion has the assuredly non-botanic effect of stimulating imagination. A tight pincushion of green with a brocade of miniscule pink flowers suggests a more whimsical realm. In the wild, moss campion adds a visual exclamation point to rocky slopes. This plant—that we did not dig—would never remind me of the desert landscape where I grew up. Instead it conjures fanciful escapades into terrain of mists and scarps, a blend of Grimm brothers and Hollywood, as if daydreams could be turned on and off like television shows, or as if I was on a quest but didn't yet know for what.

Leaving us with these minimal suggestions, Mr. Linn returned to his house. Chuck and I began to dig as if we were treasure hunters without a map. I shoveled underneath wads of faded, winter-beaten leaves and found a clutch of pale rhizomes. Lilies, perhaps, and after more digging, a tangle of roots that might be irises.

"I'll dig a potentilla," Chuck said, shoveling around a densely branched shrub and lifting it into a large pot.

Later that morning, we drove home with a mysterious collection of roots, bulbs, and shrubbery. Only after unloading the plants did we consider where to transplant them. Years earlier, a patch of lawn outside the kitchen window held a children's play fort we constructed with lumber leftover from building the barn. The raised platform with a ladder and a swing could be imagined into anything—treehouse, pirate ship, a cabin perched on stilts—but as the kids grew to teenagers, disuse and inattention resulted in disintegration. Eventually, we dismantled the backyard play area, and several years later, the new well was drilled there. A clematis vine only partially hid the well pipe that protruded from the lawn.

T I M E • Modern country living includes a septic system and a well, both marked by pipes sticking out of the ground. The septic system has clean-out pipes. Wells appear as pipes with conduit for electrical connections. A submersible pump gets lowered into the well and so eliminates the need for a well house—a small structure designed to protect the pump and electrical connections. In Cabin 135, the well house for the well drilled in 1949 was a bumped-out corner of the basement.

My parents' yard in Washington State ended up with two well houses, both constructed from concrete blocks and with sloping roofs. The second well was drilled after the first well went dry, so another well house was needed. Years later a third, and older, well was discovered underneath the floor of an outbuilding. Speculation was that that well had accidentally been drilled at a slant, and it had to be abandoned because pumps of that era needed a vertical hole in order to function.

E A R T H • "What about planting around the well pipe?" I asked.

"There's a lot of room there," Chuck agreed, surveying the expanse of lawn. "Digging up the grass will be a project, though."

Every trip between the house and vegetable garden, we walked past the new well pipe which, to me, appeared as a necessary blemish. Blooming perennials would certainly be a cheery addition.

With string, I outlined an oblong surrounding the well pipe. Over a couple weeks, we dug sod and turned over the soil. One shovelful revealed a clot of rust that, under close scrutiny, turned out to be nails. I wondered why nails would be buried a dozen feet from the house. I didn't believe anyone would dump trash that close to the house, but before being gentrified with lawn and shrubbery, the yard would have been populated by wild-growing plants and raw paths. Perhaps when the dormer was added, or the basement or garage, tools and supplies remained scattered outside when snow fell. The unexpected snow covered everything, even a box of nails. Maybe, the next spring after breakup, someone noticed a flattened box near the cabin. The cardboard was soggy, the nails already congealed by rust. The man tossed a few shovels of soil over the wet cardboard and oxidized metal. "Good enough," he muttered.

A half century later, I was working in the same place, raking composted horse manure and transplanting plants from the Linns' garden. That summer, as the plants leafed out and flowered, I identified some, but for others, I sent photographs to Jim Fox, who had designed Mr. and Mrs. Linn's garden. His additions to the list of names included *Lewisia tweedii*, *Verbascum*, *Veronica incana*, dianthus, *Iris humilis*, cut-leaf anemone, and *Silene maritima*. *Silene maritima* grows as a single clump with narrow leaves and small white flowers hitched to bladder-like pods, with an understated delicacy like vanilla flavoring added to a batch of chocolate chip cookies.

Several years later, the *Silene maritima* failed to appear. Only a patch of soil remained. This absence bothered me. Was the plant's demise due to uncontrollable circumstances? Had the winter been exceptionally harsh? Or had I failed to furnish conditions suitable for it to thrive?

The name *maritima* suggests a coastal region, but a decade later, I encountered a similar plant in a very different landscape.

I C E L A N D • North of Reykjavík, the two buses, chartered by Students on Ice, parked in a deserted lot beside a restaurant that might have been closed just for the morning or permanently shut. The group—high school students and scientists, researchers, writers, and artists—trekked along a narrow side road with no traffic. Rounding a corner, Grábrók Crater came into view with a long staircase stapled to the steep slope. As a geographic feature, the crater is actually a conical hill—a volcanic cinder cone—with a depression in the top.

I climbed slowly, favoring my knee. After what could have been a couple hundred steps, the trail curved, still upward, circling the rim of the steep-sided bowl. Gray moss, perhaps lichens, covered the inside of the crater. The bottom of the crater held a stony depression like a drain or a natural slump.

The rim of the crater provided a view of treeless slopes and, in the distance, scattered farmsteads—clusters of white buildings with red roofs. Beyond that, fields swept toward bluffs layered from ancient lava flows.

Pastures and stone-walled corrals nudged the base of Grábrók Crater. I asked the guide whether the corrals were still used. He said no, explaining that the stone corrals were part of a museum display, and the corrals used these days had wooden fences and were some distance away. The charm of stone walls includes the lack of nails and absence of rot. Repairs would have required only careful (re)fitting of rocks, which appeared plentiful across the volcanic landscape.

T I M E • In Iceland, stone corrals would have been normal a thousand years ago, after the forests were decimated by people who needed timber for building and fuel. I wonder if, so long ago, anyone worried about whether the trees would grow back. Iceland is very near the Arctic Circle, so perhaps climate affected regrowth, or maybe the forests were so thoroughly destroyed that no seeds remained. In any event, if seeds had sprouted, free-ranging sheep would have nibbled them off.

What nags me about this story of Iceland's lost forests is that a thousand years passed without major efforts to replant and nurture trees. I wonder about the effect of the absence of forests on cultural memories. How many generations of people went from birth to death without seeing a forest on their native land? There would have been no family stories featuring forests, no grand adventures in the woods. By the beginning of the twentieth century, interest in afforestation began in Iceland, and gradually, over many decades, tree planting successes mounted.

I C E L A N D • Hiking back to the buses, I skipped the stairs and instead descended along a trail. The path spiraled around the outside of the crater through volcanic crumble with a delightful scattering of pink phlox. Farther down the slope, small clumps with thin leaves and tiny white flowers hugged the ground. The blooms were attached to fat bladders and resembled the *Silene maritima* that grew in my Alaska garden for a few years. The similar-looking plant was thriving on a steep volcanic slope, in soil profoundly different from the Matanuska Valley's glacial loess.

The name I found in an Icelandic plant book, *Silene uniflora*, confirmed my notion that the plant on Grábrók Crater was in the same family as the plant we acquired from the Linns' garden. I wondered, had I misunderstood the conditions *Silene maritima* needed? Might it have needed more water? Or less? Or did it require totally different circumstances—another environmental niche entirely?

C A B I N • Unlike a car or an appliance, a house does not come with an owner's manual. Mrs. Webb filled in some history during our walk-through, including the story of the pipes freezing because the door blew open. I worried about that even though I had tinkered with the door latch, and the heating system pipes contained propylene glycol—the same antifreeze that prevents a vehicle radiator from freezing and cracking in extreme cold.

Each fall, a technician checked the health of the heating system. First an oil furnace and later, after natural gas was piped to the neighborhood, a gas furnace. The man, dressed in dark coveralls with his name embroidered on the pocket, descended into the basement lugging a bag of tools. He tested water pressure, and if the reading was low, he added water or antifreeze to the system.

I was mystified about how liquid could escape from an apparently closed system. One time I asked. "Boils off," was the terse reply, which was hardly enlightening.

Another year, a different furnace technician expressed concern about antifreeze inside the heating system.

"Why?" I asked.

"Because it can erode the copper pipes, make them thinner, more likely to break," he replied and recommended flushing the antifreeze, refilling the system with plain water, and installing a one-way valve that would automatically inject water if needed.

Later, Chuck and I discussed which had the greater risk— glycol eroding the pipes or the house freezing. We decided to get rid of the glycol. After a plumber installed a one-way valve, flushed the heating system, and replaced the glycol with water, the pipes clanked less. The new configuration evened out the pressure inside the pipes but also eliminated my notion of the house having a closed heating system.

B I O S P H E R E   2 • In Arizona, north of Tucson, Biosphere 2 was constructed as a grand experiment in closed systems. The facility, envisioned by Texas oil man Edward P. Bass, was intended to test how humans might endure an untenable environment—terrestrial or extraterrestrial—by barricading themselves inside a structure that contained everything needed for survival but not in the manner of a well-stocked bunker. Biosphere 2 was designed to be an isolated, long-term habitat—how we might visualize a settlement on Mars (except with Earth's abundant oxygen).

The design of Biosphere 2 specified that nothing, except sunlight and electronic communications, would pass through the walls and glass. In September 1991, eight people entered the lofty structures and the doors were sealed. These humans joined thirty-eight hundred species in the intensively planned and supremely isolated 3.15-acre environment.

T I M E • Fifteen years later, long after the experiment was abandoned, Chuck and I drove north from Tucson across a landscape with abundant cacti and sunshine. My first glimpse of Biosphere 2 was of pyramidal glass structures like a mid-twentieth century illustration of a futuristic city.

We signed up for a tour, which was to start in the living quarters, but to get there we first walked alongside a tall greenhouse, the inside of the glass smeared with condensation.

"Can we go in there?" someone asked.

"No," the guide replied, "it's too dangerous. The walkways are slick, and if you slipped, you'd fall thirty feet. And there have been reports of mutant animals." Whether hyperbole or poetic license, the idea of mutated creatures suggested we had entered an out-of-control world, a place where time sped up and change came more quickly than through the process of natural selection, which stretches across centuries or millennia and countless generations.

The living quarters resembled dormitory rooms with a spiral staircase up to a sleeping loft. To me the housing appeared too sterile and cramped for long-term living. Yet, inhabitants had been chosen for their ability to adapt as well as for their technical and scientific skills and knowledge. Biospherians had to be explorers, discovers, inventors, and farmers. I imagined them as astronauts or adventurers headed to unknown places. Or homesteaders—except their tasks were far more complicated than living off the land.

BIOSPHERE 2 • From the outside, a collection of glasshouse structures rose above the desert like a nascent cybernetical planet. Inside, Biosphere 2 was patterned after Earth. The inhabitants would have had to learn how to manage mechanical systems that purified and recirculated water and created tides in an artificial ocean. They would have grappled with ecologies of ocean, desert, savannah, rainforest, and marshland; they would have needed an understanding of atmospheric science; and, as if that wasn't enough, they had to grow their own food, coping with plants, animals, harvests, and cooking. The bottom line was that those who were cloistered inside Biosphere 2, potentially for years, had to maintain a livable environment and get along with each other. If anything got out of whack, their lives could be imperiled.

Successes and failures of this "closed" human-built environment would have intrigued Charles Darwin, Kenneth Boulding, and Buckminster Fuller. The hoped-for time frame of a century may have been long enough for Darwin to observe aspects of natural selection and for the others to study the isolating effects of space travel or absence of a market economy.

The experiment ended after several years, but even that short duration was long enough to observe ecological successes and failures. Hummingbirds, bees, and finches died off, but the ants thrived. The glass walls inadvertently had been embedded with an ultraviolet inhibitor, so the UV spectrum of sunlight couldn't pass through. Bees require UV light to "see" blossoms and to navigate. The bees crashed into the glass and perished.

E A R T H • I find unexpected consequences fascinating. Spending so much time in the garden, I gradually realized that my plans didn't always jibe with actual events. I had a blind spot where bad ideas lurked.

Some plants seemed like a good idea at the time, like a lupine grown from seed I collected near the swampy edge of a mountain lake. The seeds sprouted and the lupines thrived next to the house, alongside the lilac and lilies, but the blooms were an unappealing drab color, and the plants turned out to be prolific, tenacious, and deep-rooted. The lupine roots spread as a system of runners, and seeds kept sprouting for years after I disposed of the last plant.

B I O S P H E R E 2 • Unexpected consequences plagued Biosphere 2. English sparrows were the unanticipated survivors because they weren't supposed to be there. Sparrows had not been on the planners' species list and no one noticed, during construction, when three English sparrows flitted inside. They were still inside when the doors were sealed—as if Noah had neglected a species that sneaked onto the ark anyway. The sparrows thrived just like they do everywhere—backyards, train stations, airports, shopping malls.

Ants thrived—and colonized an elevator. The monkeys became so pesky that they were expelled, sent back to the San Diego Zoo. The pigs, also vexing, were slaughtered, but survival became more than just maintaining a species balance.

After two years, the Biosphere 2 experiment teetered when oxygen levels mysteriously dropped. Eventually, the low level of oxygen was traced to an oversight during construction. Concrete continued to cure after the experiment began, capturing airborne oxygen molecules and causing a change in the atmosphere as if the whole place had been transported to a valley high in the Andes or the Himalayas. Residents had symptoms of altitude sickness, and in an effort to save the experiment, oxygen was pumped in from outside.

T I M E • Touring Biosphere 2, we traversed biomes, from desert to rainforest. Each had a unique humidity, and lushness or sparseness, like themed hothouses in a botanical garden. We descended into the cool and claustrophobic dampness of mechanical systems called "the lung." The walls amplified sound, reverberating like the interior of a cathedral dome. The guide turned off his microphone and we heard him just as well. After a few minutes, I quit noticing the echo.

The short span of the Biosphere 2 experiment reminded me—like a space age parable—of how difficult it is to create and manage ecologies, and how grand plans may be dangerously derailed. I imagine the people who lived inside the experiment becoming obsessed about food because even eating depended on their own efforts, unlike astronauts who take everything with them, and the rest of us who just go shopping.

E A R T H • The loss of bees increased the Biospherians' workload. Mimicking bees, residents used small brushes to lift pollen from one blossom to another. I've pollinated cucumbers this way, wielding a thin paintbrush and lifting the broad leaves, searching for tiny yellow flowers—male blooms attached to a thin stem, female blossoms having a little green bulge that, with pollination and suitable conditions, develops into a cucumber.

My family's survival does not depend on garden vegetables or small livestock—although many of my ancestors would have had a different outlook.

T I M E • Chickens were a mainstay during the Great Depression. Hens wandered farmyards eating seeds and insects. Eggs from the hens provided food, and when a hen incubated her (fertilized) eggs, a new generation of chickens hatched. I think that chickens would have been useful in the Biosphere 2 experiment, as would small dairy animals like goats. A hundred years ago, this self-sufficiency was called homesteading.

In the early 1880s, my great-aunt Fanny "kept house" for her brother, John Graham Boulton, who was homesteading in upper Manitoba. Fanny wrote: "Graham had laid in provisions. . . barrel of pork, a 5-gallon keg of syrup, sugar, rice and porridge and good sweet flour, also, several bags of potatoes. I think possibly he had grown these."

Traveling to John Graham's homestead, besides her hand luggage, Fanny brought with her "a mattress and other bedding neatly folded in a rag carpet of [her] grandmother's making, two barrels with a tea set and other china, a folding chair . . . , [a] small chest of drawers . . . , and . . . two or three trunks."

After days of travel by train and sleigh, Fanny cooked her first meal: fried pork and boiled rice. She opened a jar of peach jam her grandmother had given her and served a loaf of bread that she had been given while traveling.

John Graham and Fanny did not worry about oxygen, or any other components, in the atmosphere. They would never have wondered, upon waking each morning, whether the air was fit to breathe. Nor would they have given a second thought if some birds disappeared because more birds always showed up.

EARTH • A less frigid winter followed by cool and rainy summer months offered perfect conditions for slugs, moist-looking creatures that cannot abide dry and hot conditions. Each hermaphroditic slug may deposit five hundred eggs—tiny translucent orbs no bigger than a pinhead—singly or in clutches, beneath debris or in holes in the ground. We set traps, plastic containers buried to the rim (like smooth sided pits) and baited with beer. We discovered cheap brands of beer from the store didn't appeal to the slugs as much as rank home brew, forgotten for a decade, in the basement.

The tiny slugs, barely an inch long and smaller than the diameter of a pencil, crawled (or fell) into the traps and drowned in the beer, as did a shrew and a vole. Difficult to say whether the shrew perished going after the dead slugs or the beer. Maybe the vole plunged into the trap after the shrew. We didn't intend to kill a shrew or vole but also didn't care much.

Several drowned slugs disappeared one morning, and we theorized that they were eaten by magpies. However, the beer-baited traps had little effect on the slug population, and our battle against slugs ratcheted up as summer transitioned to autumn. We (mostly Chuck) spent a couple hours each day hunting slugs, plucking them off cabbage leaves, carrot tops, and broccoli, and dropping them in a bucket of water where they drowned. We theorized that my large compost pile from the previous year had contributed to the slug problem because the chopped plants provided habitat.

"What about burning them? A flame thrower, perhaps?" I half-joked.

"Flame throwers need an accelerant like napalm," Chuck replied, "which is surely illegal."

"Barbecue lighter fluid?" I jested but, as sometimes happens, our zany conversation led to action. The next afternoon, Chuck borrowed a tubby propane tank hitched to a weed burner—a long contraption with a nozzle resembling a thick can that had fallen into a campfire, extreme heat having seared any coating of paint. Traipsing back and forth across the garden, Chuck loosed bursts of flame, and steam rose from the moist soil.

The next summer, as newly planted seeds sprouted in neat rows and recently transplanted beans acclimated to being outdoors, slugs again nibbled the leaves. Scorching the soil had not destroyed the slug eggs. Newly hatched slugs chomped the garden plants as voraciously as before.

T I M E • Both Chuck and I tinkered with the yard, reacting to changing circumstances with the single-mindedness of warriors yet often finding that we battled nearly invisible opponents. Over years, we gained a notion of when slugs and cutworms might begin feeding. Even so, destruction often was well underway by the time we noticed.

M O D U L A T I O N S

E A R T H • Stomping the forked spade, I rock the handle to loosen a clump of clover. Bending, I grab the vegetative mat and fling it, dribbling dirt, toward the wheelbarrow. My aim isn't very accurate and the lawn around the wheelbarrow is littered with clover, but the whole sequence of motions becomes a ritual. Tromp the spade. Rock the handle. Tug and toss until the earth beneath the lilac acquires a bare primness and the wheelbarrow brims with roots and stems. I trundle the wheelbarrow toward the edge of the woods and lift the handles, dumping the torn-up clover onto terrain formed ten thousand (or so) years ago when the ice sheet melted.

Over eons, ice scraped and gouged, lifting earth and boulders. Later, but still a millennium ago, glaciers blanketing the valley melted, releasing pulverized earth that settled into meandering moraines like those north of our house. At first, the land appeared raw—and inhospitable. Gradually, rugged low-growing plants colonized the newly exposed ground. After that, shrubs and trees sprouted from seeds carried by wind or birds and animals.

T I M E • I collect landscape images. On film, or digitally. I do this as an insurance policy against forgetting. I would hate to lose my memories—of clouds piled high above the mountains, a late autumn morning when the first snow settles on leaves yellowing but still veined with green, or on branches draped over the Little Susitna River. A long camera exposure transforms water tumbling over boulders into ropey skeins that belie turbulence, instead conveying calm meditativeness like a Japanese garden, sinuously raked with pebbles intentionally placed and a single yew tree. The long exposure with gauzy water wrapping boulders suggests stopping time—within the photo—and negates the reality of turbulence. The river roars with power and force, but in the photo it is as still and silent as a new dusting of snow—or a glacier.

No tripod or long exposure tricks are needed to photograph a glacier.

I C E • The summer of 1979, during my first trip to Alaska, Chuck and I drove in a northeasterly direction, from Palmer toward the Matanuska Glacier. After sixty miles Chuck turned the car onto an unpaved road that angled down a steep bluff. At the bottom, we stopped on a narrow wooden bridge over the nascent Matanuska River and took pictures of ourselves with the car and bridge and river. The camera used 35mm film. Pressing the thumb lever advanced the film with a satisfying thunk.

At the end of the gravel road, we parked near the forward edge of the glacier (its "toe") and walked across soggy earth, past an occasional pink-blooming dwarf fireweed, toward towering ice. Perhaps what I thought was muddy soil underfoot was actually an unfinished moraine, or we may have been treading ice hidden beneath what looked like soil. Never having been near a glacier before, I had no frame of reference and no idea what was normal for a glacier in summer, or winter.

The footing changed as we stepped across a rivulet onto nubbly ice that was speckled black like buckets of sand had been scattered. The glacier was actively melting. Water trickled, flowed, and dripped as if mocking our use of the word *glacial* to describe an occurrence that's usually thought to be extremely slow.

We trod across cleaner-looking ice toward tantalizingly blue seracs. The air became chillier, and I realized that the distance was greater and the ice more slippery than I expected.

"Chuck, the glacier is amazing. I have never seen, or walked on, anything like this. How far is it to that wall of ice?"

"Farther than it looks," Chuck replied. "We don't have the right gear either."

Not to mention we knew nothing about ice climbing. We turned around and strolled back to the car where we laid our picnic on boulders with a view of the glacier that gleamed blue with refracted sunlight. From a distance, clefts between seracs gave the ice a malleable appearance, like clay, stretchable and easily torn, yet belying the contradictory nature of ice as both hard and meltable.

T I M E • In the early 2000s, Chuck and I again journeyed to the Matanuska Glacier. This time, below the steep bluff, we drove farther along the valley to reach the glacier. After parking, we traversed spongy silt, then trod bumpy ice blackened with sand. The glacier felt alive with burbling trickles and rivulets, some flowing clear but others oozing like sludge.

In midsummer, the Matanuska River emerges from underneath the ice, already a substantial stream and murky gray, a color resembling wet cement.

Normally, the Matanuska Glacier has more freezing than thawing during the winter. Snow and ice accumulates. Summer is the opposite—with melting and runoff. River flow is prettier in winter, clear with an ethereal tinge of green because less melting occurs and ground up earth remains locked in the ice.

In an idealized world, where long stretches of time (past to present to future) blend without much change, glaciers would appear to have a sort of stasis—not much visible change within our lifetime.

Disturbing now, four decades after my first visit to the Matanuska Glacier, is the loss of ice. Besides receding, the glacier is also thinning, losing mass—or depth, like a lake that becomes shallower.

SWITZERLAND • In the town of Täsch, Chuck's cousin Irene maneuvered the car into a parking garage, explaining that personal vehicles weren't allowed in Zermatt. At the train station, Chuck and Irene waited in line to buy tickets while I perched on a low wall with Irene's dog, Salto, next to me. Salto constantly watched Irene while keeping his jaws clamped around a large stick. When the ticket line shifted and Salto couldn't see Irene, he dropped the stick and barked. I nudged the stick with my foot trying to distract him, awkwardly mimicking Irene, "Où est le bâton?" People standing in line turned and stared at me while Salto barked and pulled on the leash and I tried to calm him. Finally, Irene and Chuck returned with the train tickets, even a child's ticket for the dog. We boarded a train for Zermatt, but our ultimate destination was Gornergrat, at ten thousand feet.

T I M E • A week earlier, at the end of August, Chuck and I were on a flight from Anchorage following a Great Circle air route. Below us, sea ice in the Arctic Ocean was astoundingly beautiful, sparkling and blue-tinged, but also cleaved by channels of startling blue seawater. After landing at Frankfurt, we grabbed our carry-ons and disembarked the stale plane through a stuffy jetway, entering a crowded concourse where everyone hurried toward Customs and Passport Control. We traipsed behind a group of men wearing leather jackets and trailing cigarette smoke. They spoke a language I didn't recognize. Not English or German, French or Spanish. Our acclimatization had begun amid an alien auditory landscape. The entire trip became a lesson in becoming habituated.

S W I T Z E R L A N D • In Zermatt we exited the train station and followed Irene across a cobblestone plaza crowded with trekkers and tourists, past jitney buses and a placid dappled-gray horse harnessed to a cart. After detouring into a shop where Chuck bought a hat, we walked to another station and boarded a train bound for Gornergrat. We sat on hard plastic seats with Salto scrunched at our feet. The train got underway, but just beyond the town, it slowed and sounds of scraping metal came from under the carriage.

"What's that noise?" I asked.

"The cogs are being lowered," Irene replied. "That's how the train climbs the mountain." She explained that the cogs were rotating hooks beneath the train that clamped onto a toothed strip in the center of the track. I visualized a giant rotating zipper pulling the train up the slope.

With cogs lowered, the train climbed earnestly. My back pressed hard against the rigid seat back. The extreme slant of the windows made trees appear canted as if gravity had come unmoored, or as if we had all tipped our chairs back onto two legs.

The train heaved over the crest of a hill and windows and trees regained their flatland congruity. I realized that I'd been silently repeating "I think I can, I think I can" from the children's story *The Little Engine That Could*. We halted for some unknown reason, but a whooshing arose along with a subtle change of pressure inside the carriage. Just inches away, another train clattered down the mountain, the whole conveyance blurred as if drawn with a single swipe of chalk.

At Gornergrat we exited from an underground station onto a plaza and into brilliant sunlight. Silver-haired tourists and young trekkers swarmed the area, suspended between easy travel and wild terrain. A bored-looking young man hawked photographs taken with a jowly Saint Bernard and the Matterhorn as backdrop. In the plaza, noisy with conversations and a thumping construction machine, I felt the first thrum of a headache. Hoping to stave off a migraine, I bought coffee out of a vending machine and swallowed a dose of ibuprofen.

We skipped having our pictures taken with the Saint Bernard and the Matterhorn and marched uphill, past a large hotel and into fresh snow. We photographed ourselves perched on a rocky outcrop in the new snow, with Salto still biting the hefty stick.

I wiggled my toes tentatively inside the cramped boots Irene loaned me. Before setting out that morning, she had scoffed at my lightweight running shoes. "You need sturdy boots for the Gornergrat hike," she insisted.

Irene led the way, onto a switchbacked trail descending toward the glacier, Gornergrat, that snaked far below us, a river of ice but with a flow so slow that a lifetime would not be long enough to see movement. Across the valley, and higher up, ski lifts revolved atop another glacier.

We were the only ones hiking down the gravelly trail with views of Gornergrat and four other glaciers.

"I can't believe it," Irene said emphatically. "The glaciers are much smaller than before."

"When were you last here?" I asked

"Five years ago," she said.

"In Alaska the glaciers are also shrinking. The Matanuska too. You were there with us when you visited in 2002."

Partway down the interminable slope, beneath a perfect blue sky, we settled onto rocks and unpacked a picnic. Using silverware, we ate salad concocted of radish, fennel, and cucumber, and chunks of meat from a barbecue the previous evening. Petite and sweet Mirabella plums and cherry toma-toes plucked from plastic containers accompanied by sweet-ened herb-and-lemon tea acted as dessert.

Irene explained that trekking downhill didn't mean we'd have to climb up again. She had chosen a route that would eventually take us to a train station at a lower elevation. As we hiked down the switchbacked trail, the Gornergrat Glacier appeared near, yet we never seemed to get closer. Eventually, the trail turned and we climbed toward another ridge, leaving the glacier behind. Each step I took was accompanied by a headache drumbeat and crescendoing blisters inside the bor-rowed boots.

After climbing away from the glacier and topping a ridge, we paused beside a wind-riffled lake, on ground worn bare by tromping. Footpaths encircled the lake, and not too far in the distance, the Matterhorn loomed, streaked with snow and more precipitous than I expected. The three of us lingered, waiting to see if the wind would settle and the water calm. Across the alpine terrain, autumn-hued plants hinted at summer's last heartbeat like a slow exhale before the landscape shifts to winter. Momentarily, the air stilled and the lake reflected the Matterhorn, but I don't totally trust this memory.

Later, looking at my photos, I realized that the reflection was not as flawless as I remembered. A wispy cloud clung to the peak and a breeze skimmed the water, giving a soft focus to the mirrored peak like an artistic effect meant to conceal something.

TERRAIN • The day after we returned home, in mid-September, Chuck went to work and I packed a lunch and drove to the Reed Lakes trailhead. I wished to compare the Talkeetna Mountains to the Alps while our trek near Gornergrat Glacier remained fresh in my mind. Appearances suggest a topographical similarity, with the exception of elevation. The Talkeetnas top out several thousand feet lower than the Alps, but the landscape is decidedly alpine and the trail to the Reed Lakes would be mostly obvious.

After leaving the main road, I steered the car for several miles along a rock-studded and potholed track. At the trailhead parking, I hitched on a small pack that contained a camera, water, sandwich, and a mobile phone that was unlikely to locate any cellular signal in the mountains. At first, an old mining road cut a nearly straight line along the edge of a wet-looking valley that perhaps had once been a glacial lake. I walked quickly, keeping an eye on alders that edged the track even though, after some freezing nights, not enough leaves remained on the shrubs to hide even a spruce hen. At the end of the valley, the trail veered from the old miner's track. I crossed the tumbling stream on a sturdy footbridge, a much easier passage than ten years earlier when the "bridge" was boards balanced precariously between slippery rocks. After the bridge, I climbed earnestly along a switchbacked trail that improved immensely on the prior footpath that had blazed straight up the slope.

At the crest of that first hill, I paused, drinking water from a bottle in my pack and admiring the alpine view. Frosty nights had already rouged the tundra, a landscape that resembled slopes near the Matterhorn where we had walked a few days before. A man wearing a bright yellow jacket strolled along the path. He glanced at me and nodded.

"Nice afternoon," I said.

"Snow's coming," he replied continuing on his way down the mountain.

I shrugged on my pack and resumed walking along the well-trod trail, knowing the easy going would change. At the edge of the boulder field, I stopped and fastened the trekking poles onto my pack so I would have both hands free. With pleasant weather and evening still hours off, I scrambled onto the first boulder and scanned the complex terrain for any hint of a trail. Whether boulders piled across the narrow valley came from a rock avalanche or an ancient volcano, the spread of lichens across their surface proved they had been there a long time.

With no clear path, I jumped and crab-walked. At a daunting chasm, I doubled back, searching for an easier route. Navigating through the boulders might have taken a half hour, or an hour, but intent on safe passage, I had no thoughts of time passing. Eventually, I slid off the last boulder near the obvious trail. Again, I climbed—which is how the trek to the Reed Lakes proceeds— relatively flat trail interspersed with steep climbs. Traversing the slope above Lower Reed Lake, I glanced down at a turquoise-green pool nestled between peaks and fed by a sinewy waterfall. Above the waterfall, the angle of ascent eased, and my uphill trudge became a pleasant walk across frost-kissed tundra that, surprisingly in late September, lacked snow. Like finding a second jewel when one would have been enough, I came to Upper Reed Lake, another turquoise pool snuggled inside a semicircle of alps and where the trail appears to dead-end.

T I M E • Hiking in the Talkeetnas is different from the Alps. You won't happen upon a restaurant or pub. After I departed my car, I encountered no structures, except for a long-abandoned miner's shack, and certainly no mountain-ascending cog trains. My feet were the only transportation. Along the trail, I took a few photos of bodacious tundra and scarps. While I walked, my mind zoomed back and forth between Alaska and Switzerland as if the mountain landscape had unrooted me. Later, looking at the photos, the well-defined path and terrain in the Talkeetnas appeared similar to where Chuck, Irene, and I hiked above Gornergrat station, except the Reed Lakes Trail didn't link to any others. No signposts guided trekkers to the next village, valley, or train station.

T E R R A I N • My downhill hike back to the car was uneventful. Even the boulder field seemed less intimidating. That night the first snowfall transformed the Talkeetna Mountain's ruddy slopes from autumn to winter. The trek I'd taken the day before, to the Reed Lakes, would be impossible for the next nine or ten months.

I was glad I'd hiked to the Reed Lakes. If I had waited even a day, I would have missed that trek and whenever I went the next time, it's unlikely I would have been thinking about both the Alps and Talkeetnas—and how we are laced into the wider frame of climate, geology, history, and settlement.

ᕮᏋᏇ

I C E • Each winter, as freeze-up comes, whether practically overnight or spanning weeks, I would be the last to trust the ice. Growing up on the desert steppe, I did not encounter frozen lakes.

When the ice was a couple inches thick, our neighbor Ralph would amble across the lake as if he was the first explorer exiting onto a changeable planet. When the ice got slightly thicker, Chuck would join Ralph, whacking orange golf balls across the lake. Helen liked the ice at least four inches thick before she ventured onto it. Sometimes I reluctantly followed her onto the frozen veneer, but really, I preferred ice so thick that the lake appeared solid, the faded water lilies' heart-shaped leaves suspended as if entombed in black glass.

When the lake froze quickly without wind or snowfall or cycles of freezing and thawing, the ice appeared transparent, with few air bubbles or cracks. At first I walked tentatively, acquainting myself with the lack of friction—a slickness that promoted easy sliding. The uncannily clear ice suggested a blackness on the other side of the heavens, where gravity was reversed and we sashayed across a perpetual night sky.

Lowering myself flat onto the frozen lake, cold seeped through my clothes and skin. I stared down. The interior of the ice cradled galaxies of bubbles, constellations of tiny star-shaped birch seeds, and lily leaves, faded and papery, like inscrutable pages from an ancient book. But then, I heard a shout—and everyone was lacing on skates. We took off, kicking the blades and swooshing—faster than running—our skates cutting curlicues into the surface of the ice.

"Listen," I'd say when the temperature dropped suddenly. At any moment the ice might shift, vibrations expanding sonorously along a rift, the lake resonating like a drumhead. By spring, narrow fissures transected the ice. Cracks and tiny pushed-up ridges intersected at odd angles, suggesting a weave of fault lines, but unlike rifts in the earth's crust, ice fractures were short-lived.

C A B I N • On a sparkling winter morning, a pair of white spots appeared indoors beneath one of the living room windows. I touched the dots and felt frost mounded on screws that fastened a plastic rectangle to the wall. During the night, the temperature had dropped to twenty below zero.

Curious, I unscrewed the plastic rectangle, supposing there was a chance, however unlikely, of finding a time capsule or treasure hidden inside the wall. The plastic rectangle covered a cramped metal box wadded with tarry-black wires, likely once an electrical outlet but now a footnote to incremental addition and abandonment. The metal box embedded behind paneling, in the log wall, conducted cold from outdoors. The warm and slightly humid indoor air expedited ice crystals forming on the tiny screwheads.

T I M E • Living in this house, we discovered things we didn't want to know but that we wished we had learned sooner, like a gob of wires walled into the attic behind our bed. With a tarry coating, the wires dated to the 1950s, or earlier, and circuit junctures had been wrapped with tape. Copper showed through where mice had chewed the tape and tar coating.

Chuck and I had embarked on redoing our bedroom, replacing walls, wiring, and the window. Having hammered a hole in the attic wall, and finding the sketchy wiring, I raced to the basement to turn off the electric circuit, as if—at that moment—hurrying was crucial even though the weird connection must have been sealed behind the wall for decades. I could not guess, though, when mice nibbled the tarry insulation, whether during the previous week, or years earlier. In the basement, after flipping the breaker to cut electricity to the upstairs, I breathed easier, thinking the house safe again.

C A B I N • The wires in the metal box were dead—a wire tester proved that. With the cover off, cold air eased between sidings and chinks in the logs and flowed into the living room. I was relieved that the frosty screws hadn't led me to any dicey "live" wiring. The uninsulated wall was no surprise but more than we could tackle on a winter morning. I screwed the cover back onto the box and, after that, ignored the frosty screws.

T E R R A I N • Outside, I stomped my boots onto skis, reached down, and clamped the three-pin bindings. I shoved downhill past the barn and around the end of the raspberry patch. My skis left deep jumbled grooves in the new snow.

Breaking the ski trail after a heavy snowfall amounted to a whimsical diversion. Sometimes my skis slipped off the buried track, bogging into deeper snow. I leaned on the poles and stepped sideways, feeling through the skis for the icy firmness of the old trail. Adding to this fanciful avocation was the fact that the trail went nowhere. It looped on an oblong course with our house at the southwest corner. Creating a personal ski trail was luxury with a measure of Luddite-ness—stepping and stomping, rather than hopping into the car and driving to a park where machines groomed perfect tracks. Each fall, Chuck walked the path that would be the ski trail, clearing brush and branches with a handsaw and loppers.

Trudging not gliding, I let the landscape remind me of other times. One winter an ermine—thin and long bodied and exceptionally white—perched on a snowy log. For an instant, he stared at me, then disappeared behind the downed tree, or else he bounded away through the snowy woods, so well camouflaged that I saw nothing. The ermine offered wildness—a proof that nature exists all around us. I mentioned the ermine to Chuck and for several days kept watch for the shy, mystical creature, but I didn't see it again.

Noticing details strikes me as important, although if asked, "Why that?" I would be hard-pressed to explain. The connecting intricacies are like a jigsaw puzzle where each piece is crucial and perplexity is part of the undertaking.

Overhead, birch limbs messily thread the leaden sky. Snow crystals stack and intermesh along branches until the frozen-water weight becomes too much. A bough twitches

and snow cascades on top of me, chilling my face and numb-
ing my neck. After the frosty veil settles, the birch trunks—
some striated white, some amber—appear starker than before.
One tree with a disfiguring bulge is scarred by a horizontal
line where a wire might have been twisted. Why? For a fence?
To guy a tent? Or tie a clothesline?

T I M E • When we moved in, the backyard clothesline
slung in a continuous loop between two pulleys, one fastened to a post near the house and the other hooked to a tall
cottonwood downhill, near the raspberry patch. I suspect Mr.
Webb was the one who leaned a ladder against the cottonwood and climbed up twenty feet, balancing and reaching
to wrap wire around the thick grooved bark. He attached a
pulley to the wire and threaded a thin rope through the pul-
ley-wheel. Climbing down the ladder, Mr. Webb would have
attached the loop of clothesline to the other pulley hooked
onto a post near the house.

Summer after summer, Mrs. Webb hung laundry on that
clothesline. After fastening a garment with wooden clothes-
pins, she yanked the loop, propelling damp apparel out across
a gulf of lawn to flutter like strangely domestic prayer flags.

As if snared in a long-running behavioral loop, every summer
I lugged baskets of laundry up the basement stairs, along the
hallway, through the garage, and outside to the clothesline
slung between the cottonwood tree and the post.

Clothes dried outdoors accumulate scents that remind me of my grandma's T-shaped clothesline, her wicker laundry basket, and her routine of wiping the clothesline with a damp cloth before hanging the laundry. In fact, as far as I recall, my grandmother did not have or use an electric clothes dryer. During rainy weather, she still hung her laundry but on lines strung in the basement.

E A R T H • Cottonwoods grow fast and, as they gain mass, their shadows expand. A summer came when we blamed the stunted raspberry canes and sparse berries on the big cotton-wood's shade and greed for water and nutrients. Chuck called his friend, John Larson, who came over one weekend with a large chainsaw that he had used in coastal southeast Alaska to cut truly huge forest trees. John Larson felled the cotton-wood. Despite the tree's role as clothesline support, it did not garner any fondness from me. With the cottonwood gone, the raspberries grew more prolifically, but we had to devise a new scheme for the clothesline. Finally, I screwed a hook into the corner of the garage and stretched a line directly from the wall to the post. No longer able to yank the line and launch garments over the gulf of lawn, I sidled along, clipping one garment after another to the static line.

T E R R A I N • A whisper of tires on snow floated through the woods from the unplowed road. I imagined distance had stretched, and I was skiing across a vast wilderness, plodding and breathing, inhaling frigid air with no discernible aroma.

Stomping my skis, I ducked beneath a snag verging on collapse and glided down a short hill where my skis grated across a knot of roots. Angling uphill, the deep snow kept me from sliding backward. In summer, this north-facing slope is a tangle of highbush cranberries, currants, and prickly roses, but the snow hides all that, giving the terrain an unfamiliar open visage.

On top of the ridge, I turned east toward the road and, in a short distance, south onto an invisible trail leading toward the driveway. I hoped for easy gliding, but even downhill, the loose snow thwarted sliding. Beyond the driveway, in the abandoned pasture, my skis slid sideways, off the icy trail. I floundered onward. At the edge of the willow thicket, the trail revealed itself as shallow grooves, an echo of the prior track. Half the snowfall had caught in the branches. Beyond the brush, I turned west, laboriously ski-stomping between perpetually stunted willows favored by moose. To my left, Quonset-shaped greenhouses were silent, the business shut for winter.

Below the vegetable garden, the slope faces south, and after a few sunny days, the snow thins and the trail becomes icy, but even here, new snow still blanketed our previous tracks. At the garden, warmed by exertion, I paused and draped my jacket over a post, then continued past the candelabra birch and the two birch where birdfeeders hung from a wire tied between them. Grosbeaks, chickadees, and redpolls gobbled seeds while one startlingly red male grosbeak perched on the highest branch, surveilling the sky for predators—eagles, owls, or shrikes.

At the corner by the greenhouse, I shoved off down the slope, floating above the lawn. The deep snow slowed my speed and I rounded the corner at the bottom of the hill without crashing into the neighbor's fence. Approaching the woods, I encountered my own track where the jumbled snow was still too soft for gliding. Each circuit after that, friction from my skis packed the snow and added a glaze of ice. After several more circumnavigations, I ceased meditating on the landscape. Exhilarated, I swung my arms and poles, kicking my skis, pushing and gliding—sailing through the snowy woods and not thinking about much of anything.

EARTH • When we moved in, the driveway and lawn met in a mingling of grass and gravel. That first summer, a farmer slowly drove onto the lawn, around our house, toward his barn and hayfield—as if that was perfectly normal. That autumn, I scavenged seedpods from a caragana hedge in Palmer and planted the seeds in a row between the raspberries and black currants. Caragana, also called Siberian pea shrub, is immune to frigid temperatures and razor-sharp spines discourage ravenous moose. The seeds sprouted and, after another year, Chuck and I transplanted the tiny shrubs in a line, delineating lawn from driveway.

By the time webcam technology arrived in the early aughts, the caragana hedge blocked vehicle access to the lawn and was too tall to prune while standing on the ground. The webcam stared out the window with a monocular view. It recorded the first snow in October and the last one in April. In May the lawn sprouted green beneath blue sky and hastening clouds, and Chuck balanced on a stepladder, wielding loppers—clipping the hedge's unruly growth.

More frequently than hedge trimming, the webcam recorded the ritual of lawn mowing. The riding mower, charging like a beast, carved paths through the grass, slicing off dandelion and clover blooms and lofting pollen. Chuck sat on the mower wearing a respirator that made him look like he was planning to survive an attack of toxins rather than just breathing amid clouds of pollen.

The camera's ceaseless gaze caught comings and goings of hawk moths, mosquitoes, bees, butterflies, and birds. A robin cocked its head, trying to discern earthworms. Juncos hopped and scratched, hunting seeds and insects.

For several summers, delphiniums grew beside the window. First, a nubbin-tip of rough green appeared in a photo, the plant already five feet tall but barely above the windowsill. Over the next few days, the delphinium spiked past the camera eye, leaves unfolding like jungle foliage. A few days later, multitudes of pale lavender florets unfurled.

The lavender delphiniums creeping above the windowsill were unlike the compact clumps of sapphire-hued blooms in front of the house and behind the greenhouse. Browsing a seed catalog one winter, I noticed a picture of these more colorful delphiniums and ordered seeds. The following summer, I transplanted seedlings to the windswept patch beneath the window. A year later, the plant's own weightiness threatened to topple it. I twisted small screw eyes into the siding and used string to truss the clump to the house.

Occasionally, a darkly brindled cross fox loitered near the window, sniffing for mice, voles, or baby birds. Moose also ambled past, but not every wildlife sighting was recorded because the webcam did not know what was interesting, or even that anything had changed. It snapped photos on a schedule, every fifteen minutes or once an hour, depending on whether I fiddled with the settings.

I also have appeared in webcam pictures. Weeding the columbines, tossing stems and roots in the wheelbarrow, my tools—rake, hoe, clippers, trowel—scattered on the lawn. And when I scrubbed silt from the windows, my jeans-clad legs appeared between the rungs of the stepladder. The clean glass offered the webcam a clearer view but not intelligence.

T I M E • The expanding archive of images encompassed several years in the early 2000s but even that was only a snapshot in the timeline of the garden. As a gardener, the long term might be ten years, or twenty. I cannot imagine planning a garden for fifty years, or a century, hence. A blind spot in my imagination blocks time beyond the possible span of my own life.

Without human management (or interference, depending on point-of-view), vegetation returns to a natural state—whatever climate and terrain fosters—which may happen slowly or quickly, but will happen for sure.

)٤ ૭

C A B I N • Almost mid-September and still with relatively warm weather, I stood on a stepladder and brushed paint along a windowsill. Pop music blared from a radio haphazardly plunked on the lawn and tuned to a station that would interrupt programs to deliver critical updates. I glanced at the cordless phone, off-kilter between blades of grass, and hoped that Chuck would call.

Even while painting, I kept an eye on the sky that had suddenly, that morning, turned ominous. In Alaska's time zone, far to the west, the day has barely begun when it's lunchtime in New York City and today, when we awoke, we found the balance had shifted. Yesterday's truth was not today's.

All the planes were grounded.

S K Y • Air travel and air freight are crucial to Alaska—a lifeline really, whether flying supplies to roadless villages or transporting people in emergencies—and Anchorage is often a refueling stop for international flights. Like a bird-watcher with a life list, I notice planes, from the mundane to the unusual and spectacular—helicopters and low-flying floatplanes, oddly shaped firefighting planes, sleek fighter jets. One time a delta-winged stealth plane, looking like it had escaped from Star Wars, flew low over our house.

I glance up when I hear the rumbling piston engines of a DC-6. That plane, loaded with fuel for a remote community, climbs heavily, barely above the trees as it lumbers upward. Almost every day, passenger jets taking off from Anchorage fly above us, their gravelly roar lagging like a long audible shadow, and high in the sky contrails trace flights that skip over Alaska, following Great Circle routes to distant capitals.

Descending into Anchorage at night, I've peered out a miniature fuselage window and seen the aurora shimmering like a ragged line of colored clouds and appearing deceptively near. The plane descends over the Chugach Mountains. On final approach, we skim Cook Inlet's frigid gray water until runway lights rush past, wheels bump pavement, and the engines roar into reverse.

C A B I N • Perched on the ladder, paint dripping from the brush, I glanced up, scanning the sky for renegade planes. The phone remained silent. That morning Chuck had gone to work anyway, to one of Anchorage's high-rise office buildings. "Business as usual," the State said even though the day had become unsettling and very surreal.

When Chuck and I awoke that morning, the radio commentator, speaking in stunned tones, swept away the last sweet blackness of sleep. We raced downstairs and turned on the television. Smoke churned from the World Trade Center towers in New York City, the burning and collapsing images replayed, over and over.

T I M E • As a kid, infernos—of cities and buildings— transformed my dreams to nightmares, a symptom, I think, of the Cold War–era fear of nuclear attack that every child knew from her parents' worried conversations and schoolroom drills. These mental images reappeared, jiggled loose into a hovering wildness. Beneath the seamless autumn sky, I envisioned an endless loop of scenes, imagining worse, and knowing the worst had been clipped from Alaska's westernmost television feeds.

C A B I N • There's a limit to how many times you can helplessly watch a horrendous scene. I turned off the TV and forged ahead with what I had planned for the day—repaint the peeling windowsills. The weather was lovely, perfect for painting, yet nothing was normal.

Ringing jarred the quiet. I climbed down off the ladder and picked up the phone.

"Katie," Chuck said from an office tower in Anchorage, "There's a Korean Airlines plane, flight 85, on a course toward Anchorage, and it's being called 'potentially hostile.' The Air Force sent fighter jets to intercept it."

"Are you coming home?" I asked.

"I don't know yet," Chuck replied.

Could this be a fifth renegade plane? What was unimaginable the day before now seemed eerily possible. It had become altogether too easy to visualize more buildings burning, to believe hijackings could spread like a rash. My imagination filled the gaps—entrapment, smoke, heat. Falling, and being so afraid. And angry. And helpless.

Paint slid off the brush, giving the window a tight white outline, rejuvenating the aging wood and buffering against cold and wind, freezing and thawing. Was the KAL flight the last plane aloft? Why didn't the pilots talk to the air force? Or anyone? Say that they would arrive normally in Anchorage for refueling. Who was flying the plane? Was it on autopilot? Had it lost pressure so everyone was unconscious, the fuselage an icy tomb hurtling through the atmosphere?

Chuck telephoned again, saying they didn't know anything more about the Korean plane. He said he was sending everyone in his section home.

T I M E • We live with uncertainty. Who knows exactly when a natural disaster will hit? Forecasters, like modern-day soothsayers, warn of hurricanes, tornadoes, tsunamis, or Arctic cold sweeping out of the north. With satellite views and computer models, hurricane warnings ought to allow time to evacuate, but foreknowledge of some events, like tornadoes or tsunamis, may be measured in minutes or less—when each second counts and sirens wail, warning people to find shelter or flee to higher ground. But tsunamis are the result of what cannot be precisely predicted: crushing adjustments in the earth's crust—slips, slides, subductions. An earthquake hits, jarring and noisy, and at that moment, no one knows the outcome. Will there be deaths? Injuries? Will buildings fall? Trains derail? Dams break? Roads crumple?

S K Y • I was painting the third windowsill when Chuck called to say the Korean flight, shadowed by fighter jets, had veered away from Anchorage and was flying toward Canada.

Surely the Korean Air pilots were checking fuel supplies, calculating distance and speed, figuring how long they could stay aloft, to the last possible minute, but did the passengers know that everything had changed? Had they glimpsed the fighter jets with pilots locked inside cockpit bubbles? Looking down at the Alaskan landscape of gold-streaked forests and tough snow-topped mountains, did they realize their flight was thought hijacked and that the North American Aerospace Defense Command (NORAD), could order the plane shot down? Were they scribbling notes to their families and friends? Did the passengers realize their role in the drama (later described as "edgy and confused" with details that "remain murky") unfolding between Anchorage Air Traffic Control, the Federal Aviation Administration in Washington, DC, and NORAD?

Two American F-15s shadowed the unresponsive flight across Alaska and into Canadian air space. Along the way, the hijack code being transmitted mysteriously changed to a low fuel code, but NORAD's communication to the Royal Canadian Mounted Police was not updated. By the time the jumbo jet landed in Whitehorse, schools had been evacuated, which caused chaotic traffic while parents frantically searched for their children.

Canadian police met the Korean Air plane with their guns drawn. They allowed only one crew member to deplane, after having removed his jacket and holding his hands out. A bomb-sniffing dog was brought in and passengers were told in English and Korean the protocol for disembarking: fifty at a time, all to be searched. Anything they carried would be X-rayed.

The next day, Alaska governor Tony Knowles telephoned Yukon premier Pat Duncan and thanked her "for her cooperation" at a time that "was certainly as tense . . . for the Yukon officials as it was . . . in Alaska." Passengers on KAL flight 85, after being scrutinized and having their passports processed, improbably found themselves visitors in Whitehorse, Canada.

T I M E • On September 11, 2001, the future reoriented itself with the bitter taste of death and loss amid billowing smoke and flames, clouds of toxic fumes and dust, and a trans-Pacific jetliner forced to overfly a refueling stop. What was this stand-off really about? Saving face? Losing face? The people on the ground? The generals? People in a windowless room in Washington, DC? A tank of fuel like an hourglass steadily draining? The first trickling erosion of our high-mindedness?

C A B I N • Feeling like an automaton going through the motions of work, I dipped the brush and spread another layer of paint across the weather-blotted sills. Mass killing of Americans by foreign terrorists was beyond my comprehension, as was sending a jetliner with low fuel reserves away from its normal refueling stop and out over the Alaska wilderness.

A breeze hummed through spruce and rustled crabapple leaves.

ɩƐ ⊙

T I M E • I string together recollections according to connections I discern. On another reading, a passage reminds
me of a different occurrence that shifts what was before, or
after, as if I'm mending holes in a net of time with a thread of
memory, and logic as enigmatic as picking up a single pretty
pebble from a rocky beach. I examine the small stone, then
slip it into my pocket. Farther along the beach, I absently finger the pocket-bound pebble, and with a dismissive glance,
let it drop. The ocean does this all the time. Lapping surf shifts
stones and shells, and tangled kelp, and a conundrum of cast-
off plastic.

T E R R A I N • The deck of Chuck's brother John's summer rental in Haines overlooked Mud Bay and Mud Bay Road.
Leaning on the railing, I glanced at the last span of electric
wires just beyond the house that plunged down a pole and
disappeared underground. The wires drew lines across the
terrain, a visual interruption certainly overlooked because of
the benefits of electricity. Across the bay, like through a dingy
glass, forest fire smoke obscured the Chilkat Mountains. On
the other side of the road, alder and willow leaves rustled, a
nattering overwhelmed by each passing car. The balcony of
weathered wood was on the second floor of a small house
that had the ambience of a summer home, although I supposed someone lives there year-round, beside the silvery bay.
The water mirrored cirrus clouds streaming from the southwest, but underneath the cheery reflection, silty effluent from
Chilkat Glacier clouded the seawater.

WATER • Situated between ocean and river, water defines Haines, not just large bodies of water—frozen and liquid, salt and fresh—but also so-called domestic water.

"The water is smelly and unappealing," John warned us.

Turning on a faucet, the flow was accompanied by the stench of sulfur, like a hot springs pool. My gag reflex prevented me from swallowing the water.

"Down the road a ways spring water flows from a pipe in the rocks," John said. "People get drinking water there." Chuck and I planned to do just that before we departed on the ferry.

TERRAIN • Still a day before the ferry sailing, Chuck and I set out from the house to walk along the beach. After crossing Mud Bay Road, we strolled along a sandy trail between shrubby trees, then traversed a margin of sand, rocks, and billowing beach grass. Beyond a low hill, water lapped a changeable beach that earlier had appeared as a placid lake where a bald eagle stood, incongruously, as if he had acquired the knack of walking on water. We ambled in a southerly direction, away from the Chilkat River, treading sand and polished pebbles and large cobbles that I stepped between, as if the beach was a river and these were stepping-stones. At the upper boundary of the beach, fireweed grew in discrete clumps with dark green leaves and stems already woody even though the acutely magenta blooms had not yet reached the top.

I hoped that meaning would arise from my observations. As a matter of daily course, I watch and listen, jot notes, and wonder about causes and effects. The more intricacies I notice, the more intently I observe my surroundings. Although I had nearly always lived amid nature, I was gradually becoming more aware of how surprising details act as a repository of stories—with plots and subplots.

Fireweed along Mud Bay appeared stunted compared to fireweed along our driveway. Shaded by trees, the fireweed by our driveway grew tall, as if reaching for sunlight, or as if intending to migrate to the open pasture. This description may suggest that these fireweed growing in shade were stressed and etiolated but that was not the case. Abundant daylight plus rich soil and usually adequate rainfall bolstered their ferocious growth.

At the edge of Mud Bay, extremely dark green leaves of the fireweed attested to open habitat, but their small size suggested other challenges, perhaps related to rainfall or soil chemistry. On the other hand, maybe the tall fireweed in the Matanuska Valley were the exception rather than the rule. Considering all this, I suspect that I had adopted the disingenuous habit of considering the place I lived to be the norm.

Beyond the tidal region's squishy mud, strands of dried kelp and seaweed marked the border of high tides. Smoothly polished pebbles—black, green, red, and speckled granite and sparkly quartz—dappled the glistening sand. We proceeded along the beach until we encountered a black outcrop slapped by small surf. There, we turned and strolled back the way we had come, now with a breeze against our faces. I bent and picked up a pebble, smooth and warm, with one green edge. The sun-heated stone settled in my hand like an egg—or a medallion—that momentarily connected me to land and sea and sun.

Lowering myself onto the sand, sun-warmed pebbles pressed unevenly but not unpleasantly against my back. Where my head met the beach, I reached and pushed aside larger stones, smoothing a spot like a nest, or cradle. Cool air flowed over me even as the sun warmed my body, and beneath me, sun-warmed stones radiated heat. Lying flat, gravity felt stronger, as if the earth had clasped me more tightly than usual.

"Chuck, you should try lying on the beach." I glanced toward where he stood, perusing beach and bay and a parade of bouffant clouds. With my head turned, I acquired a more abstract perspective of a rainbow of stones splaying toward the shoreline where little waves rippled like exhalations of the North Pacific, and every other ocean, even the Arctic.

ﮩ

A R C T I C • When I mentioned to my sister Barbara that Chuck and I planned to drive to the Arctic Ocean, she laughed. "The Arctic? Wouldn't Hawaii be a nicer beach vacation?"

"Everyone goes to Hawaii," I replied. "Do you know anyone who has driven to the Arctic Ocean?"

"Not yet," she replied cheerily.

T I M E • With the purchase of Alaska from Russia in 1867, the United States became a nation with more than a theoretical interest in the Arctic. There have been many Arctic expeditions, some familiar like the race to the North Pole or seeking the Northwest Passage, others less well known like a search for land that had been speculatively reported in the Arctic Basin.

I became interested in this topic when I came across a book by Ernest de Koven Leffingwell and Ejnar Mikkelsen. These men, from the United States and Denmark, set off in 1906 to prove (or disprove) the existence of land north of Alaska. There had been reports of land and theories for verifying the presence or absence of such land related to tides, currents, and the behavior of the sea ice. In 1909 Mikkelsen wrote

> The ice which is a characteristic feature of [the] Beaufort Sea is indeed so heavy and old that it is hard to explain how ice of so formidable a size can be formed in an open Polar Sea where the ice is continually drifting out and getting renewed.

A R C T I C • Of course, an expedition needs a goal, often stated as a compelling question, such as: is there land? Or now, traveling to the Arctic, we ask: is there ice? And we can drive and look for ourselves, which is exactly what Chuck and I did during the summer of 2007. We would not be hampered by ships stuck in the ice nor would we have to kill and eat sled dogs when the going got tough. We would simply pack food and camping gear into the back of our pickup and go.

We planned to camp the first night in Fairbanks, three hundred miles north of our house. By early evening, with the sun still up, we drove slowly through the Chena River Campground. Finding every site occupied, we drove on past malls and stores. We filled the gas tank when we thought we were near the edge of the city because our traveler's guide showed only two gas stations between Fairbanks and the Arctic coast.

Continuing north, shadows deepened in the creases between forested hills, and homes and cabins became more sparse until there were none. We stopped at the Wickersham Dome pull-out and switched drivers, so I drove and peered at the sides of the road looking for a place to camp. We had no concerns about darkness because, in summer, the Far North remains a bright twilight all night. Whether a curve in the road or forest obscured my view, suddenly a wider area appeared. I braked and turned into what might once have been a wayside, or campground, but there were no picnic tables, toilets, or running water. A motor home idled nearby, and there was another car parked and a tent half hidden in the trees. After eating meat and potatoes and pitching our tent, we walked into the woods along Tatalina Creek where we discovered the steel superstructure of an abandoned bridge, faded to a sickly pink and overrun by forest.

The next morning I woke slowly, listening to the rumble of a truck engine and a motor home's generator. We boiled water for coffee, ate cereal, and repacked the pickup. We had passed Pump Station 7 but had not yet reached the turnoff from the Elliott Highway onto the Dalton Highway. Intermittently, between the hills, we saw the oil pipeline—a substantial presence constructed of tubular steel, forty-eight inches in diameter. Over its length, the pipeline is supported by seventy-eight thousand posts called Vertical Support Members (VSMs). The VSMs elevate the warmer pipe to protect the permafrost from melting.

The pipeline has a rugged grace, like an uncoiled snake, and from a distance appears like twine stretched across the variable terrain. Besides tracing topography, in places the pipeline zigzags to allow for expansion and contraction, as well as movement should an earthquake occur.

O I L • The largest oil reserves in North America were discovered at Prudhoe Bay in 1968. Five years later, OPEC targeted the United States and other countries with an oil embargo. The embargo caused shortages and rationing in the United States, along with an increase in price.

In 1974, a year after the oil crisis, construction began on the Trans-Alaska Pipeline System. Three years later, oil began to flow.

Prudhoe Bay is where the Trans-Alaska Pipeline System begins and the Dalton Highway ends. It's where oil is pumped and shipped south, on an eight-hundred-mile journey through the pipeline, to be loaded into tankers at Valdez. Deadhorse is an industrial enclave next to the Prudhoe Bay oil fields. It has few permanent residents but thousands of workers who travel there for weeks-long shifts, then return to their homes.

T I M E • During the time crews braved Arctic conditions to build the Trans-Alaska Pipeline, artists Jeanne-Claude and Christo planned and built *Running Fence*, a wall of fabric that traversed twenty-four and a half miles of California hills. *Running Fence* was constructed using 240,000 square yards of heavy woven white nylon fabric, 2,050 steel poles, 350,000 hooks, and 13,000 earth anchors.

(I am struck by the large numbers—thousands of hooks and poles and anchors—needed to build even a transient structure across miles of terrain.)

Running Fence hung across the California hills for two weeks in 1976 and then was dismantled. Whether built for art or effect, a wall has the capacity to inspire imagination and even steer us to consider other contrivances or constructs that cross the landscape. Christo's fabric fence would have made a weak border, but the effect was surely one of wonder. Even decades later, I marvel that *Running Fence* materialized at all. It suggests determination, durability of ideas, and a poetic vision.

Like poetry and art, *Running Fence* may have caused people who saw it to think about landscape differently, perhaps considering the scene to be more flexible, like when a painter adds or subtracts with the sweep of a brush, and this perhaps exactly because *Running Fence* had no practical purpose. To interpret the meaning of draped fabric that meanders across ridges and valleys is unlike contemplating an industrial object—like a pipeline—yet anything we build across the terrain is, by nature, transitory. Only the timelines differ.

A R C T I C • Where the Dalton Highway crosses the Yukon, the river is nearly a half mile wide. The road was muddy, and a large truck was gaining on us when we approached the bridge. Our pickup bounced over potholed wooden decking, and I had an unsettling view, from the passenger window, of the Yukon's fast-flowing green waters far below. The bouncing made the seat belt tighten unpleasantly, and although Chuck had a firm grip on the steering wheel, I wished he was driving slower.

T I M E • A road is like a thread with knots for memories or moments of wonder—or perplexity—and the pipeline is the reason that the Dalton Highway exists at all. They are a pair, twinned across the terrain, creating a narrow corridor of civilization. If you parked and walked away from the road, you would quickly find wilderness, something that has long fascinated explorers as well as armchair travelers. Wilderness is place and idea, and the absence of human influence. By definition, wilderness is uncultivated and uninhabited (or in some cases "unsettled"). But a definition suggests interpretation, labeling, and judgment, and you must ask what is "uninhabited"? Does a temporary hunting camp count as habitation? Does the word *settled* suggest colonizing?

In an older version of the *Oxford English Dictionary*, the definition of *wild* is less troubling. Wild is a word that can be attached to many others: wildfowl, wildcat, wildflower, wildfire, wildland. *Wild* also can represent unsound or reckless decisions; *wildness* might be a place in an uncultivated state. Evidently, going after something unlikely to be found has long been known as a wild goose chase.

Along the Dalton Highway there is certainly no cultivation so it must be wildland, yet wilderness is not so easily proved. People use the land for hunting and fishing and traveling, but it doesn't take vast tracts to meet up with the definition of wilderness. Even a city block will do—where rain seeps into sidewalk cracks and seeds sprout and, if unchecked, deterioration is speeded by roots and the frost's wedging action.

An industrial road that abuts wildland has rules, and traffic. Trucks have the right-of-way, and other travelers pull to the side each time a truck appears. Barry Lopez, in his book *Arctic Dreams*, described driving the Haul Road in the early 1980s: "For miles at a time we were the only vehicle, then a tractor-trailer truck—pugnacious and hell-bent—would shoulder past, flailing us with gravel."

Times change. In 2007 tractor-trailer rigs traveling the Dalton Highway seemed cautiously hurried rather than "pugnacious and hell-bent," and flailing gravel didn't trouble us.

A R C T I C • We cross invisible lines every day—latitude and longitude, city, state, and county boundaries—but the greatness of the Arctic Circle is that it symbolizes the earth's tilt and the timing of seasons—exemplified by perpetual daylight of a Far North summer.

With the Arctic Circle sign as backdrop, Chuck and I set up tripod and camera and were photographing ourselves when a disheveled couple approached and asked if we would take their picture. They said this photo would provide proof that ended their quest to visit all fifty states. They looked exhausted, as if they had been sleeping in their car for weeks. The woman donned a floppy brimmed hat like it was her photo-op hat and the couple, smiling tensely, posed in front of the Arctic Circle sign. I imagined the photo on Christmas cards with the caption "We did it!"

Later I learned that as a consequence of shifts in the earth's tilt, the Arctic Circle is drifting north at the rate of nearly fifty feet a year. Now I wonder whether the signage was only for entertainment purposes because the real Arctic Circle had detached from its designated latitude—and we were all being bamboozled.

T I M E • Traveling by car a long distance on a remote highway is a peculiarly isolating activity. You are ensconced inside a shell that shields you from weather and grime and chance encounters. I felt a certain detachment when I noticed two people pushing heavily laden bicycles out of the trees and onto the road and, later, a similar apathy when I glimpsed a man standing beside a long-haul truck and brushing his teeth. Inside the car, you adopt companionable rituals such as a thermos of coffee and music with a forward-driving beat or poignant lyrics. When you park, you extricate yourself from the car with the stiffness of a newborn foal and observe other travelers who have also stopped so that, should you see the same person a hundred miles farther, you might converse with common pleasantries of weather or observations of unusual sightings. It seems, in fact, to be impossible to recall an entire trip in a movie-like continuity, but the most singular incidences—the strange, surreal, or inconvenient—become well-remembered vignettes.

On a different and shorter trip, the conversation-starter was a dead moose we had seen beside the highway. It had probably been hit by a car rather than falling over the cliff and was in full rigor mortis. The image stuck in my mind was of a stiffened leg sticking straight up and a cloud of flies disturbed by our passing car. Returning the same way several hours later it was with interest that I awaited that point along the roadway only to see that the carcass had vanished.

A R C T I C • North of the Arctic Circle but still south of the Brooks Range, we passed a roadside sign indicating the "farthest north tree." The tree was, disappointingly, a dead snag, but a short distance farther, like a testament to survival or chance, or a warming climate, a fine young spruce grew.

We passed the Chandalar Shelf, an escarpment that marks the start of the steepest climb, and Chuck steered the pickup toward Atigun Pass. At nearly a mile high and with a 12 percent grade, the gravel road meandered through fantastically proportioned scenery but with a total absence of trees and, ultimately, no vegetation at all. Just talus. Through the passenger window, I had an acrophobic view into a deep canyon where the pipeline is buried. When we encountered a huge tanker or freight truck, southbound and empty, negotiating the gravelly grade in a low gear and braking, Chuck maneuvered close to the extremely crushed and probably quite useless guardrail.

Beyond Atigun Pass, we breezed downhill and, after a steep hairpin turn, pulled off at a wide area. I got out to take pictures just as a long tanker truck hurtled past. The entire vista of mountains and tundra, and the highballing truck, struck me as innately—and daringly—wild, but later the photos failed to show the grandeur, giving me the feeling that I had tried to capture a mirage.

North of the Brooks Range, we traversed treeless terrain, the human corridor anchored by road and pipeline. A scraped-earth scar in the distance, near the crest of a hill, turned out to be a rest area.

We were the only ones at the rest area when a maroon sedan raced into the lot and stopped abruptly, wreathed by dust and smoke. A young woman jumped out of the vehicle, her belly bulging in the gap between her shirt and pants. She yanked the hood open. A man with unruly black hair climbed out and stared morosely at the smoking engine. A third man, maybe a teenager, watched glumly from the back seat. The man with the tousled hair exclaimed, "She's burning up. We need oil." Chuck searched the back of our truck and handed him a spare quart of oil.

Sometimes when traveling, you adjust your ideas of the journey, and this was one of those moments. Suddenly, our trip seemed innately tame. How would it have been to be pregnant and driving from Quebec to the Alaskan Arctic in a car with mechanical troubles? These travelers had the same idea we had, to see the Arctic Ocean, but they had failed. They were stopped at the edge of the oil fields because they didn't have enough money to pay for the tour that was the only permissible way for tourists to traverse the final six miles to the coast. Perhaps it was better in the 1980s, when Barry Lopez drove to Prudhoe Bay and a travel permit allowed him to drive the entire route—all the way to the shore of the Arctic Ocean.

Departing from the rest area, we motored constantly north across the Arctic plain. On one side of the road, a landscape of verdant tundra and startlingly blue lakes appeared as if nothing much had changed for eons. Paralleling the highway on the other side, the pipeline perched atop vertical supports—offering testament to resources, investment, and motivation. Inside the four-foot-diameter insulated tube, oil flowed. Yet flow of oil is not a given. By the early twenty-first century, depletion of oil reserves resulted in flow at less than half of the pipeline capacity.

T E R R A I N • Driving across the Arctic plain, we stopped frequently to watch birds: gulls and long-tailed jaegers swooping above the tundra and an Arctic loon cavorting on a satiny-blue lake. The loon splashed, preened, dived, and rolled so his chest flashed white above the water, then he lurched upright and fanned his wings. A female loon serenely paddled nearby. On the far side of the lake, a pair of tundra swans swam, shielding four cygnets between them.

T I M E • Approaching Deadhorse, where the roadway nears the Sagavanirktok—the "Sag"—River, we stopped and looked through binoculars at a herd of musk oxen grazing along the opposite bank. Although I had seen captive musk oxen at the Musk Ox Farm (near Palmer), the wild herd offered hopefulness for long-term species survival. Like wooly mammoths, herds of musk oxen roamed the Arctic during the Pleistocene era. Unlike mammoths, musk oxen beat the survival odds—except the musk oxen foraging along the Sag were not descended from herds that migrated from Siberia across the Bering Land Bridge. In the early twentieth century, those musk oxen were hunted to extinction.

It takes will and resources to reverse an extinction. The species must still exist somewhere in order to be reestablished. The musk oxen we watched along the Sag river were descended from musk oxen transported from Greenland in 1935.

S W I T Z E R L A N D • After hiking around Le Derborence valley with Chuck's cousin Irene, we departed the same way we had come, in Irene's car, through the nerve-racking one-lane tunnel. Dodging an approaching vehicle, Irene abruptly stopped in one of the arched alcoves. We climbed out and leaned on the stone wall. Breezes welled up from the deep valley. Below us, an eagle-sized bird soared.

"I don't believe it, I really don't believe it!" Irene exclaimed, "A *gypyette!*"

"What's that?" I asked.

"Gypyettes," Irene explained, "were hunted to extinction because farmers thought the birds killed lambs. Later, they learned that gypyettes only scavenged afterbirth."

"That sounds like a vulture," I commented.

"They are a vulture. The bird is called *bartgeier* in German, which means 'bearded vulture.'" Irene continued, "A few years ago, Switzerland acquired some pairs of gypyette from Turkey, but the location where they were released was kept a secret."

While we watched, the gypyette soared upward and landed on a stony ledge across the canyon. I focused my binoculars. "Could the pile of sticks on the ledge be a nest?" I wondered aloud.

T I M E • I'm glad to hear about reintroductions of regionally extinct species, like the gypyette in Switzerland and musk ox on Alaska's Arctic plain, but I wonder about species now on the brink of extinction. The endangered list is much longer than I thought. What will future people think of us? I imagine they will be as baffled that we didn't figure out solutions as I am with past people who allowed wanton hunting and decimation of species, some well-known like the dodo and passenger pigeon, others less so, like the Carolina parakeet, aurochs, the great auk, and Steller's sea cow.

More troubling than thinking that future generations will judge us as inept or inattentive is the actual ecological impact of oceans acidifying, ice sheets and glaciers melting, sea levels rising, deforestation, and other recent ecological shifts.

Iceland's loss of forests a thousand years ago suggests both case study and metaphor. As does the migration of farmers to the Matanuska Colony in 1935.

A R C T I C • Late afternoon of our third day journeying north, we drove into the enclave of Deadhorse on a gravel road elevated above pools of water. A caribou, its hide like a moth-chewed sweater, loitered on the road berm. Breezes swirled gritty dust in front of us.

Our first stop was at the only gas station, unattended and self-serve with an unusual configuration—pump controls inside a small room presumably prevented the mechanisms from freezing during Arctic winters. We checked in at the Caribou Inn, lodging assembled from metal-sheathed modules perched atop pilings intended to avoid melting the permafrost. More foreign than I expected, Deadhorse evoked the off-kilter graininess of an old black-and-white movie but with the paradigm-shift effect of a Star Wars space station.

Later that evening, after a meat-and-potatoes dinner at the hotel cafeteria, Chuck and I tromped along gravel streets in a brisk wind that swirled dust and riffled a small lake. To the north, the sun shone weakly above low-slung clouds. Glimpsing the so-called midnight sun above the Arctic shore would clinch my idea of the Arctic as truly exotic. Seeing sea ice would offer a measure of hopefulness.

Some shorebirds—semipalmated plovers and a solitary sandpiper—behaved as if oblivious to the industrial landscape and the occasional passage of a pickup truck, but while walking, we startled a flock of red-necked phalaropes that flew up from a puddle-sized pond, circled, and alighted in the same place. Tiny sandpipers that we couldn't identify stalked the edge of a large puddle beside a boxy building.

As we trekked along the dusty berm-perched byways, to the north pink-tinged clouds grew taller until they hid the sun. Maybe under different conditions the clouds would have appeared as mirages—fabulous castles or mythical mountain ranges that might be mistaken for distant land—but these clouds were indeed real. They spread slowly inland like pink cotton, and we returned to our worn, yet warm, hotel room.

In the night, I woke to the rattle of rain against metal walls, and the next morning Chuck and I stood in the hotel's cafeteria line along with oil company employees wearing heavy work gear. We filled our plates with eggs, sausage, and toast and, after eating, waited in front of the hotel for the tour to the Arctic shore. Eventually a van showed up, and as we boarded, the driver checked our names off a list. We shared the shuttle with a couple from Alberta who said they had been camping, and we remembered seeing a tent, beaten by wind, near the Sag River. A fashionably dressed couple we had noticed at dinner in the cafeteria also boarded the van. They appeared nonplussed, as if they had stepped off the plane into a place misrepresented by the tourism brochures.

The no-frills van turned out to be a repurposed airport shuttle with towels neatly stacked on the luggage rack, and the driver introduced himself as a retired policeman from Arizona. The nighttime rain had slowed to a persistent drizzle. I rubbed steam off my window to better see rows of enormous Rolligons, vehicles with gigantic low-pressure tires that spread weight more broadly to avoid damaging the fragile tundra. The oversized rigs looked like they'd been repurposed from a science fiction movie. Or had movie designers used industrial Rolligons as inspiration for their sets?

To reach the Arctic Ocean at all, we had to submit proof of identity ahead of time, which the van driver claimed let him "vouch for us at the gate." In an odd way, that seemed apropos to the melancholy of the accelerating rain, as did the van driver's tiff with a road-grader operator regarding who got the right-of-way on the narrow road. I was certain the small van would lose in a full-fledged confrontation with the heavily bladed machine, but the van sneaked past.

After that, the tour was mostly the driver reading names of companies from signs on buildings. At the beach, he turned the van and parked facing inland. As we exited, he said, "Feel free to swim, there are plenty of towels, but no diving because the water is too shallow." Seemingly as an afterthought, he added, "Watch out for polar bears."

"Are you worried about polar bears?" I asked Chuck as I zipped my raincoat.

"No," Chuck said. "They're probably out on the sea ice."

"So you don't think we'll see a polar bear?" I asked, wondering what we would do out at the end of the long jetty if a polar bear lumbered out of the ocean.

"No," Chuck replied. "There's no sea ice here, and the van driver would surely have mentioned if polar bears were roaming the shore. Or there wouldn't have been a tour at all."

"Hmmm. I'm not so sure. I would like to see the Arctic ice pack though," I commented.

We walked through chilly rain beside seawater as somber as the misty clouds. At the end of the jetty we turned and hiked back to the van. As I recall, the Albertans went swimming.

T I M E • Cross the Arctic Basin from Prudhoe Bay and you will skirt the North Pole and eventually reach Norway. You will not see a landmass in the center of the Arctic, although you will see ice, but there is some question as to how much. In 1906 Mikkelsen and Leffingwell's expedition was plagued by ice. First they planned to commission whalers to haul their gear north, but most of the whaling ships were stuck in the ice so they bought a sailing schooner, the *Duchess of Bedford*, which was subsequently lost in the ice. Mikkelsen and Leffingwell spent nearly two months crossing ice in the Beaufort Sea with sledges and dogs, recording weather, sea depth, and describing the ice—proving the continental shelf was narrow and that no additional landmass exists north of Alaska. Mikkelsen's and Leffingwell's chronicles provide us with information and data as to the condition of the Arctic ice a century ago—like a message in a bottle from the past.

A R C T I C • In my best-case tourism scenario, glimpsing the Arctic Ocean ice pack would have symbolized hope, like a dove alighting on the railing of the ark. But we couldn't gawk at ocean ice—tongues and ridges—because in July the ice would be far offshore, and because the expanse of Arctic ice has been hugely reduced by our warming climate.

Unlike Mikkelsen and Leffingwell's expedition, our journey proved nothing.

Walking in rain on the shore of the Arctic Ocean, Chuck and I saw no ice. If we had beheld ice, not just cold rain and a flat gray sea, I would have felt more optimistic but that likely would have been because I allowed the sighting more veracity than it deserved.

GREENHOUSE • Time weighed on the greenhouse like maladies of old age. At first, the changes were subtle—a gradual decline. We didn't notice the tomato plants had become lankier, with fewer tomatoes. When we did take note, our conversation was speculative.

"Maybe it's the variety," Chuck said.

"Or the weather," I offered.

Or the soil. One spring, we replaced most of the soil in the greenhouse, heaving shovelfuls from the hip-high planting beds into a wheelbarrow, dumping each load on the rough slope beyond the lawn. We trundled composted horse manure, and loam from beside the raspberry patch, and refilled the planting beds. In early May, Chuck transplanted tomato plants that had been growing indoors since March. We hoped for luxuriant growth and plentiful tomatoes. The summer proceeded apace, the plants stretching upward but still gangly and with few tomatoes.

Our discussions repeatedly turned to the tomato situation. We looked searchingly at the little greenhouse built from recycled materials long before we arrived—lumber and plywood and windows that may have come from the house after a renovation. The corrugated roof, once a transparent fiberglass, had yellowed to opaqueness.

Would replacing the roof with new fiberglass solve the tomato conundrum?

Chuck balanced on a ladder and dismantled the old roof. He attached new fiberglass touted as unaffected by ultraviolet light and nearly transparent compared to the previous roof. Almost immediately, the tomatoes looked healthier but troubles with the greenhouse continued.

For no obvious reason, a narrow window on the west wall of the greenhouse cracked, and on the north wall putty between the panes disintegrated. I picked out the remaining chunks and messily daubed new putty.

Plastic sheeting that lined the planting beds shattered, letting moisture—and rot—seep into the wood. One of the planter walls bulged, constricting the narrow aisle even more. As a stopgap, we reinforced the protruding planting bed with planks.

When cracks appeared in the south-facing glass, I eyed the greenhouse suspiciously and vigilantly listened for creaks or groans that might warn of impending collapse. Later in the summer, the north wall split along the joint where an addition had been attached. The back of the structure had tipped slightly, as if poised to tear loose and slide down the hill.

TIME • On our walk-around with Mrs. Webb, she had pointed out a low rock wall and a patch of soil at the west end of the greenhouse. "Delphiniums grow there," she said, describing the tall and pale blue flowers that in early spring had not yet sprouted.

I was delighted by the idea of a tiny hidden garden, but neither Chuck nor I noticed that the piled-up rocks extended like a hurriedly assembled foundation underneath the end of the greenhouse.

G R E E N H O U S E • Twenty years later, both cause and effect suddenly became obvious. Delphiniums that camouflaged the rock-pile foundation hid the fact that the ground had slumped. I mentioned my discovery to Chuck.

On a peaceful summer evening, we strolled around the greenhouse, studying it like we were inspectors who had only just come onto a scene. Summer was too far along to launch demolition and construction and expect to finish that year. Besides, the tomatoes were producing deliciously.

"Maybe we can shore up the greenhouse until next spring," I said.

"I think so," Chuck replied. We shoved more rocks underneath the structure and nailed a Band-Aid of boards across the expanding crack in the north wall.

The greenhouse didn't collapse then, and throughout the winter, we discussed the possibilities for replacing it. The following spring, Chuck purchased a greenhouse kit from a local lumberyard. A few days later, a large truck dumped a load of boards and trusses, grooved plywood siding for the lower half of the walls, and UV-stabilized fiberglass panels for the upper walls and roof. The driver handed me a small box of nails and screws and a single page of instructions for assembling the greenhouse.

With a large dumpster delivered to the backyard, Chuck began dismantling the old greenhouse, and when Michael came home from college for the summer, he worked on it too. When the old structure was gone and the site scraped clean, we found an incongruous slab of cement, ten feet by ten feet, which must have coincided with the original configuration of the greenhouse. Or perhaps there had been an even earlier greenhouse—one that had rotted and been torn down to make room for one that was there when we showed up.

Michael did most of the work assembling the new greenhouse, which outlined the newly discovered concrete slab, but the "kit" greenhouse turned into a more complicated project than anticipated. The single page of instructions proved impossibly cryptic. Boards had to be recut to the correct lengths, and more nails and screws were needed than those delivered in the little box.

The tomatoes had a slow start that summer, surviving but not flourishing in pots on the patio until the new greenhouse was ready. By mid-July the structure had walls, a roof, and a door. We moved the tomatoes into the enclosed environment where both days and nights were warmer than outdoors. The cherry tomatoes ripened quickly, but the larger varieties still needed a few more weeks.

In September Chuck and I painted the lower walls of the greenhouse a Caribbean color akin to marigolds or nasturtiums, a shade with no relationship to the drab green-gray of the house, a color I had previously chosen. I suspect my subconscious of nudging me toward a bright color that would offer cheery contrast to the winter dreariness of dried grass, birch branches, and pasty sky.

)½ ♋

TERRAIN • On an errand to the Matanuska-Susitna Borough offices, what sticks in my mind is a black-and-white photograph, framed and hanging at eye level in a hallway. "An odd choice for a public wall," I thought. My first impression was of a nonsensical curio; my second thought, of a muddled impressionist artwork, but one without bold colors.

Curves and lines arched and rippled like wrinkles in a poorly shaken blanket, or an elephant's sagging skin. Gradually, details emerged forming a connection between the image and geography—dark splotches of lakes, the variable shoreline of Cook Inlet, pale earth of gravel quarries. Corrugations resolved into hills that snaked in a pattern created during ancient times when the big glaciers plastered across southcentral Alaska melted away. We know one patch of the convoluted post-glacial topography as Kepler-Bradley State Park (with deep landlocked lakes embedded in hilly terrain) and another as Crevasse Moraine. The photo, snapped from space, missed the dimension of experience—no seasons or sensations, aromas or shapes—subtleties that harbor familiarity or confusion.

CREVASSE MORAINE • Intending to spend an hour or two away from house and garden, I drove to Crevasse Moraine. Standing in the parking area, I sprayed on insect repellant, snapped on a waist pack, and jogged through forest in a westerly direction, away from the main trail system. I had in mind a more obscure route where, for an hour or so, I could imagine I had my own nature preserve, without signage or maps. I knew the lay of the land like my own skin—or at least I thought I did.

Beginning at an easy pace, I veered past the edge of the borough landfill, where windblown single-use plastic tangled tree branches. Beyond the landfill, I trekked uphill on a worn track, past several mysterious well pipes. Clouds obscured the sky, and mosquitoes hummed but didn't land on me. A trail split off and I followed it to the edge of a field. My feet tapped a course through billowing grass until the clearing yielded to aged spruce with a groundcover of fluorescent-green equisetum as floaty as a carpet of feathers. The path meandered out of the woods, and suddenly, I encountered cleared land under the new electric lines. Beneath loosely draped wires, the ground cradled corduroy tread marks of bulldozers and a willful sprouting of vetch, yarrow, and some yellow flowers that I couldn't name. Sun split the somber sky. I put on sunglasses and hunted for the interrupted trail.

T I M E • Routing a large power line across the valley had caused brouhaha and passionate discourse regarding nature and scenic values. The electric company prevailed with arguments in favor of redundancy in the electrical system but agreed to build portions of the transmission line in low areas, between the hills, in order to minimize the visual effect. I was glad the company made an effort to hide sections of the ninety-foot-tall power line.

CREVASSE MORAINE • I spotted the snipped trail, which led me into a field of knee-high grass. After cresting a small hill, I angled toward a thicket where the path again vanished, this time among alders that bristled like a disorganized—and six-foot-tall—pin cushion. After a few minutes in the alders, I abandoned my search and veered toward what I hoped was an easterly direction, where I vaguely recalled a narrow track favored by mountain bikers. The brush got thicker and taller and changed from alders to saplings—good habitat for moose and bears.

At the thought of bears, I shouted "Yo!" and "Bear!" to distinguish myself from moose. Pushing on, I swerved toward what I hoped was north and the edge of the brush, but I couldn't be sure. My only view was up at the sky. I didn't have a compass and the terrain and vegetation screened landmarks like Pioneer Peak. I kept up my obnoxious patter of nonsensical words and wished I had memorized some dramatic poems to recite at times like this.

TIME • When I was a child, my father taught me how to navigate through forests and mountains. A six-year-old without a compass, I followed paths that deer and elk trod between trees, angling downhill to cross a stream where water flowed shallowly across pale sand flecked with glittering quartz. Wherever the trail split, Dad stopped and pointed out the choices. He arranged pebbles or sticks to point the way back and emphasized noticing how the landscape looks different from each direction. On my own hikes, I watched for confusing junctures and devised directional glyphs. Dad also said, "If you ever get lost, go downhill. Find a stream and follow it until you come to the highway." If that happened, I knew he would be there, watching for a child emerging from the forest.

CREVASSE MORAINE • My father's navigational teaching offered no help in Crevasse Moraine's jumbled terrain where there were no free-flowing streams. Fast-growing trees and brush obscured less-traveled paths, and transmission line construction had severed meandering trails. The racket I made startled spruce hens that rocketed up with staccato wing beats. I peered through a netting of alder branches. The birds landed somewhere else, and I laughed as my heart-pounding adrenalin subsided. "Fight or flight," I said aloud. "Birds. Not bears." I was more annoyed than frightened when I kept losing the trail; although later I wondered at my lack of appreciation that danger might exist anywhere, even within walking distance of subdivisions and roads.

After the next hill, I still hadn't found the mountain bikers' trail, but gradually the thickets abated and I trod between elderly spruce. The dark evergreens were less dense than the alders but nevertheless blocked my view of orienting landmarks. I shied around a patch of prickly rose and angled uphill toward where I hoped to find the main Long Lake Trail, not learn that I had inadvertently circled back to the new power line.

The map in my mind was out-of-date. Embarking, I hadn't considered the effect of change on the landscape—how new electric lines sliced ad hoc trails, and trees and brush reshaped the scenery. I also hadn't entertained the thought of encountering wildlife—other than pesky mosquitoes. While shoving through the brush, I fervently hoped bears were far away, gorging on salmon in creeks or gobbling berries in the mountains.

Later I considered that, if timing had been reversed and I had already assisted on the borough's cultural use survey near the south end of Trunk Road, I would have been more concerned about wildlife.

T E R R A I N • On a Sunday morning, with rain threatening, I drove south along Trunk Road, slowing for corners where the pavement meandered around farms and forested hills. In a newly mown field, two sandhill cranes bent their long necks toward the ground. Hunting mice or voles, the tall birds lifted their knees with the careful precision of a cat stalking prey, although the cranes' dawdling gait and plumage also brought to mind tottering old men wearing identical gray suits.

Periodically, I glimpsed the new alignment of Trunk Road, still under construction and carving a straight line across the landscape rather than following contours of the terrain like the familiar—narrow and winding—old road. My destination was the park-and-ride lot near the Parks Highway where I would meet the borough's archaeologist, Dan Stone, and help with a search for evidence of prior human activity in the adjacent forest. The park-and-ride lot was slated for expansion, and in advance of clearing the forest just to the west, the borough required a cultural resources survey.

Sunday morning, the park-and-ride lot was not quite empty. I parked in a far corner, wondering who would leave their vehicle overnight? Or had early risers already met to carpool to Anchorage? I climbed out of my car. To the south, monolithic Pioneer Peak showed little relief, as if a wash of midnight blue had surreptitiously been applied during the pre-dawn hours. To the north, a field ended at the foot of a bluff.

Earlier in the summer, I helped on other borough cultural use surveys. At Point MacKenzie we traipsed through forest, searching for evidence of human use surrounding the site where a maximum security prison was to be built. My contribution was to notice anything unusual and ask questions. The borough staff liked having volunteers. We helped cover more ground and made more noise than someone working alone.

A boxy Winnebago roared into the parking lot and lurched to a stop. I stepped backward and involuntarily held my breath as a cloud of exhaust drifted off. The side door of the motor home swung open and Dan stepped out carrying an armload of maps. He wore an orange surveyor's vest, heavy canvas pants, and laced up leather boots. A fringe of gray hair stuck out beneath his Indiana Jones hat. I suspected he was younger than he looked.

"Hi," he said as he unrolled a map on the car hood, "have you been here long?"

"No. I just got here." I peered at the map that he rotated so it oriented toward north. The map verified what I could see. The adjacent forest was small, maybe ten acres—a mere postage stamp relative to the entire Alaska landscape—but still a place where people might have lived and traversed before our time of automobiles, suburbs, and shopping malls.

"We'll start over there," Dan said, looking up from the map and pointing toward the brushy undergrowth at the edge of the woods that appeared less daunting. "In the forest, we'll spread out. That way we'll see more." Dan traced his finger across the map toward the bluff where, he explained, we would turn and circle back.

"Okay," I replied, ready to be underway.

Dan rolled up the maps and stowed them in his motor home.

From my car I retrieved a pack stuffed with bug spray, bottled water, a trowel and clippers, gloves, cell phone, and a hat. As an afterthought, I had also brought a shovel. Dan reemerged from the Winnebago. He carried a shovel and a faded orange pack. He also had a pistol holstered to his leg.

My expression must have shown surprise. Or he noticed I was staring at the handgun, which seemed odd attire in a commuter parking lot.

"By the way," Dan commented wryly, "I'll be armed."

T I M E • The first thing that went through my head was people, not bears. One time, in the early 1980s, when Chuck and I were cross-country skiing through what we thought was mostly unsettled forest, a man floundered toward us through thigh-deep snow. He was wildly waving a large pistol and shouting that we were trespassing. We talked calmly—like you would to a spooky horse—and we apologized. The man wore a grimy long underwear shirt and jeans and looked like he'd been holed up for a while. He ranted that he didn't want anyone coming around his cabin. As he calmed down, he seemed to forget about the pistol. As if manipulating a prosthetic hand, he lifted the barrel and scratched his scruffy beard. Chuck apologized again, and we skied away without looking back.

T E R R A I N • Dan continued, "You know how afraid Renée is of bears?"

Like me, Renée had volunteered on the Knik archaeology dig and several cultural use surveys on Point MacKenzie.

"Yes," I said, "she told me she'd taken the Timothy Treadwell tragedy to heart."

"Last week Renée helped on a survey along the hill south of Four Corners. When we were on the ridge, we came across a large pile of bear scat."

A half hour earlier I had driven past that unremarkable ridge beside a potato field and only a couple miles from Crevasse Moraine.

"Fresh bear scat?" I asked, now wishing I had also packed a cannister of bear spray.

"Yes," he said.

"Grizzly?" I queried.

"Yes," he said, again.

Hefting the packs and shovels, and with Dan toting a pistol, we crossed the parking lot and shoved through brush. I turned and headed north, and Dan walked farther west before changing direction.

Stepping cautiously through hip-high grass and between highbush cranberry and prickly rose, I tried to avoid tripping on what I could not see—fallen branches, bulky roots, and hollows. Mosquitoes, disturbed by my passage, flew up from leafy perches. Insect repellent kept them from landing on me, but my worn jeans offered scant defense against rose thorns.

For a while I heard traffic rushing along the Parks Highway, but then trees and terrain intervened. After that, the only sounds were insects and, occasionally, a chickadee chirping.

T I M E • When I venture into the woods behind my house, I notice the growth of wildflowers, ferns, and shrubs but also more surprising occurrences like scores of tiny spiders spilling from eggs deposited on a shrubby twig and, at the height of summer, armored-looking beetles clinging to leaves already riddled with holes. I consider the habits and torturous shapes of trees. Not every birch grows straight and tall. Some have contorted limbs or splay and lean, offering lessons in growth and decay—and how to postpone the finale of gravity. The forest behind my house also contains evidence of human use—sawed-off stumps, a rusted five-gallon can, the interred remains of at least one well-loved canine companion, and trash buried prior to the 1980s. Several birch trees bear scars from twisted wires. (This evidence is twentieth century. Earlier human passage in the woods by my house is a closed book to me.)

T E R R A I N • In the forest beside the Trunk Road park-and-ride lot, the birch were large with considerable space in between—as if, just by surviving, each tree had gained the right to a certain patch of ground and sky. Overhead, leaves mingled into a cohesive canopy hinting at a single organism. I switched my attention back and forth, between ground and trees, and eventually spotted a blemish on one birch—like a gash that had healed thicker and grayer than the pale bark.

To my left, I glimpsed Dan's orange vest. "Dan," I called, "over here. A blaze, I think."

Dan strode toward me. Looking up, he said, "Yes, it's a blaze, probably used to mark a trail." Glancing around, he indicated another birch where bark had been peeled off in a four-foot section. That tree had survived girdling, but the wounded trunk healed as dark as cardboard.

Dan returned to the line he'd been following, and I shoved on, now and then climbing over a fallen tree. I tried to discern the ground, determined to notice any holes hidden by grass or shrubs. A dip might signify a place where—ages ago—Dena'ina people built a house or cached food. A cache pit—like an underground refrigerator—would have been lined with a thin layer of birch bark, the bark harvested in wide bands from living trees. If I'd found a depression, I would have gotten Dan's attention and we would have dug a hole to see if the soil revealed more evidence. But neither of us spotted any slumped earth. After more walking, I was thinking about how fast time goes and wondering who, in a hundred—or a thousand—years, will trudge through our yards and neighborhoods and piece together, from the merest scraps of evidence, our lives. Or, more troubling, conclude that there's nothing much of interest here.

CREVASSE MORAINE • During my solo trek along the western edge of Crevasse Moraine, after finally escaping the thickets, I tromped through spruce forest. Ahead of me, sun-dappled leaves shone like beacons between the shadowy spruce. Hurrying forward, I reached the edge of the woods and peered down a cutbank. Delighted, and with relief, I slid down the slope onto the well-established Long Lake Trail. Finally, certain of my geographic position and the cardinal directions, I turned and jogged toward my car, following maintained trails with maps posted at every juncture.

C A B I N • One June afternoon in 2005, I sat at my desk, listening to my mom's voice on the phone, the receiver pressed hard against my ear as if I could compress fifteen hundred miles into an arm's length. Sun beamed through the window, but birch blocked my view of sky to the north. Far off, thunder grumbled. "Mom, did you hear the thunder?" I asked. She laughed.

After hanging up the phone, I drove to Palmer to buy concert tickets and go to the gym. At the bottom of Bailey Hill, dazzling sun lit a low-slung mini-mall, and the street shone like a black lake. To the east, a deluge obscured Lazy Mountain, and as I turned on South Alaska Street, lightning gashed the cloudburst. Four blocks farther, the parking lot behind Vagabond Blues was sunny and dry. Returning to my car a few minutes later, wet pavement glistened, and a block away, backed up vehicles indicated the traffic light was out. To avoid the bottleneck, I took an alternate route.

Only daylight lit the gym. Without electricity, the place was unusually hushed. Nobody was using exercise machines, and the blaring music had stopped. An occasional grunt or mutter by weightlifters, undeterred by the power outage, cut the silence.

Without electricity, my enthusiasm for exercise evaporated. I drove home. Along Fishhook Road, in bright sunlight, hayfields gleamed like emeralds. My poor humor dissipated. At our driveway, everything appeared normal. I parked and unlocked the front door. Inside, the house was peculiarly quiet. The aged goldfish swam slowly in still water, and the old refrigerator's gimpy motor wasn't even whispering. The only sound was arrhythmic clicking of a battery-powered wall clock. I leafed through the morning newspaper while considering cooking dinner without electricity.

Wondering whether my neighbors, Helen and Ralph, still had electricity, I picked up the handset of the phone that sat on top of the microwave oven. The line was dead.

I called from my cell phone. Helen said their power had been out but came back on. After waiting another half hour, I flipped through the phone book, finding the number for Matanuska Electric and punching it into my cell phone. After listening to several recorded messages, I selected "report an outage." Instantly, a robotic voice informed me that I had called from an invalid customer number.

A few minutes later, my mobile phone rang. After I gave my address, the man with the electric company said bluntly that electricity had been restored in my neighborhood.

"But we don't have power at our house," I insisted.

"Look at the meter and see if it's spinning," he said. "Maybe the main breaker is off."

With the phone pressed against my ear, I walked outside and around the corner of the garage. Tugging open the metal cover, I pushed both breakers off then on again, then retraced my steps inside. The screen door slammed behind me.

The house remained silent. "Nothing has changed. Our power is still off," I said, irked.

The power company representative remained skeptical. Or he wanted to be certain before ordering a repair truck out to our house. "Is there a red light on the meter?" he asked.

I stomped back outside and again studied the meter. "No red light. Our power is really out."

Resignedly, he replied, "I'll send a crew over."

A few minutes later, my cell phone rang again. This time it was Ralph. He remembered that, one summer while we were on vacation, a squirrel shorted out the wires on the electric pole nearest our house.

"The squirrel tripped the breaker on the pole," Ralph said. "Does anything look different on that pole?"

Across the driveway, a chunk of metal, like a section of pipe, hung down from one of the crossbars on the power pole. I described it, and Ralph said, "That's it. That's why your power is out."

The evening was sunny and warm. Ralph drove over and we stood in the driveway looking up at the power pole. "Sure," he said, "the breaker is disconnected." Chuck arrived home from work. We retrieved beer from the silent refrigerator, and strolled around the house to the patio.

"What about dinner?" Chuck asked.

"Broccoli and salad. Lettuce and radishes, peas and baby carrots," I suggested.

We started toward the vegetable garden but didn't get very far.

"What happened to the birdfeeders?" Chuck asked.

Normally, two birdfeeders hung, between two birch trees, downhill from the greenhouse.

"Look at the clawed-up earth," I commented.

Chuck reached down and picked up a scrap of wood. "And shards from the birdfeeders."

"Maybe a bear tore down the feeders and clawed the lawn," I suggested, even though it seemed unlikely since the birdfeeders had been empty for months, and we only suspected a bear in our yard once—after finding raspberry canes crushed, with black hair snagged on the spines.

Ralph reached up and examined the end of a wire dangling from a branch. "Lightning," he said matter-of-factly, "the wire is scorched."

We began scrutinizing the yard like we were crime scene investigators. A long, charred streak coursed down the trunk of one birch.

"Lightning hit this tree, burning through the wire, and causing a steam explosion in the lawn," I postulated. Of all the things I worried about—icy roads, colliding with a moose, earthquakes, trees falling—lightning had not been one of them.

Hearing the rumble of a truck engine, we hurried to the front of the house where an electric company truck was backing up the driveway. Even folded, the lift-bucket whacked overhanging branches. Several men wearing white overalls clambered out of the cab and everyone stared up at the electric pole with the dangling fuse-arm, as if that explained everything.

"Might have been a squirrel," one of the linemen said as he walked around the base of the pole, kicking at the dry grass but not finding an electrocuted squirrel.

"Lightning," I said. "We found exploded birdfeeders in the backyard and scorch marks on a tree."

Another lineman extended a long telescoping rod and snapped in a new fuse at the top of the pole. After checking that power was flowing to the electric meter, they drove away. Ralph also departed, and Chuck and I traipsed indoors. With electricity restored, the house sounded normal. The fish tank aerator gurgled and the refrigerator motor grumbled.

I picked up the receiver of the landline phone but still did not hear a dial tone. Chuck and I discussed calling the phone company, but with evening already advancing, the after-hours technician would ask if the problem was inside the house or outside, like a coded reference. If the malfunction was inside the house, it was our responsibility. If it was outside, the telephone company would fix it.

Chuck and I decided to do our own test.

I retrieved the landline phone from my desk and Chuck grabbed a screwdriver. Outside, below the kitchen window, conduit channeled phone wires from underground to a plastic box attached to the wall. Chuck pried the cover off the box, which should have contained neatly organized bundles of colored wires. We stared, aghast. The interior of the box was sooty black, the plastic that coated the wires melted, the wires charred.

Chuck spoke first. "Lightning hit the phone wires."

"That explains the dead phone line," I said, feeling a chill-like fear. We began parsing what happened that afternoon when no one was home.

Inside, I lifted up the phone on the microwave. That phone was an old desk model with a metal base, and underneath it, the white metal casing of the microwave oven was scorched.

Electrical energy from the lightning had not stopped at the phone company's box on the side of the house but had surged through the thin copper phone wires inside the walls and exited in various places.

For once, no junk mail had been stacked on the microwave. I unclipped the phone jack from the wall socket. The miniscule wires inside the clear plastic were also burned. In the living room, another phone cord lay on the floor—exploded out of the wall jack. As we found more damage, the magnitude of the destruction gradually dawned on us. Like sleepwalkers, we drifted through the rooms, considering details of our lives and the miracle that the old log house survived at all.

The next morning, I called the phone company. A repairman replaced the box under the kitchen window and managed to get the house phones working again, but that wasn't the end of the story. Several weeks later, the Internet became unstable. Eventually, another telephone technician traced the problem to a connector by the road. He unhooked a plastic panel with several dozen wires. All were crisply burned.

The atmospheric electrical charge seeking ground was unanticipated and destructive, a near miss with devastation that haunts me. My annoyance with wrecked electronic possessions was a mere footnote when I considered how I might have returned to a house engulfed in flames, or still smoldering charcoal.

I breathed deeply, considering another scenario. If I had not finished the conversation with my mom, hung up the phone, and driven to Palmer, I would have been at home when the lightning struck. If the storm hit suddenly, without warning, I could have been talking on the landline, typing on the computer, or running water in the sink. Inadvertently, I might have occupied a moment in the path of lightning careening through the house.

◆

E A R T H • I expected freeze-blackened plants by the second week of September, but in 2008, temperatures stayed mild longer. Before the first hard frost, several warm days provided a welcome change from the cooler and wetter than normal weather that had plagued us all summer. Foliage surrounding the house was switching to an autumn collaboration of yellow and green, and every shade in between. Only ruddy cotoneaster leaves and scarlet mountain ash berries interrupted the complementary hues.

On September 28, during the wee hours, the temperature dropped to twenty-nine degrees. With the promise of a spectacular sunrise, light splayed in broad bands between the mountain peaks. When the sun finally appeared, frosted leaves glinted and windrows of frozen hay sparkled.

I put on my jacket and went outside, ambling around the yard, appreciating the glittery foliage but also assessing loss. Like an adjuster after a misfortune, I noticed which plants had died. As gardener, I mourned frost-killed plants but smiled at the snapdragons that had somehow survived, as had the dill. The marigolds, though, looked as if they had been incinerated, blackened except for mustard-yellow tufts raggedly stitched to frost-charred stalks.

T I M E • When we moved to the house that we came to know as Cabin 135, I would not have guessed that the house and garden would become like family members, characters I knew well and yet who still concocted surprises. During autumn, as daylength diminished, I expected the perennials to transition into dormancy—which protected them against frigid temperatures and dehydrating winds.

Plants that produce seed—columbines, delphiniums, lychnis, asters, clematis, calendula, and poppies—had already done so. Dried seedpods shattered, and seeds scattered at any provocation. Other seeds, attached to bits of fluff and as unintentional as escaped balloons, were carried off by breezes.

The tiger lily, though, is not a traveler. Lacking seeds, it stays close to home. A new lily sprouts only a few inches from the parent plant, possibly because the gardener hacked a bulb loose when weeding. One clump of tiger lilies was hopelessly stressed—as if root-bound in a pot—the stalks becoming smaller each year, the bulbs clustered in tight knots. Two months prior, after the lily flowers faded, I divided the clump, separating and replanting the largest bulbs—hoping for masses of blooms in the future.

In autumn, birch turn yellow quickly. The Siberian crabapple also speedily responds to shorter days and colder nights. Berry-sized crabapples dangle amid leaves colored as if a child daubed yellow and red onto a green background.

The mountain ash swaps verdant green for a ruddiness that might turn bright yellow or a fractious orange, the leaves hanging on longer than I expect. Fruit as tiny as berries cling to the limbs, even after several snowfalls, until flocks of Bohemian waxwings swoop in and devour the fruit, or a gale scatters the lipstick-red pomes.

The Amur chokecherry, a tree with stunning coppery bark, quickly sheds its knockout-yellow leaves. All the leaves fall straight down on a windless night. Even knowing this, I'm surprised when, one morning, the branches are bare and gold carpets the lawn in a circle beneath the tree.

E A R T H • Another morning, in a prior year, I perused the aftermath of the first killing frost. On my way out the door, I grabbed my camera, intending to photograph the sparkling iciness. Instead, I was distracted by masticated-looking marigolds atop blackened leaves. I squatted, studying the damaged plants. While deciding where to point the camera lens, a slight movement caught my eye.

A minuscule spider zipped along an invisible line between two plants. Had I disturbed it? I hadn't touched the marigold, or even breathed on it. My shadow hadn't fallen across the plant, although the glassy lens-disk of the camera was only a few inches away. The spider paused at one marigold then whizzed over to the next stalk.

I blinked and, in that instant, lost sight of the minute arachnid. I stared hard at the spot where it had been but saw nothing. I clicked a few pictures then stood and continued my garden ramble. Later, when I examined the photos, the spider was there, as was her silken thread. The absence was a defect in my observation—the photo proved that.

Losing sight of a spider in a backdrop of foliage is not surprising. One moment I saw it; the next moment I didn't. The passage of time both hides and reveals. I like the idea of manipulating time to see something different than what initially appears. Cameras help with this—recording the ephemeral—like when a photo freezes the appearance of turbulent river flow or, pointed at the sky, stills the aurora like an accumulation of brushstrokes.

TIME • I ponder ecologies as multidimensional—crossing terrain as well as time—and with humans too. We don't get to opt out or nonchalantly watch from the sidelines, keeping score, cheering or booing. Yet what draws and holds our attention so we don't quickly just go on to the next item? Something remarkable? An exquisite day? An unexpected conversation? Like at the seal sanctuary in Iceland where a man, well past middle age, responded to my question about whether the new tree plantings would be successful. He replied, more question than answer, "Four hundred years? Not in my lifetime."

The wrinkle is how long trees take to mature. Certainly, we're proud of planting trees but to surpass the lifespan of a woodlot (for fuel or timber) or a commercial forest (clear-cut every forty to seventy years)—to grow a forest that becomes a cultural attribute and is extensively ecologically linked—is a centuries-long undertaking. One way or another there's bound to be a discussion of markets and profits, whether for wood products or carbon offsets. And yet might there also be a conversation regarding cultural and biological benefits of ancient forests? Not just old forests that we've inherited but newly planted ones that we bestow to the future. Then the comment by the man at the seal sanctuary regarding whether the new Icelandic forest would mature ("in four hundred years?") would be made with conviction—as a statement not a question.

CABIN • My collection and planting of crabapple seeds started a period of anticipation and let the past seep back into my life, as nostalgia for homegrown apples and homemade applesauce. After a decade, the apple trees that I started from seed, grafted, and transplanted—and caringly pruned each spring—finally produced a few gallons of apples. Chuck and I stood in the kitchen, paring and slicing small apples and tossing chunks into a pot. The simmering fruit released a familiar steamy fragrance. That winter, each jar of applesauce conjured nostalgia for summer but also for my own youth and times well before—that I only imagine. Perhaps, inhabiting a nostalgic place was what I was after all along when I began indulging my inclination to experiment.

How could this small harvest, after so many years, be deemed a success? This is a reasonable question during our times that emphasize fast results. But the journey became the result. Our first harvest seemed momentous, yet it was only part of the story. I brought my expectations from elsewhere and, in sub-arctic Alaska, began to adjust my idea of normalcy.

T I M E • The life of a tree is long compared to our lives. Planting a tree is a commitment to ourselves, our children and grandchildren, and to future generations. Who argues against planting more trees? I come from tree planters, have planted (probably) thousands of trees. I'm inclined to side in favor of planting trees, but the question plagues me: can planting trees change the course of the future?

Tree planting is a transaction, sometimes sentimental but often commercial. If I embark on tree planting (in person or by surrogate) to offset my carbon use, I will have perhaps boosted the economy a bit by using transportation or making purchases (like electricity) with carbon-spewing effects that I wish to mitigate. When traveling, when buying what I need to survive but also having a home that uses resources whether I'm there or not, I might be doubling my effect on the planet—and the economy. Paying a carbon-offset fee, I may be helping employ people to plant trees in places I don't even know about, places that (hopefully) need more trees, places I hope are conducive to growing trees. But what if these newly planted trees need water? What if water is taken from another place that needs, and has traditionally used, the water?

⁀ↄ

S K Y • April 1, 2002, I lugged camera and tripod outside, embarking on a nighttime expedition to photograph the northern lights. Wind rattled trees and the aurora streamed like a sky-river. Above the fringe of forest, pale curtains drifted upward. Overhead, northern lights draped between two vortexes, seeming to wrap Ursa major and Polaris—the Great Bear and the North Star—in shimmery gauze. Constantly, the sky changed.

With the camera clamped to a tripod and pointed upward, I click picture after picture, then picked up the tripod and walked around the house. This time I set the camera to frame sky above the greenhouse. The lens-view also held an old electric pole with a television antenna perched on top like a mechanical bird—and a nod to analog technology.

Later that night when I looked at the photos on my computer, they revealed more than I expected. Auroral ribbons and stars above the greenhouse but also a streak of light in the sky to the north. Delighted, I announced to Chuck that I had caught a meteor as it burned through the atmosphere, even though chances of that were exceedingly slim. The following night, the aurora remained active. I again hauled camera and tripod outside. The new photos also showed a star trail, this time more to the west. Clearly, I had not photographed a meteor two nights in a row.

Research revealed that the streak of light above the greenhouse was a comet, the same comet discovered two months earlier, on February 1, by two amateur astronomers, Zhang

Daqing and Kaoru Ikeya. Yet really it seems that these astronomers had rediscovered a comet that was first observed (or thought to have been observed) in 1661.

The earlier comet, dubbed 153P, now has the added name of Ikeya-Zhang. Since this comet isn't expected to appear again until 2343, there's plenty of time to forget so that, perhaps, it will be (re)discovered yet again.

This idea of accumulating light (and thus time) to coax a very distant celestial object to appear intrigues me. Adding layers of light offers better vision but also requires waiting, and patience. I wonder what else I might see if I just stare harder and longer at a certain point—whether in the sky, toward the horizon, in the garden, or in the house. What am I missing?

C A B I N • With the gray plush carpet gone, the stairs—as bare as bleached bones—flaunted what twenty-some years had eased from my memory. Soon after we moved into the house, I pulled the green shag rug off the staircase. That time, I also saw the state of the stairs but only for as long as it took to have new carpet installed.

Like before, the unadorned stairs attested to the challenge of confined space and hurried construction. The bottom steps incorporated a hodgepodge of shapes and materials. Some treads were plywood, others were planks. No amount of sanding and varnishing would beautify them, but at the time, I didn't realize that each riser was also a different height.

When the carpenter who rebuilt the staircase dismantled the oddly shaped bottom steps, he found, underneath them, a low platform covered with shabby linoleum and a pile of trash—scraps of lumber, sawdust, and a broken-off whiskey bottle. The thick glass was embossed with post-Prohibition language: "Federal Law Forbids Sale or Re-Use of this Bottle."

T I M E • Prohibition ended in 1933, but the requirement that liquor bottles be marked with a warning forbidding sale or reuse was implemented in 1935 and remained law until 1964. The embossed warning was intended to discourage production of moonshine, which was against the law and resulted in lost tax revenues for the government.

I would have been surprised to find any whiskey bottle underneath the stairs, but only half of a bottle was tantalizing. The trash, entombed for decades, conveyed annoyance and frustration. Yet if this collection was meant as a message, it was on par with tossing a bottle containing a note into the ocean. The likelihood of anyone finding either seems exceedingly slim. Was the broken bottle intended as a warning about the house? A caution about relationships? Or aging? Or was it merely evidence of an evening when nothing went as expected? Surely, the house wasn't to blame for that.

With the upper stairs still intact above the tatty platform, I shined a flashlight underneath them, illuminating an outline chopped in unfamiliar wallpaper of yet another staircase, one that descended even more steeply and, at the bottom, aligned with the grubby platform.

Were the cut-out marks in the hidden wall evidence of the cabin's first staircase? Stairs were necessary to reach sleeping quarters beneath the pitched roof, where only children could stand next to the wall. I imagine, first a ladder to a loft, then stairs rising steeply because there wasn't much space. Eventually, someone dismantled and rebuilt these stairs, adding a landing and orienting the lower steps into the living room, opposite the front door—or what later became the front door. I realize that my speculative timeline has become totally murky. Had the front door been switched from the south wall to the east wall before or after the stairs were rebuilt with a landing? Of course, none of this matters except as a reminder of how convoluted actions and reactions become. And how quickly reasons vanish beneath the steamroller of time.

I suspect that the staircase with the landing was constructed in the late 1940s or early 1950s. Many years later, Mrs. Webb became desperate for more living space. She began calculating how to reclaim a patch of floor large enough for a sofa or a couple of chairs that, eventually, led her to dismantle a wall, several steps, and the landing.

The staircase we lived with for twenty-plus years proved to be a hybrid, the upper stairs from what I call the second staircase, the lower curving stairs were part of a third configuration.

C A B I N • While planning the stair reconstruction, Chuck and I drove to Poppert's Mill, north of Wasilla. From their selection of cabinet-grade wood, we chose birch for our new stairs. We liked the idea of using wood from southcentral Alaska rather than shipped from the Lower 48. After seven decades, the house harbored a medley of foreign materials, including our contributions. Twice, we chose oak (not an Alaskan tree) for floors. Prior owners had installed mahogany bookshelves and baseboards, a wood that by the mid-1970s began to be listed in international trade documents as a species at risk.

Waiting for the new stairs to be built, we bridged the gap between the linoleum-blanketed platform and the upper stairs with a ladder. The carpenter took his time, meticulously calculating and measuring, installing supports, and constructing the curving section of stairs. After that, he also replaced the upper section of rectangular stairs.

The new staircase was constructed of Susitna Valley birch that had been milled, planed, kiln-dried, and glued into thicker, wider boards, the edges bullnosed. With the platform underneath the bottom stairs cleaned and again sealed up, what remained was only our memories of debris and the ghostly outline of an entirely different staircase chopped in someone else's wallpaper.

Climbing the new, and in my estimation fourth, staircase of Cabin 135, we trod birch—creamy sapwood and chocolaty heartwood—with a long history of seasons and unpredictable disruptions of droughts, eruptions, and fires.

꿔❾

CABIN • A few years after Chuck retired, the idea of moving sneaked into our conversations. But we had lived in the house for so long that the first time the topic arose it was like treading forbidden territory. Our children had grown up there.

"It's home," the boys said even though both were pursuing their adult lives elsewhere.

The passage of time had evaporated some of the reasons we moved here in the first place. I sold the maniacal mare, Tanya, to a horse trainer who knew her well. The trainer hauled Tanya to Arizona, a place without moose or subzero temperatures. Sham had ended up with one of my sisters in the Pacific Northwest, where mild winters were easier for him as he aged.

With only two of us living there, the huge gardens and enormous lawn began to seem excessive—and too much effort. Perhaps Chuck and I were simultaneously struck with a midlife inclination for change. Yet if we decided to relocate, where would we go? When we traveled, we were like bees, always returning to the same hive.

The house had taught us lessons of improvising, and evidence hinted that residents before us also became skilled at ad-libbing and cobbling together. I wondered, though, how it would be to live in a normal house, one without so much history?

"I'd choose somewhere we could be outdoors comfortably any time of the year," I commented one evening.

"Summers are nice here, but there is a lot of yard work," Chuck said.

"Yes, the summers are wonderful. Especially all the day-light," I agreed.

"I'd spend less time mowing the lawn," Chuck said.

"I'm glad we finally got the stairs redone," I added. "I like having birch treads instead of carpet."

Another evening I asked, "Where do you want to live when you're old?"

"Somewhere with a shorter winter," Chuck answered with-out hesitation.

"Less wind would be nice," I added.

"Yes, but giving up the big vegetable garden would be hard."

"The glacial-silt topsoil is remarkable. There were no rocks in the deep ditch dug for the septic." I remembered myself, pregnant and standing at the edge of the trench, listening for the flow of water—to be certain that the contractor found the functioning drain pipe rather than an abandoned conduit.

"Don't forget the rainy season," I said, meaning rains that usually began in June when the Knik wind quit and continued like a monsoon season until nearly the middle of July.

"Not every summer," Chuck replied. "We've had really nice summers, too, but then we had to water the plants. Where would you want to move to?"

"The Pacific Northwest. East of the Cascades has drier weather and four seasons," I replied without hesitation, per-haps because that was a familiar region from my youth. I assumed that familiarity also denoted predictability.

"What about the boys?" Chuck asked.

"We don't know where they'll settle," I replied thoughtfully.

Conversations about the house and the possibility of departing continued sporadically over months. Sometimes I wondered if the house was eavesdropping.

TERRAIN • Moose amble out of the forest to browse ornamentals, crabapple a particular favorite. Plants escape from the woods. A wild rose established itself underneath the mountain ash next to the house. Each summer, that rose, a migrant with woodland parents, delighted us with masses of delicately scented pink blooms. White violets intertwine wild bluebells near the basement door and sunlight dapples tiny ferns that colonized beneath a cotoneaster hedge by the front door. I transplanted the cotoneasters from the lawn where they had sprouted on their own. (The first cotoneaster shrubs came from sprouts in Chuck's parents' yard.)

Less delightful plants also colonized niches. The cow parsnip, towering and tropical-looking—with tenacious roots, giant umbelliferous flowers, and a rank aroma—produces many large clusters of sturdy seeds unwelcome in the garden yet befitting the uncultivated slope between the greenhouse and the raspberry patch.

As if a yin and yang mode of gardening, the migrating wild plants I appreciated, like ferns, wild roses, and violets, were balanced by those I wished to eradicate.

Weeding is an artful extraction where you focus on the part of a plant you can't see—what's underground. Clover expands outward from the center. Quackgrass roots snake underground in any direction, new shoots punching upward, hunting for sunlight. Ubiquitous dandelions, with parachute seeds, anchor themselves with ropey roots.

Can a life be defined by repeating themes?

Weeding looms as a motif for me. In the subarctic summer, unwanted plants flourish. Shunning chemicals, I volunteered for the war against weeds—kneeling or sitting, using hand tools to pry out unwanted plants. Overwhelming work in even the smallest plot, but along miles of road in a national park, digging dandelions presented an exercise in perspective, ecology, and tenacity.

)ɐ○

C A B I N • For twenty-five years we cooked every meal in a kitchen as diminutive as one in a small apartment. Without a dishwasher, we washed each dish, pot, and utensil by hand. The dark varnished cupboard doors, inset with yellow plastic, were covered by impossible-to-clean wire grids. Turquoise Formica covered the countertops. Judging from the materials, the previous kitchen remodel occurred during the 1960s or early 1970s.

Failure of the refrigerator turned out to be the last straw, nudging us beyond bantering conversation. Chuck would say "We could remodel the kitchen," and I would counter "Or take a trip." Still, complete renovation was not our first plan. We hoped to simply slide out the old fridge, but the new unit ended up beside the dining table because it was too wide to fit through the narrow aisle into the kitchen.

I called the contractor, Jim, who had rebuilt the stairs and remodeled the bathroom for the second time. (The first bathroom renovation had been by another contractor who took shortcuts with the plumbing—but we didn't know that until later.)

Jim scheduled our kitchen for the following spring and advised us to decide on cabinets, countertops, and flooring. We discussed making the kitchen larger—moving the dining area to the corner of the original living room, beside the two large windows.

Several months later, Chuck began demolition by prying off the kitchen cabinets. Behind the cupboards, one wall was plywood painted an unwholesome pink, another wall was overlaid with unfamiliar geometrically patterned wallpaper in shades of black and steely blue. A harsh yellow-print contact paper above the countertops had been attached with a tarry substance. Even one layer into the dismantling, the kitchen proved to be an agglomeration of times and inclinations, as if various decades of the twentieth century had collided there.

In early April the contractor arrived. Lugging an armful of tools and extension cords, he kicked snow off his boots and stomped into the kitchen. The pace of demolition quickened. With the idea of minimizing costs, Chuck and I hoped to limit deconstruction, removing as little as necessary. We soon abandoned that strategy.

After cutting into the wall above the countertops to create a channel for new electric circuits, Jim found us outside.

"I think we should take off all the plywood," he said. "Rewiring will be much simpler and we can add insulation."

TIME • I was not surprised that insulation was absent inside the kitchen walls. Chuck and I had added fiberglass insulation each time we gained access to a wall—in two bedrooms upstairs and during the garage remodel. Even when the strange urethane roofing was replaced, the contractors built up the roof in order to add insulation. Apparently insulation wasn't a requirement or priority during the 1930s, and later when the interior walls were covered with plywood or paneling, no one added insulation except for spraying urethane on the log wall inside the garage. When we cleaned that wall, we found oakum wispily protruding between the logs. I still don't know how threads as flimsy as unwoven burlap could block the marauding gusts of the Matanuska wind.

C A B I N • "Yes. Take the wallboard off," we agreed.

The ceiling came off in layers too. Peeling off squares of acoustical tile exposed garish pink plywood interrupted by a grid-like pattern of age-darkened wood.

"Someone must have added narrow strips over the seams to improve how it looked, then painted it an uneasy pink," I mused.

"Probably someone else removed the strips to have a flat surface for gluing the acoustical ceiling tiles," Chuck added.

While the kitchen was being redone, plastic sheeting was draped between the old dining area and the original cabin living room. More plastic hung across the doorway to the back hall. We had shoved the new refrigerator across the room to the wall by the front entry. A collection of small appliances—toaster, microwave oven, electric kettle, rice cooker—occupied half the dining table, which we also had lugged into the original cabin living room.

Giving a key to the contractor and leaving for an extended vacation would have been a better plan than attempting to live in the house during demolition and reconstruction. We trusted the contractor, but we didn't trust the house. In fact, we expected contrariness and complications.

When the contractor walked out to his van to retrieve a tool, Chuck and I hurried into what had been the kitchen. After several days of demolition, the log walls were bare except for a few dangling electrical wires and furring strips that had supported the interior wallboard. The room smelled of sawdust and old wood, a scent that was both evocative and puzzling as if I should have felt nostalgia but was drawing a blank. No moment in my childhood quite fit with this one. Instead, it was as if our stripped kitchen was a time machine that had taken me back to 1935 when the cabin was new. Yet the collision of eras was complex. A patch of dark paneling remained beneath the window where the dining table had been. Above the scrap of paneling was a gap in the logs.

Leaning down, I ran my hands across the old uneven saw cuts. "Chuck, this must have been the old doorway," I said, my voice echoing between the unadorned log walls.

"Probably the original front door," Chuck replied, his voice also sounding strange, like he was talking through an overly amped microphone.

"Only a few steps through this door to the hand-dug well," I remarked. Outside, beyond the delphiniums and tiger lilies and a strip of lawn, was the plot, with two apple trees and scattered stems from the previous summer's flowers, planted where the lawn had slumped when the hand-dug well collapsed.

T I M E • The wall behind where the refrigerator had been contained the cutout shape of a narrow window, like one in the 1935 photograph of Cabin 135. That window had been boarded over with plywood on the inside and covered by siding on the outside.

I began to suspect that everyone who lived at Cabin 135 had a love-hate relationship with the house. Perhaps they found themselves living in a log cabin when they really wanted a dwelling constructed of lumber and siding, a structure that would fit in a row of cottages on a neighborhood street. I suppose Clystia and Henry LaRose liked the cabin, at least at first, since they had chosen a log house from the government catalog.

I don't have any idea which owners installed the first layer of siding, shiplap boards painted white, although years later, I suspect the Webbs added the large garage alongside the north wall of the cabin. The new garage required siding and—again I'm guessing—provided reason enough to install cedar shingles over the shiplap siding.

I began to think of changes we made as unwrapping layers. We were explorers who noticed details, but then usually covered everything up again, using a different assortment of materials. We selected contemporary flooring, cabinets, and wall coverings just like previous owners had done. In a couple of decades, I expect someone else will consider our choices quaint, or even misguided, but by then our inclinations will have blended with those of prior inhabitants—like, in the upstairs dormer room, cheery blue-and-white wallpaper that I glued on top of bland mid-twentieth-century wallpaper.

C A B I N • The clincher, proving repeating cycles, occurred as the new kitchen was nearly finished. The reconfiguration expanded the tiny kitchen across the cramped area where the dining table had been and added abundant cabinets and countertops and better lighting. We moved the dining area into the original living room, at the corner between picture windows that, before the trees grew tall, offered views of Pioneer Peak and Matanuska Peak. The only thing missing over the dining table was a chandelier.

"The center of the ceiling will be perfect," I said when the electrician came to finish the rewiring. "The upstairs attic, underneath the eaves, should allow access for wiring." While the electrician was pulling wires through the ceiling space, the contractor climbed a ladder and pared a circular shape in the center of the ceiling. Like in the kitchen, the ceiling tile was glued to plywood. With a nonplussed expression, instead of a layer of plywood above the acoustical tile, he looked up into the attic. The new aperture for a ceiling light had been cut in the same place where, once before, there had been one.

"That's a surprise," I said. "I wonder why someone would take out lighting."

The electrician strung new wires and installed a chandelier above where the dining table would be, and once again, I was left mulling the curious warp of time that threads this house.

CABIN • While the kitchen was being rebuilt, the idea of selling the house and moving remained a vague notion. "How would we even start?" I wondered, one evening.

"Start what?" Chuck asked.

"Start to get ready to sell this house," I glanced around the old living room that was cluttered with kitchen utensils and appliances. My gaze went directly to the missing trim boards that I had not replaced in the early 1980s after we installed oak over the original floor. "There's so much to finish," I said, having no idea how we would accomplish it all.

"The basement," Chuck said.

"Oh. Right." We traipsed down the stairs, turning on the lights and looking at everything—walls and ceiling, stacks of boxes, old furniture—as if we were curiously inspecting another family's situation. "The downside of a basement, I guess."

"Our storage unit," Chuck commented, dryly.

The fluorescent ceiling lights flickered and rafts of spiderwebs clung in the corners. I scrutinized the walls which, in my mind, were still as freshly painted as when we arrived. Grunginess attested to the passage of nearly three decades.

"Look at the walls. I have to paint them."

"First you have to be able to reach them," Chuck replied, practically.

A hulking office desk that had belonged to Chuck's dad held stacks of books. Bookshelves above the desk bowed under the weight of more books. Inside one of the desk drawers were pencils, notepads, and business cards—like a time capsule—from before I moved my office upstairs, following the garage remodel in 1994.

"What about all this?" I surveyed a confounding collection of boxes and tubs containing financial records, vinyl records, children's Halloween costumes, winter clothing, fabric from sewing projects, ribbons won at horse shows, and reams of computer printouts from our college days.

"See what we can throw out," Chuck said, wryly.

"Or rent a storage unit," I countered, only half-jokingly.

Outside, we continued our perusal. "The barn roof," I groaned, glancing at where roofing had been ripped off during a winter gale.

"Yes," Chuck agreed, peering into the dim interior of the barn, "there's a lot to clear out here too."

I stepped into the barn, sturdily built and still with thick rubber mats on the floor where, so many times, I'd groomed and saddled a horse. Indeed, like in the basement, items we no longer used had ended up here—horse gear packed in boxes and trunks, garden tools, a lawn mower and rototiller, children's toys, and weathered patio furniture.

TERRAIN • Turning away from the barn, we tromped up the worn path. In the woods above the driveway, we examined another jumble.

"Who needs three old television antennas?" I wondered.

"Aluminum and steel might have been good for something." Chuck picked up one of the antennas, the array of rods folded tight like a long-limbed metallic bird.

"Hmmm. We should have given away the children's picnic table before the plastic got covered with moss."

"On the list," Chuck said, "trips to the dump."

"Remember the old dump? When you could actually drive into the landfill?"

"Yes," Chuck replied. "I backed up and threw our trash onto the ground along with everyone else's. The bulldozers were right there, dragging the garbage deeper into the pit."

"Also, some people scavenged, apparently finding useful items in the refuse. It must be safer now with the transfer station," I mused as we angled downhill between trees and across the driveway to what remained of the pasture fence we had built using spruce posts from Point MacKenzie and cottonwood planks milled at the Butte. After the horses were gone, Chuck transplanted the remaining apple trees I had grafted into a corner of the pasture and mowed that area as if it was lawn. Farther from the house, I purposefully let a section of pasture go wild, hoping it would naturally change into a meadow with wildflowers that would entice butterflies, bees, and even hummingbirds. Instead, cottonwood, willow, and alders chaotically sprouted, and each summer, we chopped saplings with loppers and a handsaw. Stasis turned out to be forest not meadow—how it was before the homesteaders and colonists arrived—as if the land was actively shedding our puny attempts at settlement.

T I M E • In 1913 the government surveyor documented forest, "spruce, birch and cottonwood," and dense undergrowth, "willow, fireweed and wild rose bushes." Later, the homesteaders and colonists cleared forest for crops and gardens.

T E R R A I N • A fence with even one gap is no fence at all. Without horses, I had quit noticing precisely when a fence post rotted or a board cracked. When I did take heed, the piecemeal deterioration bothered me but I was struck by inertia. I wasn't certain whether I had given up horses for good. Perhaps I would be tempted to again rescue a young horse from poor circumstances.

Sham held a soft spot in my heart—Sham, who had truly been my equine companion. I still marvel at his unconditional trust, even after all the times I inadvertently guided him into dicey situations. When I realized that I didn't have a clue how to proceed, I let the reins go and hung on. Sham got us both to safety every time. The mare Tanya was not like that at all. Riding her was a matter of survival—my own.

Fifteen years had passed since I critically examined the barn and fence. Now, consideration of these artifacts caused me a wistfulness for the years, beginning when I was twelve, when I saddled a horse and went exploring.

As Chuck and I circled the yard, critically assessing our impact on the place, I noticed a pushback of time that might not have been as obvious if we had been more careful caretakers. If we had always, immediately, undertaken repairs, replacing every cracked fence board or wind ripped strip of roofing, the place would have appeared constantly the same, rather than succumbing to disintegration and deterioration.

"We'll have to dismantle what's left of the fence," I said, studying the discontinuous sections.

"The best course," Chuck agreed.

Considering what we would need to do if we decided to sell the house stretched over weeks, and I wondered if we had embarked on a course of interminable conversations that skirted taking action. In mid-July, the days were terribly gloomy with nearly constant rain. Our incremental assessment of clearing out and repairs implied months, or years, of toil, but the conversation had cracked open a door to possibilities and we began chipping away at outdoor jobs. It took both of us to lift and shove two rusted mowing-decks into the pickup and, at the landfill, hoist them over the high rim of the scrap-metal dumpster.

On another trip, I asked, "What was this used for?" as we leveraged a sheet of corrugated steel nailed to poles into the tall bin.

"It covered the fire pit during the winter," Chuck replied.

The rectangular pit, dug into the lawn and lined with stones and bricks, had been used for roasting hot dogs and marshmallows on sticks cut from willows in the swale below the lawn or for the more grandiose summer barbecues, with a motorized spit linked by several extension cords to an electrical outlet at the house.

C A B I N • Projects multiplied. Inside the house we noticed how worn the floors had become. The first two flooring contractors I called recommended tearing out and replacing the oak that Chuck and I laid in the early 1980s.

The third contractor had a genuine enthusiasm for refurbishing hardwood. He bid in a range we hoped for—lower than what I was willing to pay but "about right," Chuck said. The floor refinishing was scheduled and, in the meantime, Chuck hauled more loads to the landfill, even rotten fence boards.

At the landfill booth, the attendant asked what was in the pickup.

"Really ancient construction materials," Chuck replied casually.

"Any Roman coins?" the guy asked.

"Not that old," Chuck laughed.

Before the living room floors could be refinished, we had to move all the furniture out, including a piano. I called the piano tuner who'd delivered the instrument years earlier. His wife answered and when I mentioned that I was looking for help to move a piano, she replied, "He doesn't move pianos anymore. He's getting too old for that." But she took my number and her husband returned my call and carefully explained how to move a piano. The piano, an upright 1920s-era Wurlitzer, had been heavily used before I bought it. The body was marred and keys were chipped, but it had a lovely tone and stayed in tune.

Chuck bought a furniture dolly with padded trusses, and when the floor refinishers arrived, we recruited them.

"Just lift this end," I said, not certain that the ad hoc crew would succeed in moving the piano. "When you lift, I'll shove the furniture dolly under the middle of the piano." The two contractors heaved, managing to hoist one end of the piano just enough, and I shoved the furniture dolly underneath. As they lowered the end, the piano tipped and settled. Balanced on the low-wheeled platform, we rolled it along the log wall and across the hall.

After the floors were refinished, the contractors helped put the piano back where it had been. To remove the wheeled dolly from underneath the piano, they braced and heaved and the end of the piano practically flew upward. I pulled the dolly out and they gently lowered the instrument onto the refurbished floor.

"What happened?" one of them asked. "The piano got lighter."

"The strings?" I speculated. "The first time you lifted the bass end. This time you lifted the other end. The treble strings have thinner wires. Sorry. The piano tuner didn't mention to lift the treble end because it's lighter."

TIME • While shifting furniture to prepare for refinishing the floor, I found a booklet that one of my sisters compiled, in the 1980s, from fragments of family letters. The slim volume had slid through a crack behind a shelf and lodged behind a stack of videotapes. The tapes were of TV shows and movies and recordings of our children as babies, then toddlers, and in elementary school, until the era of magnetic VHS videotapes ended—and the kids grew up. The little booklet merged days from so many years, as if all our lives had drifted away from the thread of time.

In one passage, I came face-to-face with my younger self who, on May 17, 1983, wrote: "Yes we've moved! We're getting 10 acres and a Colony house that was built in the 1930s. It's a log house with siding & paneling hiding the logs. We have a lot of work to do—build a barn, some fence, an arena. Redo a lot inside the house. It has a view of Pioneer and Byers Peaks . . ."

The sentences brought to mind the entire cycle of building and creating followed by deterioration and abandonment. Barns and fences, leveling a hill into a riding arena, growing vegetables, creating new gardens, and renovating much of the house. I smiled at my younger self, wistful for the boundless enthusiasm and unflagging energy.

A quarter century earlier while touring the house with Mrs. Webb, we admired the unobstructed view of Pioneer Peak.

"We lived here when it was the best," Mrs. Webb commented.

Hardly a great statement by a seller, but Chuck and I also experienced the best times living there, in the house that started out as a colonist's cabin.

By the time the adjacent hayfield was subdivided and new houses built, the trees we had planted were maturing, providing a blend of forest and arboretum that screened the view.

E A R T H • The summer advanced, oblivious to our efforts at repairing, sorting, and disposing. On a rainy evening, I looked out the window hoping to glimpse one of the junco fledglings that had hatched in a pot of fuchsias hanging by the front door. A white-crowned sparrow fledgling, without its own family, shadowed the juncos as they hopped across the grass. A dragonfly darted toward the intensely scarlet lychnis. Or maybe it was a hawkmoth, although I hadn't seen any of the large moths for several years. Lifting binoculars, I found myself watching, not a hawkmoth but a hummingbird—only the second time I had seen one of those birds in our yard. The hummingbird, a rufous, zipped to a delphinium and hovered, methodically stabbing his long beak into one purple floret after another.

The binoculars gave me a sense of superpower vision. After a few minutes, the hummingbird zipped toward me but pulled up short, before crashing into the window. He hovered, as if inspecting his reflection in the glass, then darted sideways only to again stop and hover, facing the window, wings a blur of energy and lift. The hummingbird showed no inclination to bash into the glass like the birds that mistook it for a flyway, and whose miniscule skulls I'd unearthed in the garden below. Eventually, the hummingbird abandoned his perusal and zoomed off.

With the hummingbird gone, the overcast sky and likelihood of more rain deepened the melancholy of the evening.

All that summer, my rubber boots and raincoat stayed beside the backdoor. Weighty rain saturated the garden, and seemingly overnight, chickweed burgeoned into soggy mounds shrouding the vegetables. At least we didn't have to worry about the house flooding, or floating away, because it had been built on a hilltop, and a year earlier, the garage had been re-roofed and new gutters installed.

The nearly constant rain had not made our self-imposed tasks easier, and we still weren't certain whether we were preparing to move or just clearing out an accumulation of clutter.

When the rain finally stopped, I leaned a ladder against the eaves of the barn and clambered up, carrying a push broom and a small putty knife. On the roof my shoes sank into moss that ranged in color from pallid green to boldly fluorescent to the russet-like hue of oxidizing iron. Experimentally, I shoved the broom across the cushiony vegetation with little effect. Glad for the rain pants, I plopped down and began peeling off the damp and fibrous moss. Each thrust of the narrow blade detached a few square inches of plant material and exposed an equally miniscule patch of roofing.

Sitting on the barn roof was like being on a catawampus porch in a large treehouse. When we built the barn, we chose an opening in the forest, having no idea as to the reason for the clearing. I liked the location, which was conveniently near the house but not too close. Much later, the purpose of the clearing was revealed as the anxious mare paced along the paddock fence. Her hooves churned the soil and turned up wads of trash, even plastic bread wrappers (the smiling girl and blue checkered background nearly pristine) and clumps of rusted nails—which could have punctured her hooves. When I noticed the nails and other debris, I shut the horse inside the barn and raked and shoveled the paddock—like I was an archaeologist, or a janitor—digging up and carting off refuse from a mid-twentieth-century midden.

During the summer of 2010, a couple of afternoons scraping moss from the barn roof gave me ample time to contemplate change. In twenty-seven years, the trees had increased in height and girth. Several cottonwoods had grown too large for me to reach around. A willow that must have been an inconsequential sprout when we built the barn leaned so that its leafy branches brushed the roof.

Periodically, I stood. Stretching from my cramped posture, I used the push broom to shove loosened moss off the roof. When I climbed down the ladder and walked around the barn, ducking under willow branches and sliding between fence rails, my boots squished into heaps of moss. Later, Chuck and I scooped the loose moss into the wheelbarrow and trundled it deeper into the woods.

T I M E • In late autumn, as the weather worsened, we shifted our focus indoors, to the basement. By January, while snow drifted around the house, we sorted financial records, LPs, broken computers, and even fabric.

When I was eleven years old, I learned to sew from my mom, whose mother had taught her how to cut and measure, match plaids, stitch seams and buttonholes, and insert zippers. For years what I sewed reflected my life—suits for office work, children's clothes, curtains. But at some point, I just quit, as if sewing was a vice or compulsion easily overcome. Imports of inexpensive clothing flooded the stores, but I also had switched to an office with more casual attire, or worked from home.

In the basement, as I peeled the lid off a plastic tub crammed with fabric, each scrap of cotton or wool, pile or polyester evoked a memory. Little boys scampering upstairs wearing pajamas printed with sailboats or Dr. Seussian lions. Chuck wearing a wool bomber-style jacket. Burgundy velvet from a formal dress with V-neckline, front and back. I wondered at the apparent ease that some activities that are passionately pursued can be abandoned.

I called an acquaintance who belonged to a sewing guild and asked if she knew anyone who could use more cloth.

"Bring the fabric over," she replied.

Chuck and I drove to Palmer, the back of the car piled with bulging sacks of fabric. At Ginny's house, we lugged the bags down steep stairs to her basement where a large room overflowed with sewing projects. Ginny explained that she was creating garments for a wearable art show. One for herself and one for her daughter using patterns "with incomprehensible directions," she said, including a hoop skirt and petticoat stitched out of a brassy cloth.

A couple more hoops were still needed to shape the petticoat. The inside of the garment contained a mysterious net of ribbons.

"What are the ribbons for?" I asked.

Ginny explained the long strips would be tied around the wearer's legs, then tugged and tightened, shaping the hoops into an oval.

"How did a woman wearing such a wide skirt go through a doorway?" I wondered.

"With oval hoops, they turned sideways," Ginny replied, "or the doorways were double-wide." Peering into the bags of fabric I'd brought, she commented, "The ladies will have fun going through this fabric. We'll find uses for a lot of it."

For years, I had thought the same thing—that I would eventually find uses for all the yardage and scraps of fabric. This mode of keeping things goes back to my parents, and likely before them. When the question "Why are you keeping this?" came up, my mom repeated the adage she surely heard from her parents: "Use it up. Make it do. Wear it out." This inclination resonated with the generation who grew up during the Great Depression when jobs were scarce and "making do" was necessary.

C A B I N • Cabin 135 was built during the Great Depression, as part of a New Deal project—the Matanuska Colony—intended to help farm families who were barely making do embark on a new life. During our poking and prodding into the workings of the house, we encountered remnants of this innovative spirit sometimes taken to dangerous extremes, like the wads of taped electric wires in the closed-off attic and the wide garage roof spanned by boards of differing lengths without supporting posts. But Cabin 135 was solidly constructed and had survived the Great Alaska Earthquake and every other tremor and quake, as well as heavy snowfalls, gale-force winds, and a lightning strike.

I liked this aspect of the house—its inherent nature—although I also suspect living here would have been less complicated if we started at the beginning, with a cabin, before the accretion began, and one family after another added their concept of comfort or fashion. Finding tantalizing morsels of evidence gave me pause, whether troubling, like half of a whiskey bottle entombed under the staircase, or puzzling, like receipts for farm supplies hidden inside the kitchen doorframe.

T I M E • March 12, 1937, a receipt documents Henry LaRose's purchase of seven pounds of Swedish Putty for $1.40. (Swedish putty is a compound used to fill imperfections in wood—which seems appropriate considering all the wood in the house.) Another receipt, dated April 1, 1937, shows that LaRose owed the Alaska Rural Rehabilitation Corporation (ARRC) $1.50. The receipt is stamped "this account is payable at hospital office." I turn the receipt over and realize there's a note written in thick pencil lead on the back: "H. C. LaRose Jr. came to Alaska in 1935—May 23 from Phillips, Wis." When the Matanuska Colony began, ARRC managed the hospital, so this isn't as odd as it seems. The ARRC provided loans to new farmers, credit for purchasing feed and supplies, and health care.

The third receipt, dated April 5, 1937, documents livestock feed—two tons of timothy hay, one ton alfalfa hay, plus dairy ration, scratch feed (for chickens), rolled barley, and middlings. The hay cost $60 per ton. The total came to $224.

I'm astounded by what Henry LaRose paid for hay in 1937. The timothy and alfalfa he purchased must have been imported from Washington, where, that year, the price for a ton of hay averaged $9. For three tons of hay, LaRose paid over $150 for freight and any fees due to ARRC. Since he bought the imported hay in April, I suspect his homegrown hay was gone and he needed feed to tide his cattle over until the pasture greened up. That pricey hay likely caused hardship and tough decisions about other purchases to give up or put off.

The ARRC receipts made out to Henry LaRose were carbon copies on faded blue paper with multiple punctures where the pages had been crammed onto a spiky spindle. I try to get my imagination to conjure a scenario where filing these receipts inside the cabin wall makes sense. I'm trying to get inside Henry LaRose's head, and I'm having no luck. That the receipts were put inside the kitchen doorframe and that we found them strikes me as exceedingly peculiar. I wonder though, if the motivation was something like the broken whiskey bottle deposited underneath the stairs. If LaRose was the one framing walls and doorways inside the cabin and he'd been fuming about the cost of the imported hay, perhaps he decided this was a story that someone in the future needed to know. And he trusted the house to deliver the message.

The receipts associated with Tract 135 were indeed conveyed by the house—Cabin 135—across a gulf of time. We discovered them after the refrigerator failed and we finally redid the kitchen. And that project involved a more complete renovation than we had planned, down to the original log structure— as if the house was making sure that we glimpsed everything we needed to see.

C A B I N • The more Chuck and I sorted and disposed of things, the more convinced I became that we might actually be preparing to leave. When we first moved to Alaska, all our belongings, except a few boxes of books, fit into Chuck's Camaro, with our cross-country skis clamped on top. After that, our possessions accumulated. We furnished an apartment, then a small house, and a few years later, we really settled in at the dwelling dubbed Cabin 135. We put down our roots so that, more than a quarter century later, shedding excess belongings was like removing a stump using a small shovel.

Near the end of the twentieth century, technology arrived expensively and with obsolescence just a step behind. With the insidiousness of silt, many of our abandoned items settled into the basement. At the time, we didn't ask, "Do we need this?" Nor did we know the government rules regarding how long we ought to keep financial records. Computer disks presented another puzzle. Financial information and correspondence were saved on a mishmash of disks: 5¼-inch floppies, 3½-inch hard plastic disks, and later, chunky Zip disks. Several old computers lined a closet shelf like a museum room dedicated to obsolete technology.

Examining an inscrutable stack of disks, I asked, "What are we going to do with these?"

"What's on them?" Chuck replied.

"I don't know."

"Destroy them," he said as if that was the only course regardless of the content of the disks.

No longer having a computer that could read the old formats, I plunked the disks into a box labeled "destroy," which, along with equally enigmatic computer hard drives, we eventually dropped off at a business with the equipment to shred disks. I wondered, though, if we had transferred important documents to each new computer. I hoped that we were jettisoning junk, not thoughtlessly disposing of our own memories.

In a small cardboard box, I found a collection of obsidian, the black and orange volcanic glass cleaved to surgical sharpness. Gingerly plucking a stone from the box, I felt dormant memories flood back—from a summer camping trip across eastern Oregon where we hiked with our children and their aunts and uncles.

Opening and peering into each box (whether or not surprised by recollection), I decided on what to dispose of and what to keep. Some decisions were easy. I kept every box of photographs. Others more puzzling. Bulky winter jackets? Would we need those if we moved south? And the books? Both Chuck and I collected books, but there seemed to be no reason to keep economic texts from the 1970s or paperbacks with faded covers and broken spines.

Eventually, hoping to speed our progress, we rented a mini storage. Items that we thought we might want in the future, we hauled to the little locked room in a row of identical rooms. Finally, in late February, I had a clear view of the basement walls and the dinginess that time had wrought.

T I M E • I imagine, after living in this house for twenty-some years, Mrs. Webb also noticed how grubby the walls had become. She may have gathered paint and painting tools and put on old clothing. Circling the basement, her paint brushes and rollers transformed the dingy walls to the most enticing white.

On our first trek through the house, the basement was nearly empty and the walls gleamed beneath fluorescent ceiling lights. Nearly three decades later, as I imagine Mrs.

Webb repainting the walls before they moved, I suspect that I'm entangled in a loop of circumstances, a whirlpool of time centered on this house.

C A B I N • I vacuumed spiderwebs from the corners, spackled holes, and repainted the basement walls—white. The ceiling, though, needed more fixing than just spackle and paint. A metal grid, wired and nailed to the joists, held acoustical panels. Every electrician or plumber who needed access to the space between the joists removed at least one ceiling panel. The material was brittle and sometimes broke, leaving gaps in the ceiling, and one of the fluorescent light fixtures had quit working.

An electrician arrived to troubleshoot the broken light. After testing the circuits, he announced that the wiring in the basement ceiling was hazardous because it had been installed unsafely.

"This wiring needs to be redone," he said.

"How did we not know that for twenty-seven years?" I asked, not expecting an answer. "Please, fix it."

"This house," I grumbled, later.

"Remember the wiring upstairs," Chuck said, "without a junction box, just taped together and mouse-chewed."

"Luckily we found it," I commented.

"This house," Chuck said, as if that explained everything, like giving someone a pass for bad behavior because they didn't know any better.

"The house has ridden out earthquakes and stays warm in the winter," I said, thinking of friends who closed off rooms in their house during the Omega Block because their furnace couldn't heat the whole structure. Cabin 135 was compact and ultimately heatable. We had added insulation and modernized the heating system. Twice.

The winter continued with a pattern of dealing with situations, particularly those that we hadn't noticed before, or hadn't deemed a priority. I cleaned out drawers, reconnected phone wires in a wall receptacle that hadn't worked since the lightning strike, and cut foam insulation to cover cold water pipes where moisture condensed and dripped on the basement floor.

On Valentine's Day, Chuck took another load to the dump and returned with red and white tulips and a bottle of champagne. That evening, we took a break from sorting through our years inhabiting the log-built house.

In late March, as the snow was melting, I was still painting walls. I finished the basement and moved to the upstairs, and it seemed like a task that would never be completed. Each day, the view was the same: paint rollers and brushes and paint that, with sloppy brush wielding, slung in long arcs like worms or snakes. Finally, curls of paint adhered into a stillness.

Last, and with mixed feelings, I sanded and painted the front door, the same varnished cottage door with diamond-shaped glass panes—the door that we walked through when we first came into the house. The door offered both first impression and last impression, and more than once its operational vagaries flummoxed me.

On June 4, 2011, just before midnight and still barely dusk, a robin launched bursts of scales. A euphoria over worms? Or ecstasy for rain? The rain brought weeds; the weeds grew fast. Silt drifted onto freshly painted windowsills. I placed an ad for the house.

C O D A

T I M E • It is often the small details that we return to. I think again about seeing the small plant *Silene uniflora* in Iceland on the crumbly slopes of Grábrók Crater and its uncanny resemblance to the plant *Silene maritime,* which had perished in my garden and which I felt I had a responsibility to nurture. The disappearance of *Silene maritime* left me questioning what I might have done differently. Might I have watered it more? Or less? Or planted it in a different location. Or not even tried to move it, but then the plant might have just been spaded under.

While these thoughts haunt me, I realize that the value in thinking about all of these places and occurrences is in the echoes where, with time spent gathering and pondering experiences, I begin to see repetition. There's a glimmer of a chronology where time echoes time and place echoes place, and maybe I remember better and so adjust—and change tactics just a bit.

Although this is a small personal example, encountering a similar plant on the tough edge of a crater in Iceland brought memories back to me and loosed the same questions. And really, isn't that how it always is, whether a state-sponsored agricultural project or a home raspberry patch? Or forests that vanished a millennium ago? Or melting ice, rising sea levels, dying coral. Extinctions.

What might we have done differently? What might we do differently?

C A B I N • Cabin 135 became a character in my story, and in Chuck's. While falling in love with this place, we learned to cope with its capricious moods and inclinations. Yet, as time passed, I found myself wishing for a less complicated residence. Perhaps I was naïve, not recognizing that life needs some amount of adversity, befuddlement, and irony.

Mulling the years we lived there, what comes to mind are our battles with nature: encroaching meadows and forest, invading slugs and chickweed, moose gnawing trees and shrubs, voles and bats coming into the house. I remind myself of the enchantment of seasonal changes, cycles and rhythms of nearly perpetual daylight in summer balanced by long winter nights, sometimes with the phantasmagorical aurora borealis. Olfactory memories also recur—the rank smell of tomato plants, syrupy aroma of lilacs, licorice scent of caraway, and ambrosia of fresh-picked raspberries.

T I M E • I wonder about the future of Cabin 135 and its surroundings. I imagine the house and the well. Or perhaps the town will overtake the house, and there will be city water, not a well. In a hundred years, the raspberry patch will be something else. Or the raspberry patch will still be a raspberry patch, but the raspberries will be different. I hope the startling flavor of the raspberries never changes.

Each summer, no matter where I am, when I bite into the first raspberry, memories flood my mind of city gardens and country gardens—my mother's garden, my grandfather's, and mine, but also generations of gardens. Indeed, even centuries of gardens. Gardens that no one remembers, well-tended or gone wild, and that hint at what comes next.

REFLECTIONS ON WRITING THIS BOOK

Cabin 135 exists as place and idea, abode and quirky companion. As place, the house offered abundant opportunities to explore and contemplate decisions made by previous residents. As an abstraction, the log-built cabin both anchored and propelled my speculative notions of time and place. Eventually I looked outward, beyond the house toward the microcosms of garden and yard and on toward a wider terrain. Nature meanders through my life as an ongoing theme, whether semi-tamed garden, national park, or wild-seeming forest.

Much is outside the world of this book, not because it is unimportant but because it is not part of my experience, or I did not find an appropriate connection. Human history in Alaska stretches back more than a millennium to the last Ice Age and migrations across Beringia. Oral histories tell that Native people inhabited and traveled the Matanuska Valley for many centuries. Yet written histories tend to begin in the eighteenth and nineteenth centuries when Russians drifted north and settled along what would come to be known as Cook Inlet. Later, after the United States bought Alaska, explorers and surveyors arrived. I pick up some of the surveyor story because I became acquainted with the same terrain.

As the book evolved, I learned that I'm twitchy about time. My thoughts jump between present and past and, sometimes, sneak into the limitless possibilities of the future. How an idea or event brings forward a memory is both mysterious and fascinating and offers many possibilities—like an ecology of the mind. The easiest writing solution would have been to adhere to a timeline, but that experiment resulted in tedious storytelling and more limited narrative possibilities. (Repeating headings create a structure that accommodates my flexible notion of time and, hopefully, provides a roadmap for readers.)

Some events, especially seasonal or annual occurrences, are conveyed as a composite rendering when it allowed for more compelling storytelling. Other occurrences, those connected to a certain year or date, are indicated as such. Dialogue is recreated from journal notes, or when based on memory, I try to faithfully convey the tenor of the conversation. In the absence of personal experience or documentation, I have inferred certain stories and invented dialogue. One example is a conversation I imagine colonist Clystia LaRose having with a friend. That exchange is totally invented on my part, but from evidence offered by the house and yard, I believe something like it could have occurred.

My narrative journey samples history, gardening, and nature and grapples with a many-faced house. Within the thematic structure of this book, I learned to pay more attention to my surroundings—sometimes with a broad-brush approach, other times, contemplating only a small plot of forest or garden or a patch of wall. I also hunted for telling moments in locations away from Cabin 135, searching for themes that highlight different perspectives—like glancing sidewise into a mirror—or through a prism. While searching for narrative larger than myself, everything I experienced, pondered, and tinkered with became part of my story. I puzzled over how we change places in both minuscule and wide-ranging ways.

I write iteratively, one revision after another. Each version exists, however briefly, as a quasi-meditation. Delving into observations, experiences, and ideas, I watched for linkages between events, places, and situations, heeding instances where stories percolated.

Writing provided a framework to explore place as both a literary construct and abstraction. Later, engulfed in scores of revisions, my biggest frustration became finding language that conveyed the inherent character of place, yet I suspect words will never be wholly adequate. There will always be uncertain moments and missed context of what came before. The overlap between multitudinous narratives plus motivations, lucky breaks, and weird confluences proved fascinating, but the stories in this book represent only one possible route across a dimensional terrain that's spatial, biological, societal, temporal, and laced with ideas—and where a small log-built house occupies a certain plot of land. As is the case with any memoir, much has been left out—omitted, ignored, or forgotten.

ACKNOWLEDGMENTS

Cabin 135 would not have been completed without encouragement from many people—mentors, editors, writers, and friends. Whenever I considered abandoning this project, I would recall an encouraging comment from Dawn Marano or Peggy Shumaker—both of whom I thank for their suggestions and support. To have written this book at all, I had to find my way into the writing community of the Rainier Writing Workshop. At the Kachemak Bay Writers Conference in 2006, Stan Rubin encouraged me to apply to the Rainier Writing Workshop's MFA program. As a mentor, Judith Kitchen encouraged all my writing explorations as if there were no limitations, just possibilities. Thank you to everyone who read and offered suggestions on parts of this book.

I'm grateful to Helen and Ralph Hulbert for sharing years of friendship and experiences in the neighborhood of Cabin 135. I appreciate that, in 1983, Mrs. Webb told us stories about the house. Thank you also to Irene Hildebrandt, who organized some surprising excursions into the Swiss Alps, and to Bernice and Alan Linn, who generously shared their plants, and Jim Fox who provided names for those plants.

Thank you to the Matanuska-Susitna Borough and Denali National Park for recruiting and encouraging volunteers. I particularly wish to thank Fran Seager-Boss, Mat-Su Borough cultural resources specialist, and Dan Stone, archaeological assistant, for explanations and insights into valley history, archaeology, and cultural resources when I volunteered in 2008; and Wendy Mahovlic, who was Denali National Park's invasive species coordinator when I volunteered for the deveg crew that same year.

Besides people who appear in this book, there are others who helped me expand my experience, often because of quite random conversations. I particularly appreciate the interest and support for my writing by Bridgette Preston (former executive director of the Palmer Arts Council), Alaska lieutenant governor Mead Treadwell, and Geoff Green, founder and director of Students on Ice (Ottawa, Canada).

I'm grateful to my parents for their choices of places to live and for sharing stories about their families and ancestors. I truly appreciate my grandfather, Clare Boulton, for his sensibility and my grandmother, Violet (née Gregorious), who told and retold stories from her youth enough times that I remembered them, and for her love of gardens and her perfectionist nature. I'm also grateful to my sister Barbara, who has shared music and Alaska with me. My most enduring appreciation goes to my husband, Chuck Logsdon, who was on the Cabin 135 journey with me and who, with much understanding and patience, follows my considerable forays into new ideas.

Early versions of several stories in this book—"Cabin Fever," "The Fragrance of Memory," and "Negotiating Spring Creek"— first appeared in *Cirque, A Literary Journal for the North Pacific Rim*. I greatly appreciate the encouragement of the *Cirque* editors.

My chapbook, *Unbound: Alaska Poems* (Uttered Chaos Press, 2013), includes poems rooted in the terrain surrounding Cabin 135 as well as elsewhere in Alaska. One poem, "The Place Where You Go To Listen," covers territory similar to one of the narratives in this book.

REFERENCES AND NOTES

This list of references is not meant to be exhaustive but includes resources with intriguing ideas, historical perspectives, and data.

ARCTIC

Alyeska Pipeline Service Company. *Trans Alaska Pipeline System: The Facts*. Anchorage: Alyeska Pipeline Service Company, 2016.

Lopez, Barry. *Arctic Dreams: Imagination and Desire in a Northern Landscape*. New York: Charles Scribner's Sons, 1986.

Mikkelsen, Ejnar. *Conquering the Arctic Ice*. London: William Heinemann, 1909.

ART AND LANDSCAPE

Christo and Jeanne-Claude: Remembering the Running Fence, *April 1, 2010 – September 25, 2010*. Smithsonian American Art Museum.

BIOSPHERE 2

Broad, William J. "Paradise Lost: Biosphere Retooled as Atmospheric Nightmare." *New York Times*, November 19, 1996.

Fuller, Buckminster. *Operating Manual for Spaceship Earth*. Carbondale: Southern Illinois University Press, 1969.

Kelly, Kevin. "Pop Goes the Biosphere." Chap. 9 in *Out of Control: The New Biology of Machines, Social Systems and the Economic World*. Boston: Addison-Wesley Publishing Company, 1995.

Walford, Roy L. "Biosphere 2 as Voyage of Discovery: The Serendipity from Inside." *Bioscience* 52, no. 3 (March 2002): 259–63.

Warshall, Peter. "Lessons from Biosphere 2: Ecodesign, Surprises, and the Humility of Gaian Thought." *World Earth Review* 89 (Spring 1996): 22–27.

COLD WAR

O'Neill, Dan. *The Firecracker Boys.* New York: St. Martin's Press, 1995.

HOMESTEADING

Willis, A. F. *The Days of My Pilgrimage.* Hong Kong: Christian Book Room, 1972. Anna Frances Boulton lived from 1859 to 1929. I refer to her as "Great-Aunt Fanny."

ICELAND

Eysteinsson, Thröstur. *Forestry in a Treeless Land,* 4th ed. Egilsstaðir, Iceland: Iceland Forest Service, 2013.

Kristinsson, Hörður. *Flowering Plants and Ferns of Iceland.* Reykjavík: Oddi, Eco-labelled Printing Company, 2010.

LITERATURE

Stein, Gertrude. *Tender Buttons: Objects, Food, Rooms.* New York: C. Marie, 1914.

MATANUSKA COLONY AND THE MATANUSKA VALLEY

Alaska Rural Rehabilitation Corporation with Willis T. Geisman, official photographer. *Official Photographic Album, Alaska Rural Rehabilitation Corp., Matanuska Colonization Project.* Mary Nan Gamble Collection, 1935–1945. ASL-PCA-270. Alaska's Digital Archives, accessed May 26, 2015. https://vilda.alaska.edu/digital/collection/cdmg21/id/3142/rec/3.

Cole, Vickie, Pat O'Hara, Pandora Willingham, Ron Wendt, and Mary Simpson. *Knik, Matanuska, Susitna: A Visual History of the Valleys.* Alaska: Matanuska-Susitna Borough, 1985.

Hill, Paul, and Joan Juster, dir. *Alaska Far Away, The New Deal Pioneers of the Matanuska Colony.* 2011. San Francisco: Juster Hill Productions. http://alaskafaraway.com/.

Johnson, Hugh A., and Keith L. Stanton. *Matanuska Valley Memoir, The Story of How One Alaskan Community Developed.* Palmer: University of Alaska, Alaska Agricultural Experiment Station, 1955.

Williamson, F. W. *Field Notes of the Survey of the Seward Principal Meridian through Township No. 18 North, Between Ranges 1 East and 1 West; Field Notes of the Survey, East Boundary of Township 18 North Range 1 East, Seward Meridian.* Cook Inlet District Alaska, 1913.

MUSEUM OF THE NORTH

Adams, John Luther. *The Place Where You Go to Listen.* Installation at the Museum of the North, Fairbanks, Alaska.

9 / 1 1

Brown, Sarah Elizabeth, and Chuck Tobin, "Aircraft Hijacking Initially Feared," *Whitehorse Daily Star,* September 11, 2001.

Demer, Lisa. "Fears That City-Bound Jet Was Hijacked Are False – Anchorage: Korean Jumbo Jet Diverted to Yukon Territory." *Anchorage Daily News,* September 12, 2001.

Korenko, Jeff. "Confusion Reigns as Schools Emptied," *Whitehorse Daily Star,* September 11, 2001.

Levin, Alan. "Korean Air Jet May Have Narrowly Missed Disaster." *USA Today,* August 12, 2002.

Small, Jason. "Bomb-sniffing Dog Flown In," *Whitehorse Daily Star,* September 12, 2001.

Tobin, Chuck. "NORAD Suspected Plane Was Hijacked," *Whitehorse Daily Star,* September 12, 2001.

Tobin, Chuck. "Yukoners Receive Alaskans' Gratitude," *Whitehorse Daily Star,* September 13, 2001.

Tobin, Chuck, and Stephanie Waddell. "A Day Never to Be Forgotten," *Whitehorse Daily Star,* September 11, 2001.

RAILROAD

"Curry Hotel," an article posted on https://www.alaskarails.org/historical/curry/. Accessed February 15, 2019.